WHAT

JOINING THE MOVEMENT

JESUS

CHANGING THE WORLD

STARTED

Steve Addison

IVP Books

An imprint of InterVarsity Press
Downers Grove, Illinois

InterVarsity Press
P.O. Box 1400, Downers Grove, IL 60515-1426
World Wide Web: www.ivpress.com
E-mail: email@ivpress.com

InterVarsity Press® is the book-publishing division of InterVarsity Christian Fellowship/USA®, a movement of students and faculty active on campus at hundreds of universities, colleges and schools of nursing in the United States of America, and a member movement of the International Fellowship of Evangelical Students. For information about local and regional activities, write Public Relations Dept., InterVarsity Christian Fellowship/ USA, 6400 Schroeder Rd., P.O. Box 7895, Madison, WI 53707-7895, or visit the IVCF website at <www. intervarsity.org>.

All Scripture quotations, unless otherwise indicated, are taken from the THE HOLY BIBLE, NEW INTERNATIONAL VERSION®, NIV® Copyright © 1973, 1978, 1984, 2011 by Biblica, Inc.™ Used by permission. All rights reserved worldwide.

While all stories in this book are true, some names and identifying information in this book have been changed to protect the privacy of the individuals involved.

Design: Cindy Kiple
Images: fish in nets: Jeff Rotman/Getty Images
         swimming fish: © Predag Vuckovic/iStockphoto
Interior design: Beth Hagenberg
Maps: Peter Bergmeier

Published in association with the literary agency of WordServe Literary Group, Ltd., 10152 Knoll Circle, Highlands Ranch, CO 80130.

ISBN 978-0-8308-3659-8

Printed in the United States of America ∞

Library of Congress Cataloging-in-Publication Data

Addison, Steve.
  What Jesus started : joining the movement, changing the world / Steve Addison.
     p. cm.
  Includes bibliographical references.
  ISBN 978-0-8308-3659-8 (pbk. : alk. paper)
  1. Christianity—Origin. 2. Church history—Primitive and early church, ca. 30-600. I. Title.
  BR129.A33 2012
  262—dc23
                                                                                     2012038557

P   19   18   17   16   15   14   13   12   11   10   9   8   7   6   5   4   3
Y   28   27   26   25   24   23   22   21   20   19   18   17   16   15   14

To my parents

Joan and Bruce Addison

CONTENTS

PART THREE
What Jesus Continued to Do: *Paul and His Team*

PART FOUR
What Jesus Is Doing Today

Simon Peter . . . fell at Jesus' knees and said, "Go away from me, Lord; I am a sinful man!" For he and all his companions were astonished at the catch of fish they had taken, and so were James and John, the sons of Zebedee, Simon's partners.

Then Jesus said to Simon, "Don't be afraid; from now on you will fish for people."

LUKE 5:8-10

FOREWORD

Jesus started the Christian movement with the Great Commission.

So, why is the Great Commission great? Well, for many reasons. Jesus says, "Go therefore and make disciples of all nations," and at that very moment, Jesus' mission shifts from a centripetal mission of the Old Testament (to bring the nations "up to Jerusalem" to worship) to a centrifugal mission—to go out "from Jerusalem" to the nations. Jesus tells the disciples they'll go out from Jerusalem to Judea, to Samaria, to the uttermost parts of the earth. Because of his death and resurrection, he moves the mission in a new direction: victory over death, sin, the grave, and hell, to the uttermost parts of the earth. He sends them out to proclaim his death on the cross, for our sin and in our place. That's pretty great.

Recently I traveled to Turkey, burdened to see a fledgling church with so few workers. It's a slow work in Turkey, and there are challenges to working in a predominantly Muslim context, but I couldn't help but grieve over seeing the church struggle. There are seventy million Turks around the world and just a few thousand believers. Yet this is where we find the seven (long gone) churches in the book of Revelation. This is where the first seven "ecumenical councils" of the church were held, where things like the Nicene Creed were birthed. This place, this formerly thriving center of Christianity, now has only a few thousand people who would claim the name of Jesus Christ. What is God's plan there?

Steve Addison helps us see a little more clearly, pointing believers to Scripture as the roadmap for what Jesus expects us to do. In the New Testament, we meet a Jesus who sees spiritual poverty, overwhelming need like I experienced in Turkey, and responds with a message and a mission. I'm reminded that, even in a land with so few Christians, the Jesus message and movement can go forth. Like it did in the church's earliest days.

Learn from Jesus. Jesus connects with the lost, shares the gospel, trains disciples, gathers them in communities, and multiplies them to go out and do the same. Steve's insight into this process is clear and communicable. This book will challenge you to think more like a movement and less like an institution.

God wants your church, your community of mobilized disciples, to join the mission. There are six thousand unreached people groups in the world today. Somebody brought the gospel message to you; to whom are you taking the gospel?

The Great Commission is great because the One who gave it to us is great. If you desire to obey Jesus' command to make disciples of all nations, baptizing and teaching them as you go, first you should get to know him. Don't ask yourself, "What would Jesus do?" Ask the Scripture, as Steve does, "What did Jesus do?" Do that. Don't let your church be a cul-de-sac on the Great Commission highway.

Ed Stetzer
President of LifeWay Research
www.edstetzer.com

ACKNOWLEDGMENTS

In the 1980s I was working as a youth intern at my local church when I stumbled on a pile of dusty old books, laid out for the church staff to pick through. I found two gems by Roland Allen: *Missionary Methods: St Paul's or Ours?* and *The Spontaneous Expansion of the Church*. The titles got my attention, and a free book is always a good book when you're a youth intern, so I grabbed them and tucked them away for future reference. It was years before I read them and even longer before they worked their magic in my mind and my heart, yet they changed me.

Twenty years later a friend sent me an unexpected gift—Eckhard Schnabel's two-volume *Early Christian Mission: Jesus and the Twelve* and *Paul and the Early Church*. These two volumes extend to over nineteen hundred pages. I read and marked every page.

I want to acknowledge my indebtedness and gratitude to Roland Allen and Eckhard Schnabel. These two great writers have deeply influenced my understanding of Jesus as the founder and living Lord of the Christian movement.

I would also like to acknowledge the practitioners and trainers whose example and thinking have enabled me to see how Jesus continues to call and equip us as workers in his harvest field—Bill Smith, David Garrison, Steve Smith, Grant McAllister, Jeff Sundell, David Watson, Nathan Shank, Dave Lawton and Tim Scheuer.

Thank you to Val Gresham who has patiently and skillfully worked with me as my writing coach and initial editor, and to Grant Morrison, trainer and coach of church planters, who has consistently and fearlessly provided helpful insights. Thank you to Peter Bergmeier, my designer, who worked with me to create and simplify the *Movements* diagram. Thanks to Dave Zimmerman, my editor at IVP, for bringing the project to completion.

Finally, I am deeply grateful for the support of my wife, Michelle, in this project. Michelle, thank you most of all for leading the way in our local ministry among migrants from all over the world. Our experience there has helped shift the biblical principles from my head to my heart and my hands.

IN THE BEGINNING WAS JESUS

Without Jesus there would be no Christian movement. Peter would never have stood before thousands on the day of Pentecost to proclaim that God had revealed himself in the crucified and risen Jesus of Nazareth. Communities of disciples would never have been formed in Damascus, in Syrian Antioch, in Corinth, Ephesus, and Rome.[1]

Many theories seek to explain the astonishing rise of this new faith. Only one will do: Jesus is the founder and living Lord of the movement that bears his name.

The world had never seen anything like it. By A.D. 300, long before Christianity became a favored religion, Christians made up around 10 percent of the population throughout the Roman Empire—five to nine million followers of Jesus.[2]

As first century Christianity was advancing west throughout Europe, thriving centers of faith also sprang up in North Africa, in the Middle East and in central Asia. Much of what we call the Islamic world today was once Christian. There is credible evidence that the apostle Thomas established churches in northwestern and southern India.[3] Courage and faith were all that the apostles and other missionaries needed to spread the gospel along the trade routes of the ancient world.[4]

A missionary movement was something totally new in human history. Outside of the faith of Israel, no one believed in one universal religion or one true God. There were no missionaries and no conversions. In a world over which many gods ruled, new gods didn't replace old ones; they were just added to them.

In contrast to the surrounding pagan nations, Judaism taught that there is one God who is the Creator and Lord of all. He chose Israel to be his witness to the world. Through Israel the nations would be drawn into God's salvation. In the "last days" or "end times" God would send his servant, the Messiah, to bring salvation to the nations. Individual Gentiles could be accepted into the people of God if they converted to worshiping Yahweh, submitted to circumcision and adopted the Mosaic Law. To convert, a Gentile had to become a Jew. Individual Gentiles did convert (or at least become "God-fearers") on the fringe of the synagogue. Yet

Judaism never became an expanding missionary movement. There was no organized, sustained attempt to convert Gentiles to Yahweh.[5]

The Christian movement was something new in human history. Jesus' first public act, recorded in three Gospels, was the calling of Simon, Andrew, James and John to leave their fishing nets and join his band of mobile missionaries. From then on, he told them, they would be fishing for people.

Jesus continues to lead the way. Every new generation of his disciples sits at the feet of Jesus and learns from his example as founder and living Lord of the movement. No movement that bears his name can rise above his example and his leadership. The mission of Jesus was universal. It knew no bounds. No one was excluded. There were no outsiders. There were no borders. The mission was to the ends of the earth and to the end of history. Jesus' early followers were convinced that forgiveness of sins was possible for Jews and non-Jews, for the educated and for the barbarians, for men and women, for rich and poor—through faith in Jesus, the Messiah and Lord.

Missionary movements communicate the truth about God and salvation to others. They teach followers a new way of life that accords with that truth. The purpose of a missionary movement is that people accept the message, begin to follow Jesus, share him with others, and form new communities of faith that become partners in the spread of the gospel.[6]

What does that look like? What do missionary movements do? These are the six activities we will refer to as we examine the ministry of Jesus as it began in the Gospels and as it continued through his followers in the book of Acts.

Six activities—simple enough and interconnected enough that you could sketch them out on a napkin, yet intricate and all-encompassing enough that they merit the full attention and devotion of all Jesus' followers throughout history.

1. **See the end.** Missionary movements obey God's call to join his mission. They submit to the leadership of Jesus through the Holy Spirit and the power of his living Word. They are moved with compassion for lost people and do not rest until the good news of salvation through Christ is proclaimed and communities of disciples are gathered throughout the inhabited world.

2. **Connect with people.** Movements cross boundaries (geographic, linguistic, cultural, social, economic) to establish contact with non-Christians. They seek out responsive people who have been prepared by God.

3. **Share the gospel.** Movements share the good news of Jesus the Messiah and Savior through proclamation, preaching, teaching and instruction. They equip new disciples to become the means by which the good news spreads throughout their communities.

4. **Train disciples.** Movements lead people to faith in Jesus Christ (conversion, baptism, gift of the Holy Spirit) and teach them to obey what Jesus has commanded, including the command to make disciples of others.

5. **Gather communities.** Movements form new believers into the local communities of the followers of Jesus (featuring the Lord's Supper, transformation of behavior, love, service and witness). Each community of disciples is responsible to reach its region in depth and to contribute money, prayer and workers who take the gospel to unreached regions.

6. **Multiply workers.** Missionary movements release mobile apostolic or missionary teams into new, unreached fields to advance the spread of the gospel.

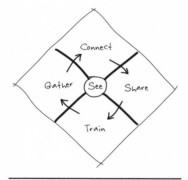

Christianity did not thrive in the ancient world because the social, economic, religious and political conditions were right. There was nothing inevitable about the spread of the gospel. Christianity thrived because all authority was given to the risen Lord who commanded his followers to go into all the world and make disciples. Their mission thrived because Jesus is Lord. He still commands us to follow him, and he still promises to teach us to fish for people, make disciples and multiply communities of his followers—everywhere.

The six elements of the movement Jesus started: see the need; connect with people; share the gospel; train disciples; gather communities; multiply workers (represented by the X).

WHAT TO EXPECT

This is a book written for those who want to follow Jesus and to have him train them in his movement. There is a job for everyone to do. The movement Jesus founded advances because we are all called to connect with people who are far from God. We are all called to share our story and share Jesus' story, the gospel. We can all open the Scriptures and begin learning together how to follow Jesus in loving obedience. We can all form communities of disciples that gather to worship, to learn, to love and to witness. We can all play our part in the multiplication of disciples and churches, both locally and throughout the world.

First we'll look at the mission of Jesus of Nazareth, and then at how as the risen Lord, he continued to pursue his mission through his followers— the Twelve and the early church, and then Paul and his coworkers. Along the way there are stories of how Jesus is at work through his people around the world today. Finally, we'll ask the most important question of all—how can we respond to the invitation to follow him and to let him teach us to fish for people?

Jesus' example alone is not enough. As the disciples learned, without his Spirit, none of us has the capacity to fulfill his command to take the gospel to the ends of the earth. Jesus Christ, the Savior of the world who died and rose again—although now exalted to the right hand of God and later to return in glory to judge the world—is also present through the Holy Spirit, inviting us to share in the spread of the gospel throughout the world.

PART ONE

What Jesus Began

1

WHY JESUS CAME

To fulfill what was said through the prophet Isaiah:
"Land of Zebulun and land of Naphtali,
the Way of the Sea, beyond the Jordan,
Galilee of the Gentiles—
the people living in darkness
have seen a great light;
on those living in the land of the shadow of death
a light has dawned."

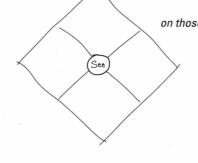

—MATTHEW 4:14-16

JESUS WAS BORN IN BETHLEHEM around 5 B.C. He grew up in Nazareth, a town of just a few hundred people in lower Galilee.

In Jesus' day, the region of Galilee was a Jewish enclave surrounded by centers of pagan Greek culture left over from the conquests of Alexander the Great in the fourth century B.C. Rome was now the ruling power, but the Greek language, culture and religion continued to dominate. The population of the region was mixed, with most Jews living in the countryside and Gentiles living in the cities and border towns.

Galilee was no backwater. It had two major Greek cities—Sepphoris and Tiberias—of 10,000 to 20,000 people each. A few miles from Nazareth was the great highway that stretched from Egypt to Syria. Along it flowed a constant stream of Greeks and Barbarians, as well as Roman soldiers. Sepphoris, an

hour's walk from Nazareth, was rebuilt by Herod Antipas as his capital in 4
B.C. Tradesmen were in high demand. Jesus would be apprenticed to his
father, a tradesman who worked in timber, stone, and metal.

Jesus was raised in a devout Jewish home. As a boy he attended the synagogue each Sabbath with his parents, brothers and sisters. Jesus grew up
speaking Aramaic and at age five probably began learning to read the Torah
(first five books of Moses) in Hebrew at the village synagogue school.[1]

Galilee was fertile and supported a population of 200,000 people living
in 175 towns and villages.[2] The region was the breadbasket of Palestine, and
wheat was a major commodity. Wine from Galilee was exported to Phoenicia; northern Galilee produced and exported olive oil. Tiberias was known
for its textiles, pottery and glass, while Gennesaret was noted for its date
palms and fruit trees. Fishing was a thriving business in Galilee, and salted
fish was exported far and wide.

Despite this abundance, however, most Jews in the countryside lived a
hard life. Roman rule meant that agricultural land was hard to retain. The
problem began back in 34 B.C. when the Romans installed Herod I ("the
Great") as king over Judea and Galilee. Herod was corrupt. Wealthy and
ruthless, he murdered anyone he suspected of opposing him: two high
priests, an uncle, his mother-in-law, three of his sons and his favorite wife.[3]

Within one generation Herod I had rebuilt Jerusalem and transformed
the holy city into a Greco-Roman capital. Under the rule of Herod and his
sons, Israel was a divided society. Herod surrounded himself with nobles,
wealthy landowners, military commanders and the religious ruling families who controlled the Temple in Jerusalem and the position of high
priest. This local elite submitted itself to Roman rule and promoted Greek
culture and values.

Supporting the elite were their officials—bureaucrats, tax collectors, military officers and judges. These men enforced Herodian rule over the rest of
society, which was divided into roughly three groups. The first group included self-employed merchants, craftsmen, fishermen and farmers who
owned their land. Then there were the landless peasants who had lost their
land through taxes, crop failure and debt. On the very outer fringe of society
were the beggars, prostitutes and bandits.

Herod the Great's sons perpetuated these divisions. Herod Antipas (c. 20
B.C to A.D. 39) controlled Galilee during most of Jesus' life. He introduced
Greek culture and values, to the dismay of the ordinary people who sought

to be faithful to Israel's covenant. Herod Antipas' luxurious palace in Tiberias was filled with Gentiles and decorated with idolatrous images.

The rural Jewish population longed for Yahweh to bring deliverance for his people. This was the setting of Jesus' mission.

The Spirit of the Lord is on me,
because he has anointed me
to proclaim good news to the poor.
He has sent me to proclaim freedom for the prisoners
and recovery of sight for the blind,
to set the oppressed free,
to proclaim the year of the Lord's favor. (Lk 4:18-19)

Jesus came proclaiming "good news to the poor"—not just the economic poor but also those rejected as "unclean," including camel drivers, shepherds, shopkeepers, butchers, goldsmiths, tax collectors, peddlers and tanners.[4]

In A.D. 28 Jesus submitted himself to baptism by his cousin John, identifying with sinful Israel, in need of cleansing and restoration. Jesus' baptism also marked the time when Jesus would leave his carpenter's workshop and take up the mission he was destined for. In his baptism Jesus committed to fulfill his mission, even if it meant persecution and death.

Before he could plunder Satan's kingdom, Jesus would have to defeat Satan. The Spirit thrust Jesus out into the Judean desert on the western side of the Dead Sea, where Jesus faced his adversary for forty days and forty nights. Satan offered Jesus the kingdoms of the world, if only Jesus would bow down and worship him. Would Jesus use his power and unique status as God's Son to serve himself, or would he accept the "cup" God had called him to drink?

Satan offered Jesus the chance to fulfill his mission and establish the kingdom without the cross. Instead Jesus saw his mission as saving people from their sins and from the just judgment of God. He chose to willingly follow the path laid out by his Father, even at the cost of his life.

ON THE MOVE IN GALILEE

Jesus returned to Galilee in the power of the Spirit,
and news about him spread through the whole countryside.

Luke 4:14

Jesus issued a compelling call to a small band of disciples and took them throughout Galilee proclaiming the arrival of God's rule, casting out demons

and healing the sick. From town to town, in the synagogues, by the shores of
the lake, in the open fields, in the market places and in homes—every settlement in the region—Jesus declared that the kingdom of God was present.

Matthew records that Jesus' ministry touched "all" 175 towns and villages of Galilee. To reach them all Jesus could rarely have stayed in one place
for more than a few days; he would have been constantly on the move. By
the end of his ministry, most of Galilee's 200,000 people would either have
met Jesus or have known someone who had.

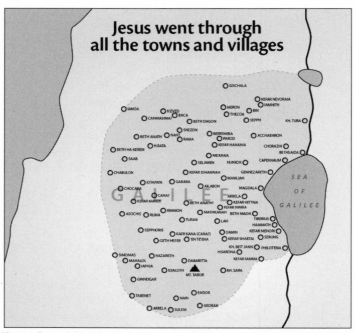

Map 1.1. Some of the 175 towns and villages of Galilee that, according to Matthew, Jesus
visited. See Eckhard J. Schnabel, *Early Christian Mission*, Vol. 2, *Paul and the Early Church*
(Downers Grove, Ill.: IVP Academic, 2004), p. 1592.

Jesus left his home in Nazareth and made Capernaum his base. This
harbor town of a thousand people was on the northwest shore of the Sea of
Galilee and was known for fishing, agriculture and trade. From Capernaum
Jesus and his disciples could reach dozens of small towns and villages within
one or two days' travel.

Jesus' central concern was the kingdom, or reign, of God. Since childhood

Jesus was taught that there was one God, Yahweh, who is Creator and Lord of all. He learned that through Abraham, God had chosen Israel to be his witness to the world. Through Israel the nations (Gentiles) would be drawn into God's salvation. As he studied the prophet Isaiah, Jesus learned how in the last days God would send his Servant to suffer and die for the sins of his people. God would restore Israel through the obedience of his Servant, and the nations would hear the good news of salvation.

The kingdom could not be advanced or established by human effort. The kingdom of God was God's act of breaking into history through this Servant Messiah's life, death and resurrection to save sinful humanity. Jesus identified himself as the Son of Man who, according to Daniel 7:13-14, will be given universal dominion. He also identified himself as the Servant of Isaiah (Is 40–55) who will suffer and be rejected by men. Yet God's purpose is that his innocent death will be as a ransom for many (Mk 10:45).

As Jesus set out on his mission, he concentrated his ministry on the "lost sheep of Israel"—the people chosen through Abraham to be a blessing to the world. Israel was Jesus' priority *because* the whole world was his concern. During his ministry, he prepared his disciples for a worldwide mission; the time would come when he would send them to the ends of the earth.

Jesus' fame spread from Galilee to Judea and into the surrounding regions of the Near East (Mt 4:24-25). Palestine itself was home to over a million people—at least eight hundred thousand Jews and half a million Samaritans, Greeks and Nabateans.[5] People came to Jesus from all over Galilee and the surrounding regions. They came from the south—Judea, Jerusalem, Idumea and Samaria. They came from the east across the Jordan, from Perea, Batanea and the Decapolis. They came from Syria in the north, and from the Phoenician coastal cities of Tyre and Sidon. This fulfilled Isaiah's prophecy— Galilee of the Gentiles had seen a great light (Is 9:1-7; Mt 4:14-16).

ON THE MOVE IN JUDEA AND JERUSALEM

When Jesus had finished saying these things, he left Galilee and
went into the region of Judea to the other side of the Jordan.
Matthew 19:1

After their campaign throughout Galilee, Jesus and the disciples traveled south into Judea, visiting towns and villages, and preaching in the synagogues. Since the death of Herod the Great in A.D. 6, Judea had become a Roman province under the authority of a military governor based in Caesarea. The Romans ruled through the Jewish Sanhedrin in Jerusalem, which was responsible for government administration and tax collection.

Jesus' ministry brought him into conflict with the Pharisees. They were zealous for God's Law, as interpreted by their scribes. Their traditions defined correct behavior. Their concern for ritual purity separated them from the majority of Jews who they described as "the people of the land."

The Pharisees' power base was in the local synagogues scattered throughout Judea and Galilee. Seeking to remain true to the covenant with Yahweh, they rejected the influence of Greek culture. They were popular among common people but enemies of Herod, his sons and their wealthy supporters, including the Sadducees, a small but powerful sect of Judaism made up of wealthy, aristocratic families. The Pharisees controlled the temple in Jerusalem and the ruling body of the Sanhedrin.

The Pharisees rejected Jesus as the Messiah and regarded him as a blasphemer in league with Satan. Jesus intentionally broke the Pharisees' rules and embraced the very people they considered unclean. He rejected the legalism of the Pharisees that undermined the true meaning of the Law and excluded sinners from God's mercy. Jesus was concerned with the evil that polluted people's hearts, not the contamination that comes from neglecting ritual.

Jesus also clashed with the Sadducees. They accepted Roman rule and embraced Greek culture, and chose the high priest who ruled with the permission of the Roman governor. The Pharisees sought to kill Jesus, but it was the Sadducees who eventually used their influence with the Romans to get the job done.

A year before Jesus' death, around the time of Passover, John records that a great crowd tried to make Jesus their king (Jn 6:15). Jesus withdrew from them and left Galilee for ministry in the surrounding Gentile regions, out of the reach of Herod Antipas. His public ministry in Galilee was at an end (Mk 9:30). Much of his time was now spent with his disciples, away from the crowds.

During this period Jesus and the disciples visited Caesarea Philippi, twenty-five miles north of the Sea of Galilee. Caesarea was a pagan city built by Herod the Great to honor Caesar Augustus. It was at Caesarea Philippi that Jesus asked Peter "Who do you say that I am?" Peter's answer acknowledged Jesus as the Messiah (Mt 16:13-21). Jesus said he would build his church upon the truth of Peter's confession. Jesus would build a new temple made up of the restored people of God, including the Gentiles. He told his disciples that he must go to Jerusalem where he would be rejected by the religious leaders and killed. After three days he would rise again.

Ever since Herod the Great rebuilt the Temple, Jerusalem was the most-visited city in the Roman Empire. It had a population of 25,000 people within the walled city and up to 100,000 in the immediate vicinity. That number could swell to a million people during a major festival.[6] The pilgrims came from the 800,000 Jews in Palestine and the two to seven million in the Jewish *Diaspora*, or Dispersion, scattered throughout the Roman Empire and beyond. The people of Jerusalem were dependent on the business generated by the Temple and the thousands of pilgrims who traveled there. Most of these visitors stayed in tents on the hilly country surrounding the city.

Jesus' mission was approaching its final stage. In the holy city the nation's leaders would reject his claim to be the Messiah. During the Passover of A.D. 30, Jesus would be arrested and interrogated by the Temple authorities, then handed over to the Roman governor who would execute him for treason against Rome.

FROM ISRAEL TO THE ENDS OF THE EARTH

> *Therefore I tell you that the kingdom of God will be taken*
> *away from you and given to a people who will produce its fruit.*
> Matthew 21:43

God chose Israel through Abraham to be a blessing to the nations. Jesus' ministry to Israel opened the way for that blessing to be realized in full. By rejecting the Messiah, the holy nation sealed its own fate. Except for individual Israelites, God would pass over the nation Israel and gather the nations of the world into his kingdom.

During his lifetime different Gentiles sought Jesus out. They came to him from the Gentile regions east of the Jordan and from Syria, the Decapolis, Tyre and Sidon. He never turned them away. Jesus was astonished by the faith of one Gentile military officer and told him, "I have not found anyone in Israel with such great faith." He said that many Gentiles would enter the kingdom while those who rejected him would be cast out.[7]

In Jerusalem Jesus overturned the tables of the moneychangers and drove out everyone who was buying and selling because God intended the Temple to be a "house of prayer for the nations"—a holy place where the Gentiles could meet with the God of Israel. This prophetic act signified the end of the sacrificial system and the beginning of a new era in which the nations would be drawn into the new people of God—the worldwide community of Jesus' disciples.

CONCLUSION

Jesus came to seek and save what was lost. His mission focused on the people of Israel, chosen by God to be witnesses to the world.

1. **Jesus saw the end.** He was moved with compassion. He looked out over Israel and saw sheep, lost without a shepherd. He wept over Jerusalem's rejection of God's messengers. He prepared his disciples to take the gospel to the whole world.

2. **Jesus connected with people.** Jesus crossed whatever boundaries stood in the way and connected with people. No group was beyond his care. Jesus spent a lot of his time ministering to people, looking for the "sick" not the "healthy," "sinners" not the "righteous." He sought out people who knew they needed God's mercy.

3. **Jesus shared the gospel.** Jesus proclaimed the good news of salvation in words and deeds. In him, God's rule had become a present reality. He preached, he taught, he rebuked, and he invited everyone he met to repent and believe. He gave his life as a ransom for many.

4. **Jesus trained disciples.** Jesus led people to put their trust in him and to learn to obey his commands. He modeled and taught them a new way of life.

5. **Jesus gathered communities.** Jesus formed his disciples into communities characterized by faith in him, love for one another, and witness in word and deed.

6. **Jesus multiplied workers.** Jesus equipped his followers to make disciples of all nations. He sent the Holy Spirit upon them so that they would continue his ministry in his power.

Jesus fulfilled God's promises to Israel. Wanting to reach as many people as possible from every level of society, in every town and village, he focused on Israel, God's chosen witness to the world. He chose and trained the Twelve who represented a restored Israel and became the nucleus of the restored people of God who would take the good news of salvation to the ends of the earth. Jesus prepared his disciples for a worldwide mission following his death and resurrection, and the outpouring of the Holy Spirit. He began to build his church, and the gates of hell will not prevail against it.

2

LET'S GO SOMEWHERE ELSE

Simon and his companions went to look for him,
and when they found him, they exclaimed:
"Everyone is looking for you!" Jesus replied,
"Let us go somewhere else—to the
nearby villages—so I can preach there
also. That is why I have come." So he
traveled throughout Galilee,
preaching in their synagogues
and driving out demons.

—MARK 1:36-39

JESUS CONNECTED WITH a bewildering array of people—religious scholars, greedy tax collectors, unclean lepers, military officers, rulers, beggars, a rich young noble, a demonized pagan, hard-working fishermen, wealthy women, shamed prostitutes and adulterers.

Jesus didn't wait for people to come to him. He walked from village to village looking for people—on the road, in the marketplaces and synagogues, in private homes and in public places, by the lake and in the Temple, at a wedding feast and at a funeral, at a banquet with sinners and a meal with Pharisees. Wherever the people were, Jesus went. The good shepherd was looking for lost sheep.

Jesus taught, and he debated. He listened, and he asked questions. He rebuked, and he forgave. He healed the sick, raised the dead, cast out demons and cleared the Temple. He taught thousands on the hillsides of Galilee and talked with a lone Samaritan woman by a well. He preached in village synagogues and to multitudes of festival pilgrims in Jerusalem.

Jesus shared meals with all sorts of people. He accepted invitations to eat with sinners, with the rich and the poor, with the Pharisees and with Gentiles. His meals were associated with the joy that comes from the forgiveness of sins. A meal with Jesus was a life-changing event.[1]

Jesus withdrew occasionally—to rest, to pray, to be safe, to be with his disciples. Mostly he was on the move, rarely staying in one place for long. He was always moving on to the next settlement, the next crowd, the next person, the next opportunity. He covered the length and breadth of Galilee. He made repeated forays into the surrounding Gentile regions and down into Judea. He sought people out, and thousands came from afar seeking him. The Pharisees complained, "Look how the whole world has gone after him!" (Jn 12:19).

Why did Jesus keep moving? He told his disciples that this was why he came. He was saying something important about his mission. He had a message, and he was going to keep moving to reach as many people as possible—in every town and every village.

Wherever Jesus went, the people came. The scribes and the Pharisees regarded the common people with contempt, but they were the objects of Jesus' love and mission. Even though he loved these people, however, Jesus knew their faith was fickle. He never identified the crowds with his band of disciples. Jesus called his disciples out of the crowds to follow him. The crowds stood between faith and unbelief, between acceptance and rejection.

Jesus' compassion drove him on. He refused to live a settled existence. His mobility was strategic; he was laying the foundation for a missionary movement. He was training his disciples to do what he did.

REACHING ALL KINDS OF PEOPLE

Jesus touched the least and the greatest. He said the kingdom of God was like a dragnet in which all kinds of fish would be caught (Mt 13:47). He did not limit his mission to any one section of society. There was no one who was outside of his concern.

His family. Nazareth was home to Jesus' family and his other relatives. Jesus ministered in his hometown with mixed results.[2] During his lifetime his family did not understand his mission. They even came to take him away, fearing he had gone mad.[3] Following Jesus' death and resurrection, however, his mother and brothers put their faith in him and joined the movement.[4]

The "people of the land." Jesus ministered among the common people in the villages and countryside of Galilee. The crowds that flocked to Jesus were made up of day laborers, farmers and fishermen. Jesus also sought out the lepers, blind and crippled beggars, the sick and those tormented by demons.

The powerful. The Gospels and Acts identify a number of people connected with Herod who were touched by Jesus' ministry. There was the royal official who came to Jesus at Cana seeking help for his sick son. There was the centurion at Capernaum (probably a Roman military officer serving in Herod Antipas's forces) who sought healing for his sick attendant.[5] One of Jesus' disciples, Matthew-Levi, had been employed by Herod as a customs official to collect tolls on the highway joining Mesopotamia and Egypt (Lk 5:27-28). Also among Jesus' disciples was Joanna, whose husband, Chuza, was an important official of Herod Antipas. Jesus had healed Joanna "of evil spirits and infirmities." She was one of a group of wealthy women who traveled with Jesus and supported the ministry financially. She was in Jerusalem at the time of the crucifixion and was one of the women who found the empty tomb (Lk 8:3; 24:10).

The "righteous." Jesus maintained contact with the Pharisees despite their hostility. At least twice he accepted an invitation to share a meal with them. On both occasions he used the situation to demonstrate and teach about the grace of God. His parables of the Lost Sheep, the Lost Coin, and the Lost Sons served to invite the Pharisees to join in the celebration of God's love for sinners. Following Jesus' death and resurrection, the Pharisees and the religious leaders in Jerusalem maintained their opposition to the Jesus movement that emerged after Pentecost. Yet large numbers of priests became obedient to the faith, and there were believers even among the Pharisees.[6]

Women. A number of women became disciples of Jesus through his healing ministry. They followed him in Galilee and to Jerusalem. Luke mentions three by name—Mary Magdalene, Joanna and Susanna—but there were many others like these women among Jesus' followers. We also have three examples of Jesus accepting and forgiving women who were guilty of sexual sin: the Samaritan woman, the woman caught in adultery and the woman who washed Jesus' feet with her tears.[7]

The prosperous. Jesus ministered to the small portion of society that lived in comfort. Some of Jesus' disciples were prosperous fishermen who owned their boats and employed workers. Mary, Martha and Lazarus had sufficient means to host Jesus and his disciples in their home and hold a dinner in Jesus' honor, during which Mary poured expensive perfume over his feet. After the crucifixion, Joseph of Arimathea, a rich man and prominent member of the Sanhedrin who had access to the Roman military governor, secured permission to bury Jesus' body.[8]

The despised. The Pharisees and experts in the law accused Jesus of being a glutton, a drunkard, and a friend of tax collectors and sinners. "Tax collector" was a term of abuse in both Jewish and Roman society. The Romans sold the right to collect taxes to the highest bidder, who then extracted as much as he could from the people. Tax collectors represented a system of greed, dishonesty and oppression of the poor. Zacchaeus was a chief tax collector and a wealthy man, but Jesus sought him out. When the crowds complained, Jesus told them he had come to seek and save the lost.

Gentiles. Jesus focused his ministry on Israel, yet Gentiles were drawn to him, and he never turned them away. The crowds that flocked to Jesus included both Jews and some Gentiles from Galilee and the surrounding regions of Judea, the Decapolis, Trans-Jordan, Tyre and Sidon. Jesus agreed that Gentiles were sinners, but unlike his opponents, he regarded them as objects of God's grace and mercy. He healed them and preached the gospel to them. He invited them, along with the Jews, to repent.[9]

WHO WILL I MEET TODAY?

How did Jesus find responsive people? It was simple. He began every day with the expectation that God had prepared people for him to meet. Let's look at one example.

Jesus and his disciples were traveling from Jerusalem to Galilee.[10] It was a three-day journey on foot, and the most direct route was through Samaria. In the heat of the day they stopped at Jacob's well near the town of Sychar. Jesus sent the disciples to get food while he sat down to rest.

Middle Eastern wells did not have buckets. A traveling group would carry their own rolled up leather bucket for drawing water. Yet Jesus sat by the well without a bucket. The disciples had probably taken it with them.

Jesus sat down, waiting for someone to appear.

Village women avoided the heat of the day by going to the well early in the morning and just before sundown. They normally went as a group. Yet one woman arrived at the well in the middle of the day. She was alone. Middle Eastern culture dictated that as she approached, Jesus should withdraw to a distance of at least twenty feet. Only then could she move to the well, unroll her small leather bucket, and lower it into the water. From the bucket she would fill a clay jar, place it on her head and return home. As she approached, Jesus stayed by the well and asked her for a drink.

A Jewish rabbi would not even talk to his wife in public, let alone a woman he'd never met. Jesus ignored these customs, along with five hundred years of hostility between Jews and Samaritans. He was thirsty and had no leather bucket. In humility he placed himself in her debt.

They talked. Jesus took this woman seriously, and he allowed her to lead the conversation. He listened and responded using her words and her questions as his starting point. At first she saw a thirsty man, then a Jew, then a rabbi, eventually a prophet, and last of all the Messiah, the Savior of the world.

Overwhelmed with her discovery, she left her water jar and rushed back into the village where she begged her friends and neighbors to come and meet the man who could be the Messiah. Jesus knew her past, and yet he had offered her living water, eternal life, salvation. The whole town came out to meet Jesus because of this woman's story. She became the first missionary to her own town.

Jesus could have gone into town himself. He could have sent in his disciples. Instead Jesus chose this woman. Why? In that culture, a woman's testimony had no authority. The whole town knew about her reputation with men. Her knowledge of Jesus was based on just one conversation. Why did Jesus choose her?

God had prepared this woman as a bridge over which the gospel would enter her community. She was a "person of peace" who welcomed Jesus and welcomed his message (Lk 10:5-6). What qualified her for this task? She could tell her story of how she met Jesus. She could ask people, "Could he be the Messiah?" That's all.

The whole town came out to see Jesus because of the change in the woman. They put their faith in Jesus as the Savior of the world. They pressed him to stay, and even more villagers believed. Then after just two days, Jesus and the disciples left for Galilee.

This story shows us how Jesus entered an unreached town and connected with people he had never met before—something he did frequently. Jesus came looking for people who knew they needed him, and through them the gospel spread to their community of relationships. The Gerasene demoniac is another example. After Jesus delivered him, he begged Jesus to be allowed to join him; instead Jesus sent him home. He went away and began to proclaim what Jesus had done for him throughout the whole region of Decapolis (Mk 5:18-20).

There are no examples of Jesus refusing an invitation to a meal. He would even invite himself to people's homes. Jesus told Zacchaeus, "I must stay at your house today." At Zacchaeus's home, Jesus met his family and friends and extended household. By the end of his visit Jesus was able to announce that "salvation has come to this house" (Lk 19:2-9).

Jesus called Matthew-Levi, a tax collector in the employ of Herod, to follow him. Later Matthew held a great feast and invited his friends and associates. When Jesus was criticized for attending, he said he wasn't looking for good people but for sinners. What better place to find sinners than at Matthew's feast? What better way to reach them than through their friend Matthew?

Jesus' disciples were with him at the banquet that night. He was showing them how to connect with lost people. When he sent them out on mission later, he told them to go into a village looking for a "person of peace" (Lk 10:5-7). They knew what he meant. They had seen him do it so many times before.

RULES OF ENGAGEMENT

Jesus trained his disciples to connect with people. Jesus sent the Twelve in six teams of two throughout Galilee to preach, heal the sick, and cast out demons. Assuming each pair spent two days in each settlement, they could have finished their mission in two months.[11]

Jesus told them not to take anything for their journey but to trust God to provide through the people who welcomed them and their message. If they found no household of peace, they were to shake the dust off their feet and move on. If the disciples were welcomed, they stayed long enough to connect with a household of peace and plant the gospel before moving on to the next town. In each location they sought at least one household of peace that could become the means of the gospel spreading to the whole community.

Jesus and his disciples were strangers in most of the towns they visited. They went looking for people who, as insiders, spread the gospel of the kingdom in their community.

Jesus and his disciples worked on multiple fronts at one time. They did not settle down and focus on one location. Everywhere he and his disciples went they lit fires that would spread beyond their direct control and influence. Everything Jesus did on mission was reproducible and sustainable. Moving on meant new disciples had to take responsibility to reach their community.

At the heart of Jesus' ministry was the conviction that, since the Father is Lord of the harvest, he will provide the workers. God alone initiates the mission. So in each location the disciples' assignment was to find the people that God had prepared. In this way Jesus laid the foundation for a missionary movement that would reach the world.

3

JESUS' GOSPEL

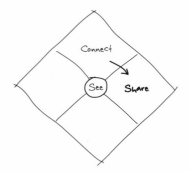

But go and learn what this means:
"I desire mercy, not sacrifice."
For I have not come to call the
righteous, but sinners.

—MATTHEW 9:13

JESUS TAUGHT LIKE NO OTHER RABBI. Jesus' sayings and stories were alive with color and meaning. Their vivid images left people hungering for more. As he moved from place to place, he told and retold the stories and his teachings so that his disciples could remember them and pass them on to others.

Jesus told stories about camels jumping through needles, treasures buried in fields and a battered traveler rescued by a hated Samaritan. He spoke about God as a loving Father who won't give you a scorpion when you ask him for an egg. He shocked his listeners when he told them haters might as well be murderers.

Jesus didn't just teach about the kingdom of God, he made it happen. What the prophets predicted was happening. The kingdom of heaven was present. Everyone was to turn back to God and believe this good news. Salvation was not way off in the distant future; it had arrived. Sick people were healed. Demon-possessed people were freed. Sinners were welcomed at God's table.

JESUS ANNOUNCES HIS AGENDA

Jesus was in the local synagogue at Nazareth when he outlined his agenda. Reading from Isaiah, he spoke about good news to the poor, release to the captives, liberty for the oppressed and sight for the blind.

Jesus announced that as Isaiah predicted, God would rescue his suffering people who were humble and who sought him (Lk 4:16-20; cf. Is 61:1-2). The poor that Isaiah wrote about were the people of Israel, humiliated and broken by conquest and exile. They had returned to the ruins of Jerusalem and were waiting for salvation. The poor were the true people of God who depended on him when they were in trouble. These were the people Jesus came for, not the "healthy" who didn't need a doctor.[1]

Jesus said the blind would receive sight, and he healed the blind. But Jesus' healing ministry pointed to a more desperate need. His healing ministry demonstrated his authority to bring salvation that would open eyes and turn people from darkness to light. Jesus said those who are crushed would be liberated, and he went about freeing everyone who was oppressed by Satan (Acts 10:38). Jesus promised "release for the captives." The word *release* everywhere else in the Bible refers to the forgiveness of sin, whereas the word for *captives* normally refers to prisoners of war. So, Jesus seemed to be saying, he came to free those who were bound by sin and held captive by the prince of darkness.[2]

Jesus relied on the realities of poverty, blindness, captivity and oppression to describe people in need of salvation. Salvation was offered to all those who humbly turned to God in faith and repentance. Humility was required because salvation was impossible for the rich, for sinners, for the "righteous"—for any person. The only way to enter the kingdom of God was to become a helpless child. Entering the kingdom of God required humble acceptance of one's sinfulness, a dependent trust in Jesus alone and the abandonment of confidence in any other hope.[3] When Jesus spoke about the purpose of his mission, he said that he came to call sinners and to give his life as a ransom for many. Those who answer Jesus' call and accept the sacrifice of his life belong to the restored people of God.[4]

Jesus dramatized his message with a story of two lost sons and a waiting father. It is a story of extravagant love.[5]

TWO LOST SONS

A father had two sons. One day the younger son came to his father and demanded his inheritance immediately.

Such a thing did not happen in the Middle Eastern culture of Jesus' day. There was no law, custom or precedent that allowed a son to take his inheritance while his father was alive. This young man wanted his father's property, but not his father. He might as well have told his father to hurry up and die.

The father would have been expected to maintain his honor and answer his son's demand by beating him and driving him from the family home. But in an act of costly love, the father granted his son's request. The son sold everything and left in a hurry for a far-off land. By his actions the young man broke the relationship with his father, his brother and his community. He was lost.

Once he was away from home, the son descended into a hell of his own making. He was alone in a strange land with no friends and (soon enough) no money in a time of famine. He attached himself to a local farmer who offered him work tending pigs. He was starving and wanted to eat what the pigs were feeding on. Even if he did, it wouldn't be enough to keep him alive.

Desperate, the son decided to go home. He had a plan to save himself: he would become his father's hired servant. A hired servant was a free man who could live independently in the local village, but he was also an outsider. Such a servant got work when he was needed, but when there was no work, he was put off. The son's plan was to return home, keep his independence and work to pay his father back. This was the plan he would announce to his father.

Back home were the younger son's extended family and community, all of whom had been deeply offended by what he had done. He had insulted his father, sold his inheritance and wasted it living among Gentiles. Middle Eastern landowners lived in town and went out to their fields to work. When the son came home, he would not arrive at an isolated farm; he would walk into his village and face the community he had offended. He would not be welcomed home. Yet he must go back or he would die.

A man of distinction in this culture did not run; it was considered to be undignified. Yet when the father got his first glimpse of his son, he gathered up his robes and ran through the village like a boy. Before the whole community, the father embraced his son. This father, who had been humiliated, offered his son love and forgiveness.

The father commanded his servants to dress his son in fine clothes and to place a ring on his finger and shoes on his feet. There was to be a feast of celebration. A fatted calf—not just a sheep or a goat—was chosen. This was a rare and costly honor. The family would need over a hundred people to feast on the animal, so the whole village was invited. The son had broken their relationship, dishonored his father and squandered his inheritance, but before the son did anything to repay his father, the father welcomed him back. Forgiveness came freely to the son, though at a great price to his father.

The calf was slaughtered, cut into pieces and baked in ovens. The feast began in the early evening as the workers came in from the fields. When the first of the meat was ready, the musicians started to play. The sound of the pipes and the drum announced to the village that the food was ready. The people came to sing, to dance, to drink, to eat and to celebrate into the night.

Now comes the climax of Jesus' story. As the older son returned from the fields and heard the music, he was outraged. He refused to go in to embrace his brother, greet the guests and honor his father publicly. Instead, as the guests were arriving, he bitterly confronted his father. He reminded his father that he had served faithfully. He had always been obedient. "But when this son of yours who has squandered your property with prostitutes comes home, you kill the fattened calf for him!" (Lk 15:30).

The older son had never left home, but he was just as lost as his younger brother. He was lost, and yet he was convinced he had done nothing wrong. Like his brother, he wanted his father's possessions, not the father himself.

The two brothers were both lost to their father, but the older son was in greater danger. Like the Pharisees, he believed his good behavior gave him a claim on his father. He found it harder to face his sin and his need for the father's love and forgiveness. The story ended with the father humiliated again, this time seeking out the older son and urging him to come inside and join the celebration.

Jesus left the story open ended. We don't know if the older son relented.

Like the father in the story, Jesus demonstrated costly, forgiving love to those who were lost. He bore the cost of humiliation and forgave. His offer was for sinners who had run away to far-off lands, but he also offered forgiveness to those who considered themselves "righteous." Jesus radically redefined what it meant to be right with God. Sin is much deeper than breaking the rules. Sin is putting ourselves in the place of God as Savior, Lord and Judge.[6]

To enter the kingdom, both the "righteous" and "sinners" must become like children—totally dependent on God's mercy through Jesus. Repentance means acknowledging failure and sin, returning to God and accepting his extravagant love. Like the father in the story, Jesus forgives freely and welcomes back sinners with joy.

Jesus wanted the Pharisees to see the reality of God's mercy for sinners. He wanted them to face their own self-righteousness and receive the message of the kingdom as trusting, dependent children. If not, they would remain outside of the kingdom under the judgment of God.

TWO MEN AT PRAYER

Jesus had no time for those who approached God on the basis of their moral or spiritual superiority. Sinners are saved only because they are more ready to admit their need before God.

Jesus told a parable which was also a true story to explain what was required to enter the kingdom.[7] Two men go up to the Temple to pray; one a Pharisee, the other a tax collector. The Pharisee stood apart from other worshipers. In his own mind he was righteous, and he despised those who weren't like him. The Pharisees had a name for the unrighteous: *Am ha-aretz*—people of the land. They were defiled. To touch such a person would render the Pharisee unclean. So he stood apart.

It was customary to stand and pray quietly aloud. This Pharisee stood and prayed so he could instruct the unrighteous around him. He did not offer thanks or praise to God for his good gifts. He asked God for nothing. He prayed and in doing so paraded his righteousness. The Pharisee thanked God that he was "not like other men—thieves, swindlers, adulterers . . ." In contrast to Moses' command of a fast for the Day of Atonement (Lev 25:29; Num 39:7), this man fasted twice *every* week. Moses limited tithes to certain foods; this Pharisee tithed everything. Here was a man sure that he was acceptable to God.

He glanced around and thanked God that he was not like the nearby tax collector—a wretched and despised man. In Jesus' day, collecting taxes for the Romans or for Herod could make you a rich man; in fact, you had to be rich to even apply for the job. The right to collect taxes went to the highest bidder, who then had to recoup his costs and his profits from the people. It was a system that fed corruption and was a cruel reminder to the Jewish people of their oppression. To a Pharisee any house entered by a tax collector was defiled.

The tax collector stood apart not because he was superior but because he was unworthy to stand with God's people before the altar. A broken man, he wouldn't lift his eyes or his hands to heaven. Instead in grief he pounded his chest within which beat his heart—the source of evil. He offered nothing to God but asked everything of God—for mercy, to "make atonement" for his sin.

The Pharisee and the tax collector went up to the Temple to pray at the same time. They left at the same time. They were probably at the Temple for the morning or evening sacrifice of atonement. The tax collector returned home accepted by God. The self-deceived Pharisee returned home under even greater condemnation. The sacrifice of the lamb for the sins of the people had been made—but only the broken hearted, who trust in God's gift, are made right with God. The tax collector expected nothing of himself and everything of God.

What is required to enter the kingdom? Only God's grace and faith on the part of a sinner. Tax collectors who cast themselves on God are acceptable to God. Pharisees who pride themselves in their achievements are not.

GETTING THE WORD OUT

Jesus' stories stay with us—a father waiting anxiously for his lost son, a shepherd searching for one lost sheep, a man lying beaten on the ground while "good" people pass him by. They are memorable, and their appeal is universal. Jesus used vivid stories and unforgettable sayings to communicate his message. Those with ears to hear and eyes to see could readily understand and share them with others.

Jesus' miracles were not just individual acts of compassion; they were real life parables that revealed the truth of who he was. He gave sight to the blind and proclaimed, "I am the light of the world." He gave food to the hungry and announced, "I am the bread of life." Before he raised Lazarus from the dead, he told his sister Martha, "I am the resurrection and the life. The one who believes in me will live, even though they die" (Jn 11:25).

For those whose hearts were open, Jesus' message was simple, memorable and easily passed on. He intended that the good news of the kingdom would spread like a contagion throughout Israel from person to person, village to village, and ultimately to the whole world. The disciples were not the only ones to become his messengers. As Jesus' ministry touched the lives of people, they became the messengers to their own communities. Jesus' encounters with Zacchaeus, the Samaritan woman and the Gerasene demoniac resulted in whole communities hearing and seeing the reality of the gospel.[8]

Jesus crafted his message and its delivery so that it was readily understood, remembered and passed on to others. He trained his disciples to follow his example. He expected the newest believers to immediately begin sharing what he had taught them and what God had done for them. Everywhere Jesus went, he left behind people who had understood and experienced enough to become messengers to their community. The news about Jesus spread from person to person throughout the whole of Israel and surrounding regions, touching Jews, Samaritans and Gentiles.

By the end of his ministry, Jesus had imprinted his message on the disciples' minds and hearts. His profound but simple sayings and stories were easily transmitted as the missionary movement advanced.

4

FOLLOW ME AND
I'LL TEACH YOU

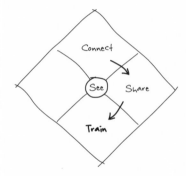

JESUS WAS TEACHING BY A LAKE, with a crowd of people pressing in around him. Nearby fishermen were cleaning their nets; they were exhausted after a night out fishing on the water without anything to show for their efforts.

To avoid the crush of the crowd, Jesus stepped into a boat owned by Simon Peter and asked him to row out from the shore so he could use the boat as a platform. Peter agreed, and while Jesus taught, Peter manned the oars to prevent the boat from drifting out of earshot of the crowd.

Peter used his boat to catch fish. Jesus used Peter's boat to fish for disciples.[1]

When the teaching was over and the crowds began to drift home, Jesus the carpenter told Peter the fisherman how to catch fish. What Jesus was asking him to do made no sense. At night the fish would come out from hiding under the rocks to feed where the freshwater streams and springs flowed into the lake. The dragnets Peter used at night in deep water were useless during the day when the fish could see and avoid them. Peter finally agreed, however, and they rowed out into deep water. Suddenly, the nets began to strain under the weight of a great catch.

Peter waved frantically for help. As the fishermen hauled in the fish, their nets began to rip, and their boats started sinking. This catch could earn Peter and his crew some good money, but Peter was no longer thinking about the fish. He was overwhelmed with wonder and fear. Peter the fisherman was caught in Jesus' net. So too were Peter's partners, James and John, the sons of Zebedee.

Jesus told them, "Don't be afraid, from now on you won't be catching fish, you'll be fishing for people." The call—a phrase unique to Jesus—was absolute and compelling. Peter, James and John left everything to follow Jesus and to learn how to fish for people.

Jesus focused his ministry on two groups of people: the disciples and the crowds. From the crowds came both opponents and disciples—those who obeyed Jesus' call to follow him.

TRAINING TO DO

Jesus taught his disciples that a genuine love for him would be shown in their obedience to what he commanded. Love and obedience are two sides of the one reality of being a disciple. He taught them what it meant to express their love in concrete acts of obedience. They did not always live up to his expectations, but they knew what discipleship looked like.

Jesus taught that the first and greatest command was to "'Love the Lord your God with all your heart and with all your soul and with all your mind.' . . . And the second is like it: 'Love your neighbor as yourself'" (Mt 22:37-40). Here are seven commands that Jesus expected his disciples to follow and to teach others to obey.[2]

1. Repent and believe the good news (Mk 1:15). Discipleship began with repentance and faith. Before Peter could fish for others, he had to learn to follow Jesus. Before Peter could respond to Jesus' call to follow him, Peter had to face his helplessness in the world he thought he controlled. Jesus stepped into his world with God's absolute authority, and Peter was unraveled. He fell at Jesus' feet and confessed his unworthiness.

Discipleship began with God's initiative. It cost nothing, and yet it cost everything. Jesus was not afraid to lose followers, and he allowed them to walk away if his teaching offended them. When a large group turned back, he asked Peter whether he also wanted to leave. Peter answered, "Lord, to whom shall we go? You have the words of eternal life. We have come to believe and to know that you are the Holy One of God" (Jn 6:68-69).

2. Baptize them in the name of the Father and of the Son and of the Holy Spirit (Mt 28:19). When Jesus submitted himself to God in baptism, he set an example he expected his disciples to follow. Baptism normally signified forgiveness and cleansing from sin, yet Jesus' baptism was unique in that he was without sin. In his baptism he identified with sinners and demonstrated his willingness to be the Suffering Servant (Is 53) who would bear their guilt.

Jesus expected and commanded his disciples to be baptized. Jesus did not baptize those who followed him, but he did teach his disciples to baptize (Jn 3:22; 4:1). In Matthew 28, Jesus' central command to make disciples is supported by two activities: baptizing and teaching new disciples to obey.

3. As I have loved you, so you must love one another (Jn 13:34). On the eve of the crucifixion, John tells us, Jesus gave his disciples a "new commandment": they were to love one another as he had loved them. Not love as an abstract principle but love as he had loved them. They had experienced Jesus' love for them. He was the model for how they should love. Jesus' love was sacrificial and involved laying down his life for his friends. Jesus' love was demanding—it would not tolerate evil. Jesus' love was forgiving. He forgave the disciples when they let him down. He forgave his enemies and taught the disciples to do the same. During his final night with his disciples, John 13 records how Jesus "loved his own who were in the world" and that "he loved them to the end." Jesus rose from the table, took off his outer garment, wrapped a towel around his waist, and began washing their feet, including those of Judas.

Jesus summed up the whole teaching of Scripture with two commands: love God with all your heart, soul, and mind, and love your neighbor as yourself. This was the example he set and what he taught his disciples to do.

4. Do this in remembrance of me (Lk 22:19-20). Jesus had shared many meals with his disciples, but his last meal with them was different. Jesus died at the time of Passover, when the Jewish people met in homes to remember how God delivered them from slavery in Egypt. So Jesus' last meal with his disciples was a Passover meal. As host, Jesus took the bread, broke it and shared it with his disciples, telling them, "This is my body given for you." He took the cup and told them, "This is my blood of the covenant, which is poured out for many." Then he instructed them, "Do this in remembrance of me." This was a clear command to continue to remember his sacrifice in the celebration of the Lord's Supper.[3]

Jesus' death as a sacrifice for sin sealed the new covenant between God and his people. The command to celebrate the Lord's Supper stands for as long as his disciples wait for his return in glory and the coming of the kingdom in fullness.

5. **Always pray and do not give up (Lk 18:1).** The disciples learned how to pray both by watching Jesus pray and by hearing him teach about prayer. Jesus repeatedly withdrew to be alone with the Father in prayer—early in the morning in a lonely place, up on the mountainside, in the desert, sometimes for a whole night. He prayed when he was under great strain. He prayed when he had important decisions to make. He prayed as he faced the prospect of crucifixion. He prayed on the cross itself.

The love of God was so real and so compelling to Jesus that when he turned to God in prayer, the cry that naturally came to his lips was *Abba,* the Aramaic word for "father." No other Jew had ever spoken of God as *Abba,* yet Jesus almost always addressed God as his father, and he taught his disciples to do the same.[4]

6. **Give, and it will be given to you (Lk 6:38).** Jesus warned that "the worries of this life, the deceitfulness of wealth and the desires for other things come in and choke the word, making it unfruitful" (Mk 4:19). Jesus challenged his disciples to find lasting treasure in heaven, not on earth. He expected his disciples, like Zacchaeus, to respond to God's generous offer of forgiveness with generosity to those in need. Jesus promised to reward those who provided for his disciples on mission. He told his disciples, "Anyone who welcomes you welcomes me, and anyone who welcomes me welcomes the one who sent me" (Mt 10:40).

7. **Go and make disciples of all nations (Mt 28:19).** The disciples accompanied Jesus to watch, learn and assist. Then he sent them out to do what they had seen him doing and to teach what they'd heard him say. The instructions he gave them were extraordinary: take nothing for the journey; go from town to town preaching the gospel, healing the sick, and casting out demons; look for the person or house of peace; and if you and your message are not received, wipe the dust off your feet and move on to the next place. They were to expect rejection and opposition. Signs of healing and deliv-

erance from Satan's power would accompany their proclamation. They were to leave their money behind and trust God to provide through people's hospitality. If they were arrested, they should trust "the Spirit of your Father" to speak through them.

HOW DID JESUS TRAIN?

Jesus taught by setting assignments: cross this stormy lake, feed these thousands of people, go out on mission, watch and pray, cast out this demon, and so on. The learning began once the disciples discovered how much they didn't know.

Jesus taught by repetition. The disciples would have heard many "Sermons on the Mount" as Jesus taught in different places. They would have known his parables by heart. Jesus taught using stories and memorable sayings. His teaching style—especially his stories and the questions he asked—encouraged self-discovery. The disciples were first century Jews, and from age five they were taught in the local synagogue to memorize large sections of the Torah. Jesus trained them to memorize and pass on his teaching, even if they did not grasp its full implications.

Jesus did not teach his disciples merely to add to their knowledge. He taught them to obey. A storm on the Sea of Galilee became the opportunity to teach them about faith. An argument about who was the greatest became a lesson in humility and leadership. A hungry crowd prompted a teaching on God's provision and the true bread of life. The depth of Jesus' relationship with the Father led the disciples to ask Jesus to teach them to pray.

Jesus taught as they traveled from place to place. He taught them in the middle of life, mission and relationships. This was not a classroom approach to learning. The focus was on obeying the truth. Jesus' teaching was profound, but it was also simple and therefore readily passed on from person to person.

The Twelve were a part of a larger group of Jesus' followers. There were the seventy disciples that Jesus also sent out on mission. There was a wider group that included Mary Magdalene, Joanna, Susanna and many other women. There were also Mary and Martha of Bethany, along with their brother Lazarus, whom Jesus raised from the dead. There is no record that they traveled with Jesus, but they opened their home to provide hospitality for Jesus.

Following Jesus began with the response of repentance and faith in Jesus. It led to a life of loving obedience to Jesus' commands. Jesus' training in discipleship took place in the midst of challenging assignments. Learning did not begin until the disciples discovered how much they didn't know. His teaching methods were easily transferred to others as the disciples were sent out on mission. Those same disciples became the nucleus of restored people of God who were sent to make disciples of all nations, baptizing them and teaching them to obey everything Jesus had commanded.

I WILL BUILD MY CHURCH

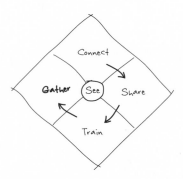

IT WAS JESUS' LAST NIGHT. Soon they would come for him. He would be arrested, tried, convicted, beaten and crucified.

Jesus planned a meal together with his closest followers. He chose the location, and he was the host who presided at the meal. He knew Judas would betray him and the others would desert him. He knew the fate that awaited him, yet he wanted to share the Passover meal with them.

As Jesus and his disciples drank the wine and ate the unleavened bread, he taught them the significance of the meal: Jesus' poured-out life and his broken body would form the basis of a new covenant between God and his people. After the meal the host became the servant, as Jesus washed the disciples' feet one by one. As he had loved them, they were to love one another. Following his death and resurrection, they would become the nucleus of the renewed people of God.

This meal was typical of Jesus' actions. Wherever Jesus went, he collected people. One of his first public acts was to gather a group of disciples to be with him. Soon others joined as members of a close-knit band of followers who had laid aside other loyalties to be with Jesus and each other.

Most of the time Jesus traveled with at least some of his followers— the twelve disciples, a larger group of around seventy, and others, including women. At Capernaum we find Jesus staying with Peter at his mother-in-law's house. In Bethany near Jerusalem he stayed with Mary, Martha and Lazarus.

The old symbols that had defined the identity of God's people—the Law, the Temple, the Sabbath, the land—no longer applied.[1] Jesus had redefined what it meant to be part of God's people. Through faith in Jesus, anyone who came to God as a child—sinners, Gentiles, outcasts—was welcome.

Jesus came for lost people, but he didn't want to just save individuals. He built communities of disciples wherever he went. Jesus could do nothing less, because God is community—Father, Son and Holy Spirit. He always intended that his disciples would become a people for God's own possession.

CAESAREA PHILIPPI

> *I will build my church, and the gates of Hades will not overcome it.*
>
> Matthew 16:18

The first time Jesus spoke about building his church, he was in Gentile territory (Mt 16:16-18). Caesarea Philippi lay twenty-five miles north of the Sea of Galilee at the foot of Mount Hermon. It was a place where Jesus and his disciples could withdraw to rest. Jesus would soon set out for Jerusalem where he would be arrested, tried and crucified. This was an opportunity for Jesus to make clear to his disciples who he was and to prepare them for his rejection and death.

Jesus expected his followers to continue meeting as a group following his death. The word in Matthew 16:16-18 that we translate as *church* could be used of any gathering of people, but in the Greek translation of the Old Testament the word was used for the people of God.[2] Jesus intended his people—his church—to be the new temple of God's presence, replacing the Temple of Jerusalem built by Herod the Great. In his final days, as Jesus drew near to the great city of Jerusalem, he wept over its rejection of the prophets and messengers God had sent.

> Jerusalem, Jerusalem, you who kill the prophets and stone those sent to you, how often I have longed to gather your children together, as a hen gathers her chicks under her wings, and you were not willing. Look, your house is left to you desolate. (Mt 23:37-38)

Through his death and resurrection Jesus would destroy and rebuild the Temple as God's dwelling place with his people. The Twelve represented the hope of a restored Israel incorporating the nations. The Gentiles would be gathered into the new people of God (Mk 14:58; Jn 2:19-21). Jesus' fellowship with his disciples pointed forward to the birth of the early church. Their fellowship did not end with his death but continued after the resurrection and the coming of the Holy Spirit. At Pentecost, Jesus' disciples formed the first church in Jerusalem.

The fruit of Jesus' ministry were communities of disciples. The kingdom is about God's rule; the church consists of those people who have come under his rule. The goal and intention of Jesus' ministry was the formation of a missionary movement that would make disciples and multiply communities of his followers throughout the world.

There would be no discipleship without community. Wherever the gospel went, new disciples would be made and new churches formed around their common faith in Jesus. The true church of Jesus Christ exists where his disciples live in relationship and together seek to follow him. There are no disciples without church and no church without disciples.

How will Jesus build his church? We'll learn more about that when we look at the book of Acts. But Jesus of Nazareth was already at work gathering disciples and teaching them what it meant to be his followers together. He taught them obedience to his commands. He taught a new way to live, based on his example—a life of love, forgiveness, generosity and service. He taught them to be witnesses in the world by proclaiming the good news of God's reign and making disciples. He taught them to pray and expect God to answer. He taught them not to fear persecution. He taught them to baptize new disciples and to celebrate the Lord's Supper. Most of all, he taught them who he was—the Savior of the world.

6

TIME TO GO

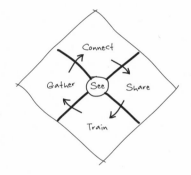

*This is what is written:
The Messiah will suffer and rise from the
dead on the third day, and repentance
for the forgiveness of sins will be
preached in his name to all nations,
beginning at Jerusalem.*

—LUKE 24:46-47

IF IT HAD BEEN LEFT TO THE DISCIPLES to take up the mission of Jesus, the movement would never have survived.

Following Jesus' trial and execution, his disciples were defeated, scattered and afraid. As far as they were concerned, when Jesus cried out, "My God, my God, why have you forsaken me?" and died, it was all over. The movement died with him.

Peter and Andrew would have rebuilt their fishing business. Matthew might have returned to collecting taxes. The others would have drifted back to their former way of life. That didn't happen. Just when the Roman and Jewish authorities were sure the crisis was over, it was upon them again in a new form. There were reports that the crucified Messiah was among his followers—alive.

The risen Lord resumed his mission in a new way. Over forty days, Jesus drew his disciples together, picked up the pieces, resumed leadership and taught them. He charged them to take the gospel from Jerusalem to the ends of the earth. He promised his presence and power through the Holy Spirit. Their mission was to continue his mission, under his leadership.

Jesus always intended that his followers would continue the movement he founded and multiply communities of disciples throughout the world. Having been called and trained, the disciples would now form the spearhead of an international missionary movement. At the heart of their mission was the proclamation of the forgiveness of sins through Jesus' death on the cross.

The death and resurrection of Jesus was the turning point in God's plan of salvation. Jesus was now revealed as Lord over all people and all nations, over heaven and earth. What was hidden during his earthly years must now be proclaimed throughout the earth. There is no person, no town or city, no nation, which does not need to hear this good news.

The Gospels and Acts each have their own account of Jesus' missionary commission. Each report is different. They all add something to the overall picture. Here are the common themes.[1]

1. **Jesus is Lord.** The starting point for the mission is the risen Lord's authority over all things, authority given to him by God the Father who is Creator and Lord. Jesus shares entirely in that complete authority over heaven and earth.

2. **Jesus sent his disciples to the ends of the earth.** They will reach people in Jerusalem and Judea and in the nations beyond with the message of salvation. They must go to people who have not heard of Jesus or his message. The disciples should tell them the good news of the salvation that Jesus has won. They must make disciples and teach them to obey what Jesus commanded. Their mission is not limited to Israel or even the Roman Empire. The boundaries of God's people's mission have been extended to include the whole world.

3. **Jesus will be with them as they go.** Jesus was leaving the disciples physically so that he could be present in a different way. Jesus did not command that they follow a particular missionary method. He promised his continued presence through the Holy Spirit who would guide and empower them. Heaven and earth will pass away, but his words will never pass away.

CONCLUSION

This chapter concludes our look at the ministry of Jesus. We have seen that Jesus began his ministry with the intention of founding a missionary movement. He chose his disciples so that one day they would continue his ministry throughout the world in the power of the Holy Spirit.

Jesus was not someone who waited for people to come to him. He took the initiative and went looking for them in most, if not all, of the towns and villages of Galilee and in Jerusalem, the major city of Judea. Jesus proclaimed the good news of God's reign to all people: the simple and the educated, the pious religious leader and the shamed prostitute, the rich man and the beggar, the condemned criminal and the expert in the law. The kingdom was like a net that caught all kinds of people.[2]

As the disciples served with Jesus for three years, he trained them to "fish for people"—to catch all kinds of people who were willing to listen to their message and put their faith in Jesus. When the disciples received Jesus' command to continue his mission, they would have assumed this meant reaching as many people as they could in the towns and villages of the regions they visited.

Jerusalem and the Temple were no longer at the center of God's plan of salvation, drawing the nations in. Jesus' death and resurrection had fulfilled the Law; now Jesus' followers must take the good news to the world beyond Jerusalem and beyond the borders of Israel. The word must travel to Damascus and to Antioch, to Athens and to Corinth, to Rome and beyond.

The disciples followed Jesus' example as they preached and healed, made disciples, and taught them to obey what Jesus had commanded. They proclaimed the gospel as the very Word of God and the only hope for the forgiveness of sins. They established communities of Jesus' disciples. Without Jesus, however, there would be no New Testament story. He was not just the inspiration of a missionary movement. He began the movement, and as the risen Lord he became the driving force behind it.

Before moving on to look at the story of the church in Acts, we'll pause to hear an account of Jesus at work through his followers today.

Church on the Porch

Jeff Sundell spent ten years of his life spreading the gospel among Tibetan Buddhists in northern India and Nepal.[1] He soon discovered that as a tall, blond American, he stood out in the politically sensitive and remote villages of the Himalaya Mountains.

There was no way Jeff could reach this people group alone. He began training local believers to make disciples and plant churches. Jeff learned to ask five questions:

- How do I enter an unreached region and connect with people?
- How do I share the gospel?
- How do I make disciples who disciple others?
- How do I form groups in the community that will reproduce?
- How do I develop and multiply local leaders?

Jeff sought out examples of the best practices from anywhere in the world where he could find a church planting movement. He then applied these lessons to his setting. He learned that a church planting movement is a work of God through his Spirit and his dynamic Word.

Jeff learned to teach new believers to obey Christ. He learned to identify leaders, not by their knowledge and gifts but by their obedience, because obedience is at the heart of any church planting movement. Local believers with little or no education faced persecution with courage and boldly declared the gospel. They learned to obey what they knew. Jeff discovered that a disciple who is obeying the little he knows is on the road to maturity.

Over the years Jeff and the leaders he trained equipped thousands of local believers to share the gospel and plant churches. Across the region tens of thousands of new disciples formed new simple churches—many of them in regions where there is official hostility toward Christianity.

In 2009 the Sundells moved back to the United States and began applying what they had learned to their new situation. They moved to an old mill town in North Carolina that had been in economic and social decline since the 1970s. Unemployment was high, and drug and alcohol abuse was a problem. With help from the police, Jeff identified the three toughest neighborhoods in their county—Henrietta, Alexander Mills and Spindale—and chose them as his mission field.

Jeff met with pastors in the wider area to cast vision and offer training to anyone who was interested. He gathered a small group of men and women on Monday mornings and began training them how to share their story and Jesus' story. Then they went out prayer-walking in one of the three neighborhoods, expecting God to lead them to persons of peace. They walked, they prayed, and they looked for opportunities to connect with people who were far from God.

These areas are known for their pit bull dogs and methamphetamine labs. As Jeff and his coworkers met people, they asked, "If God could do a miracle in your life today, what would it be?" Then they prayed for people on the spot.

Jeff recruited his mom and dad, Norm and Paula, to the team, and they began walking and praying. On their first day, Jeff's parents visited an African American neighborhood. The day didn't begin well when Jeff's "Yankee" father asked two middle-aged women, "How are you guys?" They thought he was addressing them as men and began cursing him. (A real Southerner would have asked, "How are y'all?")

Norm and Paula persisted in the conversation, however, and eventually one of the women, Ruth, asked them to pray for a severe pain in her chest. The other asked, "Just pray I'll get through the day." Jeff's parents prayed for them and promised to visit again.

A week later Jeff's parents returned and met a man named Randy sitting out on his front porch drinking even though it was only 10 a.m. Randy's porch was the place to hang out if you wanted to party. He invited them to come back to share some stories about Jesus.

Norm and Paula moved on and visited Ruth to pray for her. Word spread that they had returned, and a woman called Annie came looking for them. She'd heard there were some folks praying for people and wanted them to pray that God would provide a stove for her and her family. They prayed for her—and for a new stove. A few days later a friend of the Sundells heard about the need and donated a stove.

The next week Jeff's parents were at Annie's house enjoying the cookies she had baked on her new stove when Ruth came banging on the door. She wanted prayer. The doctor had just told her that the pain in her chest was breast cancer. They prayed for her.

Norm and Paula began a simple discovery Bible study with Randy and his drinking buddies on Randy's porch. They read stories about Jesus and asked, "What does this say about God? What does this say about people? Is there a command to obey or an example to follow?" Norm had them reading the story of the four friends who lowered the paralytic through the roof so that Jesus could heal him when Randy realized he needed to do something about Ruth's condition. Since Ruth had been diagnosed with cancer, she had missed all her medical appointments out of a combination of fear and her drinking problem.

Randy and his buddies knew this, and when they read the story of the four men who brought their friend to Jesus, they knew what they had to do. Before Ruth's next appointment, they stayed up all night to make sure she didn't get drunk. The next morning she arrived at her appointment on time.

The Bible studies on the porch continued until one day Jeff's dad got a call from Randy saying, "I believe! I believe!" Ruth also gave her life to Christ. Six weeks after his conversion, Randy told Norm, "You know I'm an alcoholic. Would you pray that I'd get healed?" Today Jeff's mom and dad have a ministry on the porch praying for people; they ask "that alcohol would taste bad in their mouths." They also pray for people to find work, and God answers.

Randy, Ruth, and other new believers in the community consider that porch as their church. The porch used to be the place where the parties happened. Now no one is allowed to drink on the porch. Instead those who are still drinking bring their bench as close to the porch as possible so they can listen in while the church meets around God's Word. Over twenty people have been baptized, and disciples are meeting in three simple neighborhood churches. One of the groups meets in a hotel room.

Jeff and his coworkers continue to prayer-walk the community. They pray for needs, share their story, share the gospel and make disciples. Discipleship can be a challenge as new believers grapple with drug and alcohol addiction and fractured relationships. Some of them are still using drugs or living together. Jeff never compromises what the Scripture teaches; he knows that making disciples takes time.

Sometime later Jeff met with Neil Perry, pastor of a growing church in nearby Forest City. After planting the church, Neil found himself preoccupied with counting "butts on seats." Over a three-hour cup of coffee, Jeff helped Neil discover how he could get back to making disciples. One of the new believers in Neil's church was Chuck, a former crack cocaine dealer who had run a prostitution ring in his basement. With Jeff's help, Neil taught Chuck to make disciples and plant churches. Now Chuck runs a simple church for his former friends and associates in the basement where he once sold cocaine and ran prostitutes. A pastor in Spindale, Andy Evans, has also connected with Jeff and is training anyone who wants to learn how to make disciples. One of the new believers is a former cocaine addict who has formed a church in a trailer park with twenty baptized new believers.

It's a long way from the Himalayas to North Carolina. Jeff has been able to adapt the principles he learned in Nepal to a very different context. He still asks himself the same five questions.

1. **How do I enter an unreached region and connect with people?** Jeff prayer-walks the community, looking for opportunities to connect and praying for needs. His purpose is to find households of peace that connect him and the gospel to relational networks.

2. **How do I share the gospel?** Jeff shares his story, and he shares Jesus' story. He offers a series of simple, discovery Bible studies called *Seven Stories of Hope*.[2] He trains new and existing believers to do the same.

3. **How do I make disciples who disciple others?** Jeff and his coworkers do not do anything their disciples cannot copy. They teach new believers to share their story and to share Jesus' story. They teach new disciples to ask, "If God can do a miracle in your life today, what would it be?" Then they ask, "Can I pray for you?" They train new disciples how to take a friend or family member through the *Seven Stories of Hope*. All they need are the stories and four simple questions: "What does this teach us about God? What does this teach us about humanity? Is there a command to obey? Is there an example to follow?" All of the learning is obedience-oriented. At the end of every study, the leaders ask, "How can you obey what you have learned today?" At the beginning of every study is the question, "How did you obey what you learned last week?"

4. **How do I form groups in the community that will reproduce?** Jeff believes that churches come from disciplemaking, not the other way around. He teaches communities of new disciples the basics of church life from the book of Acts—worship, ministry, fellowship, evangelism and missions, and discipleship.

5. **How do I develop and multiply local leaders?** Houses of peace become church communities. Multiple churches are formed simultaneously. Jeff trains existing believers and new believers to make disciples and form groups.

After two years, over 350 people are gathering in 73 groups. Over 250 people have been baptized. Jeff has identified 45 people in the network who are effective in connecting, sharing the gospel, and reproducing disciples and churches. Seventeen of them have equipped groups to reproduce between two and four generations of new groups.

Jeff's example and training is inspiring a growing number of people to apply simple church planting methods across the United States and Australia. Those he has influenced are identifying houses of peace, baptizing new disciples, and forming new neighborhood churches in their communities. In doing so they are imitating Jeff, but Jeff himself is imitating Jesus, because Jesus is the Lord of a missionary movement that Jeff and his friends have joined.

PART TWO

What Jesus
Continued to Do

THE TWELVE AND THE EARLY CHURCH

7

ACTS OF THE RISEN LORD

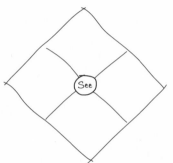

When we consider the rise of Christianity there really is only one question: How was it done? How did an obscure messianic movement on the fringe of the Roman Empire dislodge classical paganism and become the dominant faith of Western civilization?

—RODNEY STARK,
*THE RISE OF
CHRISTIANITY*

ACTS IS THE ONE NEW TESTAMENT DOCUMENT dedicated to telling the story of the rise of the Christian movement. From beginning to end, Acts has one major theme—the missionary expansion of the movement Jesus founded. The Gospel of Luke and the book of Acts show us that it is God himself who leads, directs, energizes and carries out his plan of salvation. God moves the mission forward and connects all the elements of the story. The spread of God's Word is the decisive factor in the advance of God's mission as the message of salvation moves from Jewish to Samaritan to Gentile audiences.

The Gospel of Luke and Luke's book of Acts are two parts of the one history of Jesus Christ. The Gospel of Luke tells the story of what Jesus *began* to do and teach. Acts tells the story of what Jesus *continued* to do through his disciples, by the power of the Holy Spirit.

PENTECOSTAL POWER

Without the coming of the Spirit there would be no prophecy, no preaching,
no mission, no conversions, no worldwide Christian movement.

Ben Witherington,
The Acts of the Apostles: A Socio-Rhetorical Commentary

It was early in the morning of the fiftieth day since the Passover. One hundred twenty people were gathered in the upper room of a large house when the Holy Spirit came with a sound like the blowing of a violent wind from heaven. Tongues of fire came and rested on each one. These disciples were filled with the Holy Spirit, and they began declaring the wonders of God in languages they had never learned.

The disciples' joyful and unrestrained worship attracted a crowd of foreign Jews who were attending the feast. These Diaspora Jews were the descendants of those who had been driven into exile when Jerusalem fell to Babylon in 586 B.C. They were from the regions of Mesopotamia, Asia Minor, Egypt, North Africa, Italy, Crete and Arabia. Some were pilgrims visiting Jerusalem for the feast; they would eventually return home. Others lived permanently in Jerusalem. Together they represented the whole Jewish world. They were surprised to hear these Galileans, who normally spoke a dialect of Aramaic, speaking in languages they could understand.

Peter reassured the crowd that the disciples were not drunk. He told them that the Holy Spirit had been poured out, as promised by the prophets. The last days had begun. God was restoring his people. He had established a new covenant. Peter called Israel to repent or face God's judgment. He told them that anyone who called on the name of the Lord Jesus would be saved. Jesus' death had atoned for sins. Now risen and exalted to the right hand of God, the Lord Jesus poured out his Holy Spirit.

The response to Peter's message was staggering. Three thousand believed and were baptized, possibly in the pool of Siloam. Eventually the pilgrims returned to their distant homes to proclaim the good news of Jesus the Messiah. They were the first fruits of the gospel going out from Jerusalem to the world. Those new believers who lived in Jerusalem were added to the 120 Galileans, and the church in Jerusalem was born.

These events reveal that the church is God's creation. Without the coming of the Holy Spirit, there could be no worldwide mission. Every attempt to explain the rise of the Christian movement from purely natural causes breaks down. The exalted Lord Jesus poured out his Spirit on his people as a foretaste of their final salvation. The Holy Spirit descended, and the mission began.

Through the Holy Spirit, Jesus was present with his people in a new way. Jesus' resurrection and the coming of the Spirit transformed the disciples from a group of bewildered individuals into a missionary movement.

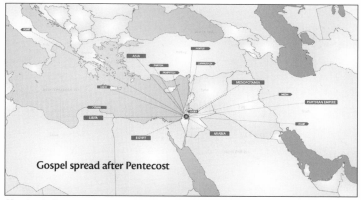

Gospel spread after Pentecost

Map 7.1. At Pentecost there were Parthians, Medes and Elamites; residents of Mesopotamia, Judea and Cappadocia, Pontus and Asia, Phrygia and Pamphylia, Egypt and the parts of Libya near Cyrene; visitors from Rome (both Jews and converts to Judaism); Cretans and Arabs (Acts 2:9-11).

Luke describes the mission of the Christian movement as a work of the Holy Spirit. Peter, filled with the Spirit, boldly declared the gospel before the same people who crucified Jesus (Acts 4:7-13). The Spirit filled the perse-cuted believers as they prayed, and they spoke the Word of God with boldness (Acts 4:31-32). As needed, the young church chose leaders who were filled with the Holy Spirit. One of them, Stephen, by the power of the Holy Spirit courageously faced a violent death (Acts 7:55). Philip took the gospel to the Samaritans, and God poured out his Holy Spirit on them (Acts 8:14-17). The Holy Spirit guided Philip to an Ethiopian who became one of the first Gentile believers. Luke explained the spread of the gospel into new regions by pointing to the activity of the Holy Spirit (Acts 9:31).

In Acts, the Holy Spirit brings the blessings of a relationship with God to those who put their faith in Christ. The Spirit works through those who have put their faith in Christ, enabling them to make disciples and form believing communities. The Spirit initiates breakthroughs and new phases in the mission. The Spirit empowers Jesus' followers to witness, and new churches rise out of their witness.

THE UNSTOPPABLE WORD

As Acts unfolds, Luke provides reports on the spread of God's dynamic Word. In Scripture the Word of God is a powerful, living force through which he achieves his purpose (Is 55:10-13).[1] Luke reports that the Word spreads, increases, multiplies and grows in power, producing new disciples and new churches. The Word of God travels to the ends of the earth, conquering the world in the process.

The apostles and other believers are threatened, beaten, jailed, even executed. Despite these things, the Word of God continues to advance. Wherever the Word goes, the world is turned "upside down" (Acts 17:6). Households believe. Thousands are converted. Cities are in uproar. Vast regions are reached. Communities of disciples are formed.

Table 7.1. Acts is structured around a series of reports that describe the unstoppable progress of the Word.

Acts	Progress Reports
6:7	So the word of God spread. The number of disciples in Jerusalem increased rapidly (ESV "multiplied greatly"), and a large number of priests became obedient to the faith.
9:31	Then the church throughout Judea, Galilee and Samaria enjoyed a time of peace and was strengthened. Living in the fear of the Lord and encouraged by the Holy Spirit, it increased in numbers (ESV "it multiplied").
12:24	But the word of God continued to spread and flourish (ESV "increased and multiplied").
16:5	So the churches were strengthened in the faith and grew daily in numbers.
19:20	In this way the word of the Lord spread widely and grew in power.
28:30-31	For two whole years Paul stayed there in his own rented house and welcomed all who came to see him. He proclaimed the kingdom of God and taught about the Lord Jesus Christ—with all boldness and without hindrance!

At the end of Acts, Luke describes Paul, in custody in Rome but unhindered as he proclaims the gospel of the kingdom (Acts 28:30-31). This open ending shows that the Word will continue to progress. The book of Acts ends, but the missionary expansion does not. Luke doesn't tell us what happened to Paul, but he leaves us in no doubt that despite the obstacles and the suffering, the Word will continue to grow, spread and multiply. The Word will prevail. God will do it.

HOW DID THEY DO IT?

Following the crucifixion, the disciples had no vision. All their dreams were shattered. All their hopes dashed. The risen Lord stepped into their midst and revealed his victory over sin, death and Satan. He gathered this band of dispirited followers and commanded them to fulfill a task they could not achieve without his presence and power. They saw the end because they saw the risen Lord.

Their contribution to God's mission began with a fresh determination to obey Christ's command and a dependence on his Spirit and his Word. There were no existing models for an international missionary movement. They would have to learn as they went.

The fulfillment of Jesus' commission required travel. For journeys on land, the disciples could use camels, donkeys, mules, horses or carts. Most of the time the missionaries would have traveled by foot, twelve to twenty miles a day.[2]

On the road the disciples would have encountered government officials, marching soldiers, merchants, couriers, pilgrims, philosophers, poets and entertainers. Accommodation in run-down inns along the way was unclean and crowded. The disciples who came from devout homes would have had a solid basic education, gained at home and in the local synagogue school. Language would not be a problem in the eastern half of the Empire if they spoke Greek. Matthew-Levi, the former tax collector, would have been fluent in Greek. Peter, Andrew, and Philip came from Bethsaida, close to the Gentile city of Julias. They probably spoke Greek.[3]

Natural entry points in unreached regions were the Jewish communities and synagogues throughout Israel and in most cities of the Empire. The disciples could also meet Gentile God-fearers at the synagogue. These Gentiles proved to be some of the most responsive people and the bridge to the wider pagan or polytheistic Gentile community.

What the disciples had learned on mission with Jesus could be adapted in new situations among the Samaritans and even among Gentiles. The first new believers could become the bridge by which the gospel spread to family, friends and neighbors. The communities they formed became places where others could be drawn in by the life, worship and teaching of the group as the missionary moved on to new locations.

As they pursued their mission, the disciples learned through experience. They learned that in cities like Jerusalem there were many people who were responsive to their message. Eventually, they learned that even Roman military officers with their family and friends could be converted. They learned that persecution could lead to a greater spread of the gospel. They learned about the importance of meeting with God in power through prayer. Most of all, the disciples learned that they could not manufacture the success of their mission. They knew they were totally dependent on God, through the Holy Spirit, to convince people of the truth of the message of salvation through Jesus, the crucified and risen Messiah.

8

MISSIONARIES
WITHOUT BORDERS

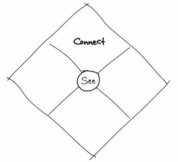

*The suffering and even death of disciples, like
their Master, doesn't lead to the squelching
of the Jesus movement, it leads to
its success and expansion.*

—BEN WITHERINGTON,
*THE ACTS OF THE APOSTLES:
A SOCIO-RHETORICAL
COMMENTARY*

PENTECOST MARKED THE BEGINNING of the mission to make disciples
and establish communities of believers in Jerusalem, Judea, Samaria, and
throughout the inhabited world.

The crowd that day was made up not only of locals from Jerusalem but
also Jews and Jewish converts who were Parthians, Medes, and Elamites.
In addition, there were residents of Mesopotamia, Judea, Cappadocia,
Pontus, Asia, Phrygia, and Pamphylia; Egyptians, Libyans, Romans,
Cretans, and Arabs also were represented. Many new believers returned to
their homes and families and took with them their newfound faith in the
Messiah Jesus. In this way, churches in cities such as Rome were founded
soon after Pentecost without any evidence of apostolic involvement.

Meanwhile in Jerusalem, the religious authorities tried to contain the growth of the Christian movement with threats, beatings and imprisonments. The gospel spread from person to person and through the preaching and healing ministry of the apostles. Soon the number had grown to over five thousand, and the movement was spreading from Jerusalem to the cities and villages of Judea, Galilee and Samaria.

OUT OF JERUSALEM

In the early chapters of Acts, Jerusalem was still at the center of the movement. In the next phase (Acts 6–12), the mission moves into Samaria and the coastal region of Judea, around the cities of Gaza, Azotus, Lydda, Joppa, and Caesarea. The Word spread beyond the borders of Israel to Ethiopia, Phoenicia, Cyprus, Tarsus, and the Syrian cities of Antioch and Damascus.

These advances came as the result of persecution, not careful planning. Earlier there had been clashes with the Jerusalem authorities over the apostles' preaching and healing ministry. The death of Stephen by stoning in A.D. 31/32 was the signal to the religious leaders for a more coordinated crackdown. Saul of Tarsus led the attack.

The believers in Jerusalem were scattered to other regions. The apostles, however, remained in Jerusalem; possibly they were not targeted due to their popularity with the people. Perhaps the persecution was only directed at Greek-speaking Jewish Christians such as Stephen and Philip. The vast majority of Jews lived outside the Holy Land in what was known as the Diaspora. They were Hellenists—they spoke Greek and had been influenced by Greek culture.[1] Thousands of Diaspora Jews returned every year to Jerusalem on pilgrimages. Many remained permanently and set up their own synagogues (Acts 6:9). Barnabas, Stephen, Philip and Saul/Paul were Diaspora Jews who lived in Jerusalem. It is no coincidence that these men led the way in taking the gospel to the nations.

At his trial, Stephen explained that Jesus' atoning death brought an end to the central role of the Temple and its system of sacrifices for sin. Righteousness and holiness could only be attained through Christ. The Jewish Law and the Temple had found their fulfillment in Jesus. God had opened the door for the Gentiles to approach him directly through Christ.

Stephen was executed before he could take the gospel beyond the borders of Israel, but his death opened the door for others. What Saul and others intended for the destruction of the church resulted in the spread of the gospel into unreached regions. Philip led the way in taking the gospel first to the Samaritans, then to an Ethiopian, and then to the Gentile cities on the Mediterranean coast.

Map 8.1. Even before Paul came on the scene, God was at work unsettling the believers in Jerusalem and sending them out to reach both Jews and Gentiles with the gospel.

PHILIP ON THE FRINGE

Philip fled Jerusalem and went to Samaria, a journey of two or three days. This was not a mission planned or sanctioned by the apostles, yet God was at work to launch a mission into an unreached field.

The Samaritans lived in what was once the northern kingdom of Israel. The Assyrians invaded the north in 722 B.C. Thousands of Jews went into exile in various parts of the Assyrian Empire. The rest remained and inter-married with the pagan Assyrians. Their descendants became the Samaritans. They established their own temple on Mount Gerizim; they also accepted the first five books of the Old Testament and looked for the coming of a Messiah who would be a prophet like Moses. The Jews regarded the Samaritans as heretics and half-breeds.

Philip proclaimed Jesus as the Messiah with great success in a city of Samaritans. Like Jesus, Philip spoke with authority, cast out demons and performed works of power. A great number of people believed and were baptized. The apostles in Jerusalem sent Peter and John to investigate. When John (who earlier wanted to call down fire from heaven on a Samaritan village that rejected Jesus) arrived with Peter, they prayed for the converts to receive the Holy Spirit. They also dealt with Simon the magician, whose new faith in Christ was motivated by greed and the desire for spiritual power. After a short time, Peter and John returned to Jerusalem, preaching the gospel in many Samaritan villages along the way.

The Holy Spirit then led Philip to go down to the desert road between Jerusalem and Gaza. He met an Ethiopian returning home from Jerusalem. This royal official was the treasurer of Queen Candace and had a deep attachment to the Jewish faith. He had traveled to Jerusalem as a pilgrim, and he owned a scroll of Isaiah, probably in Greek. As a castrated male, he could not become a full convert to Judaism despite his deep devotion (Deut 23:1). Yet Isaiah had prophesied that one day even eunuchs would join the assembly of God's people (Is 56:3-5). That day had come.

When Philip arrived on the scene, the Ethiopian was reading Isaiah 53, about the Servant of the Lord who suffered and was rejected yet was vindicated by God. Philip explained that through the Servant's suffering, outcasts like this eunuch could be included among God's people. On the desert road, the first black African to put his faith in Christ was baptized and welcomed into the community of God's people. The Ethiopian continued on his way home to tell his friends and family what God had done for him through Christ.

The Holy Spirit snatched Philip away to Azotus where he continued to preach in the Greek settlements along the coast to Caesarea. We can assume that in each place Philip began by connecting with the local Jewish population and through them to the Gentiles who, like the Ethiopian, had been attracted to the God of Israel.

Philip's unplanned missions demonstrated how God ensured that the gospel spread to those on the fringes of Judaism. There was still no mission to pagan Gentiles, but that was about to change. Again, it is the Lord who led the way.

Philip and Peter established churches in the Gentile cities of the coastal plain to the west of Judea and Samaria—in Lydda, Joppa, Caesarea, Ptolemais and maybe Ashdod. Luke reported that the churches in Judea, Galilee and Samaria were strengthened and encouraged by the Holy Spirit and were growing in numbers and living in the fear of the Lord (Acts 9:31).

ANTIOCH BREAKTHROUGH

Philip was one of many Jerusalem believers scattered by persecution in A.D. 31/32. There were other Greek-speaking Jewish Christians forced out of Jerusalem. They evangelized among the Jewish communities on Cyprus and in some Phoenician cities. Some fled to Antioch in Syria where the next breakthrough occurred.

After Rome and Alexandria, Antioch was the third most important city of the Roman Empire. It had a population of 500,000 people and included a well-established Jewish community. In Antioch the refugee believers continued the mission among Jews. Then some disciples from Cyprus and Cyrene began sharing with Greek-speaking Gentiles. Luke doesn't tell us the names of these missionaries. They probably began by sharing the message of Jesus in the synagogues of Antioch with Jews and Gentiles. Soon the gospel was spreading from these Gentiles to their pagan relatives and friends. The gospel was going beyond the synagogue. Immediately it met with success. God was with them, "and a great number of people believed and turned to the Lord" (Acts 11:21).

The church in Jerusalem sent Barnabas up to Antioch—not to control what was happening but to add momentum to it. Many more people were added to the Lord.

PETER'S CONVERSION

Meanwhile, Peter was traveling further and further away from Jerusalem into Gentile territory. One of the cities he visited was Joppa where "many believed in the Lord" (Acts 9:32-43). In the coastal city of Caesarea, the angel of God appeared in a vision to a Roman military commander named Cornelius.

Caesarea was a fitting location for a major shift in the mission of the early church. After Jerusalem, Caesarea Maritima on the Mediterranean coast was the second most important city in Palestine. It was the center of Roman military and commercial power. Built by Herod the Great to honor Caesar Augustus, it was the headquarters of the Roman governors such as Pontius Pilate, Antonius Felix and Porcius Festus. Caesarea was a pagan city.

Cornelius was a centurion, a commander of eighty men. He was a man of status and rank who earned sixteen times the pay of a regular soldier.[2] Cornelius and his family were devout people who feared God, gave generously to the poor and prayed continually. He was greatly respected in the Jewish community. Like the Ethiopian official, Cornelius was on the fringe of Judaism. He was one of the many Gentiles who rejected pagan gods and were drawn to the faith of Israel in the one true God.

In Cornelius's vision, the angel told him to send for Peter. Meanwhile, Peter went up to the rooftop to pray and fell into a trance, where he saw something like a great sheet lowered down from heaven. In it there were all kinds of animals that were ritually unclean for a Jew. The Lord commanded Peter to kill and eat, but he refused. This was not the first or the only time that Peter had talked back to Jesus. This is also not the first or only time that Jesus pushed at the barriers that excluded people from the kingdom.

The vision was repeated three times, and each time Peter refused to eat. Finally, the Spirit told Peter to get up and go with the men who were about to arrive. The next day Peter traveled with them to Cornelius's house. When he arrived at Caesarea, he found Cornelius waiting for him with a house full of his relatives, servants and close friends. The group probably also included his military and business associates; in the culture of the day they could all be included in his extended "household" or *oikos* in Greek.[3]

In Caesarea Peter realized that his vision was not just about food; it was about people! Peter shared the good news about Jesus with Cornelius and his household. He told them of Jesus' ministry, his death and resurrection. Peter declared that God had appointed Jesus to be the judge of the living and the dead. Finally, he assured them that everyone who believes in Jesus would receive forgiveness of sins.

Before Peter had time to finish his message, the Holy Spirit fell on all those listening, and they began speaking in tongues and praising God. The Jewish believers who came with Peter were amazed that the Gentiles had received the Holy Spirit just as the Jewish disciples had at Pentecost. At Pentecost Peter had announced that everyone who calls on the name of the Lord would be saved. Now Peter understood the implications of his own preaching. God shows no partiality, and he welcomes people from every nation.

Peter was not the mastermind of the Gentile mission. He was a reluctant missionary to the Gentiles. This breakthrough was not an initiative of Peter, or any of the Twelve, or of the church in Jerusalem. It was not the result of a carefully coordinated plan. God himself was responsible for the conversion of Cornelius and his household. God had determined that the Gentiles would be included in his people. They were welcome not because they were ritually pure but because of their faith in Christ as evidenced by the presence of the Holy Spirit in their lives.

At Pentecost the Holy Spirit was poured out on the first Jewish believers. The Samaritans had also received the Holy Spirit with power. Now the Gentiles had received the same Holy Spirit. God was gathering his people from all the nations of the world.

Just as God had accepted these Gentiles, Peter recognized that he must accept them into the church. He commanded them to be baptized in the name of Jesus. A few days later Peter returned to Jerusalem, leaving behind a new community of disciples that probably continued to meet in the home of Cornelius.

The example of Cornelius showed that although there were many Gentiles in Palestine who could have been the focus of missionary outreach, no deliberate attempt had yet been made by the leaders of the Christian movement to reach them. The Lord intervened. He prepared Cornelius; he overcame Peter's objections. He sent the Holy Spirit upon the Gentiles with visible signs to confirm the reality of their salvation without submitting to the Mosaic Law. Through Cornelius, a person of peace, the gospel spread to his family, servants, friends and colleagues.

NOT WHAT YOU KNOW BUT WHO YOU KNOW

For the Christian movement to spread into unreached fields, believers had to travel. Some traveled intentionally as missionaries. Others traveled for business or family reasons. God also used persecution to move believers from Jerusalem to the wider world.

How did these early followers of Jesus connect with people in a new location? We know that God led Philip to the Ethiopian and led Peter to Cornelius. They were people God had already prepared. They were responsive. Peter was an outsider, but Cornelius was a respected insider, so the gospel spread quickly.

It's reasonable to assume the same dynamic was at work when the new believers at Pentecost and the Ethiopian official returned to their homes in distant lands. When the believers who fled the persecution in Jerusalem arrived in Cyprus or one of the Phoenician cities, they would have initially made contact with members of the local Jewish community. They may have done so through personal or family relationships. Through those ties, the gospel would spread into the local Jewish community and to the Gentiles connected with it. In Antioch it went even further, and pagan Gentiles were converted.

When they arrived in a new location, *outsiders* such as Philip and Peter relied on responsive insiders to spread the faith into their community. Philip did not settle in Samaria. Peter stayed just a few days with Cornelius. They shared the gospel widely. They found responsive people. They provided them with basic instruction and trusted them to carry on the ministry. They returned at later times to strengthen and encourage the new churches.

LEARNING ON THE JOB

The methods of the early church were surprisingly haphazard. Jesus' commission to the disciples was clear, but there were no instructions on exactly how the task was to be completed. Other than the example of Jesus, there were no precedents for what they were trying to achieve. The followers of Jesus had to learn on the job.

The gospel moved out in ever widening geographic circles from Jerusalem. As it did, it reached people further and further from the heart of Judaism.

Here are just some of the lessons these early missionaries learned.

1. **God took the initiative.** The missionary expansion of the Christian movement was not a natural process. There was nothing inevitable about it. Without exception, every major advance and every new breakthrough resulted from God's intervention.

The twelve apostles were active participants in the spread of the gospel. What is surprising is their lack of central control of the mission. It was Philip and some unnamed believers who led the way in crossing cultural and geographic boundaries. The apostles did not send them out. The church in Jerusalem didn't plan these missions. The mission came to them when they were unexpectedly driven out of Jerusalem by persecution. God challenged the attitudes of Peter and the church in Jerusalem so that they could embrace the believing Gentiles as full members of the people of God.

2. **God worked through his people.** Many Diaspora Jews converted at Pentecost returned home and took the gospel with them. The message about Jesus filled Jerusalem, and thousands were added to the church.

Unnamed believers fleeing persecution took the gospel to Judea, Galilee, Samaria, Caesarea and other towns on the southern coast, Cyprus, Phoenicia, and Antioch.

God worked through the apostles, church leaders and ordinary believers. We hear the stories of Peter and Paul, but we also read of Philip, Barnabas, Apollos, Priscilla and Aquila, Tabitha, and Lydia. The Holy Spirit worked through a variety of people.

3. God prepared persons of peace. Jesus had trained his disciples to enter a new town looking for a "person of peace"—someone who would welcome the messenger and the message into their community. In Acts, there are many examples of the gospel spreading through relationship ties: Cornelius, Simon the tanner, the merchant Lydia in Philippi, the Philippian jailer and Crispus the ruler of the synagogue in Corinth.[4] God had prepared these people to be bridges into their communities.

4. God moved them on. There was an urgency about the early Christian movement. Many new believers at Pentecost returned to distant lands where they shared their faith and formed communities of disciples. God scattered the believers in Jerusalem, and they took the gospel with them to the Samaritans, to the Jewish Diaspora, and eventually to the Gentiles.

Whenever the disciples settled down, God unsettled them. Despite the success of the Samaritan mission, Philip, Peter and John did not stay to shepherd the new believers. They kept moving, just as Jesus had done. After their initial instruction, they left new believers behind who formed new communities of disciples and took responsibility to reach their region in depth. The person most likely to be the leader of the new church gathered in Cornelius's home was not Peter but Cornelius.

5. God used unqualified, inexperienced, under-resourced people. Think about what this missionary movement didn't have. Funding was limited. There was no central organizational structure. There was no professional priesthood. No schools for training missionaries. Galileans were not well thought of throughout the rest of Israel. Jews were cultural outsiders in the dominant Greco-Roman culture. The political and religious powers of the day were against the disciples. There were no historical precedents for what they were trying to achieve.

The disciples only had Jesus' example, his teaching, the message of his death and resurrection, his authority, and the power of the Holy Spirit. Otherwise, they had very little to aid them in their mission.

The unifying thread that ties together the advance of the gospel from Jerusalem to the world is the work of God. Every advance is the result of his initiative. There are human factors, but these are secondary causes. The Word advances despite the failures of the disciples, despite the violent opposition, despite the reluctance from within the church to include the Gentiles. Nothing can stand in the way of the gospel's advance. Jesus still leads the way.

EYEWITNESS NEWS

*The gospel of the kingdom as we find it in Acts is the
announcement of forgiveness and the gift of the
Spirit that flow necessarily from the throne
of the crucified and risen Savior-King.*

—CHRIS GREEN,
GOD'S POWER TO SAVE

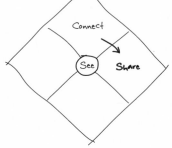

CLEOPAS AND HIS FRIEND SET OUT on the two- to three-hour journey from Jerusalem to Emmaus. It was three days after Jesus' crucifixion. These two disciples were struggling to understand the news that morning that Jesus' tomb was empty.

Along the way a stranger joined them. He appeared to know nothing about these events. Cleopas and the other disciple shared their confusion with him. They may have expected sympathy. Instead the man rebuked them for their unbelief and gave them a Scripture lesson, explaining how Moses and the prophets predicted the Messiah would suffer before entering his glory.

At Emmaus the stranger agreed to share a meal with them. As he broke the bread for the meal, their eyes were opened, and they recognized the resurrected Lord. He vanished. They ran back to Jerusalem to tell the others that Jesus was alive. As they spoke, Jesus appeared to the group. He told them the Scriptures had been fulfilled that the Messiah must suffer and rise from the dead on the third day. Repentance for the forgiveness of sins must be proclaimed to the world, beginning in Jerusalem. But first they were to wait in Jerusalem for the Holy Spirit to clothe them with power.

There were many encounters like this in the days after the resurrection. As far as we know, during that time Jesus didn't heal anyone. He didn't cast out any demons. He didn't dispute with the Pharisees. There was no mission to Jerusalem or to the towns and villages of rural Palestine. Instead, Jesus prepared his disciples for their mission.

Over forty days he taught the disciples that he was the promised Messiah, that he died on the cross for the sins of the world, that he was raised from the dead on the third day, that he was exalted at the right hand of God, and that he would return to establish God's victory in a final and visible way. Meanwhile, salvation from God's judgment could only be found by confessing faith in him (Acts 4:12).[1] Jesus made sure his disciples were clear on their message, their mission and their need for the power of the Holy Spirit.

Notice how powerless and defeated these disciples were. The gospel did not originate with them. Between the resurrection and the ascension, Jesus had to remind his disciples of their mission and their message. He promised them his presence and power through the Holy Spirit. He called broken, sinful, defeated followers to trust in him and to follow him in obedience.

WHOSE GOSPEL?

When Peter rose to speak on the day of Pentecost, he did not preach *his* gospel. He spoke for the Twelve and for the 120 disciples gathered in the upper room, but it wasn't *their* gospel either.

Jesus had spent three years teaching and training his disciples. They knew him, and they knew his message and the significance of his death and resurrection. Risen from the dead, he had spent forty days with them explaining from the Old Testament about the suffering and victory of the Messiah. He taught them about the gospel of the kingdom and how they must proclaim it throughout the world in the power of the Spirit.

When Peter stood at Pentecost, filled with the Holy Spirit, this Galilean fisherman from Capernaum proclaimed the gospel of Jesus Christ. From his Pentecost message and other messages in Acts, we can identify the major themes of the gospel proclaimed by the early Christian movement:

- Jesus is the promised Messiah sent by the God of Israel.

- Salvation has come through the life, death and resurrection of Jesus.

- Jesus has been exalted to the right hand of God as the head of a restored Israel.

- He is now present among his people through the Holy Spirit.

- Jesus will return in glory to judge the world and restore all things.

- God commands everyone to repent and to put their trust in Jesus, to receive forgiveness of sins, be baptized and receive the gift of the Holy Spirit, and eternal salvation.[2]

The proclamation of the early church reveals a consistent message about the person and work of Jesus. That one gospel was adapted for different audiences and contexts.

The heart of the disciples' faith is the story of the life, death and resurrection of Jesus who now sends the Holy Spirit. The speeches in Acts to Jews and to Gentiles reveal a belief in one God and Creator of the world who is Lord over all and who will one day judge the world. Jesus, who offers forgiveness of sins today, is the one who will be our judge on the last day. Everyone must repent and believe the gospel no matter what their religious background.[3]

Jesus commands both Jews and Gentiles to return to the living God. The Jews must return to Yahweh, who has revealed himself in Jesus the Messiah. The Gentiles must turn to the only true God, whose revelation in Jesus Christ, the Savior, provides the only possibility to receive forgiveness for sins.

Jesus was the source and originator of this one gospel. In the first decades of the early church, before the Gospel accounts were written down, the teaching and stories about Jesus spread by word of mouth. People learned about Jesus through the preaching and teaching of the apostles; they memorized the message and passed it on to others. This took place under the supervision of the eyewitnesses of the ministry of Jesus. First among the eyewitnesses were the apostles appointed by Jesus. They were chosen to witness his deeds and master his teaching. After the resurrection they passed on the tradition they had received from Jesus. They became the authoritative witnesses to the gospel.[4]

The apostles' teaching became the foundation of the Christian movement, but the gospel's origin and power to save lay with Jesus. The gospel was something the early church received from the Lord.

THE LOST KINGDOM?

The kingdom of God was the central theme of Jesus' ministry, yet the book of Acts appears to neglect it. The term *kingdom* occurs forty-two times in Luke's Gospel but only eight times in Acts. How could such an important theme of Jesus' message almost vanish?

The references to the kingdom of God in Acts are few, but they are significant. Acts opens with Jesus teaching his disciples about the kingdom (Acts 1:3) and closes with Paul under house arrest in Rome boldly proclaiming the kingdom of God from morning to evening (Acts 28:17-31). For Luke, the story of the spread of the Christian movement demonstrates the reality of the kingdom.

When Philip went down to Samaria to proclaim Christ, heal the sick, cast out demons and baptize new believers, Luke tells us he preached the good news of the kingdom. When Paul and Barnabas returned to strengthen the disciples they had made and the churches they had planted, they reminded the believers that they must go through many hardships to enter the kingdom of God. In Ephesus, Paul entered the synagogue and for three months spoke boldly about the kingdom of God. In his farewell speech on the beach at Miletus, Paul reminded the Ephesian elders how he had gone among them preaching the kingdom and thus proclaiming the whole will of God.[5]

In Acts, kingdom ministry is expressed in pioneer evangelism, making disciples, and planting and strengthening churches. The kingdom will come in its fullness at the end of time. Meanwhile, disciples must persevere through many hardships (Acts 14:22). Right now the reality of the kingdom can be experienced through a life of discipleship in community that begins with repentance and faith in Jesus. The proclamation of the kingdom has become the proclamation of the King whose life, death and resurrection mark the beginning of God's victory. Jesus is the active ruler over his kingdom.

The gospel of the kingdom in Acts is the announcement of the forgiveness of sin and the gift of the Spirit, both of which flow from the throne of the crucified and victorious Savior-King. The building and equipping of his church is exactly what Jesus' kingly rule is designed to produce. The gospel of the kingdom is not an alternative to the gospel of Christ crucified for our sin. Jesus came to announce the reign of God and to perform the decisive act through which God will bring in his reign. Talking about the kingdom of God requires us to talk about the cross, the resurrection and the coming of the Holy Spirit.

The disciples continued to proclaim the good news of the kingdom, but the emphasis shifted from the kingdom to the King who brings forgiveness of sins and the gift of the Spirit. Wherever people respond to the Word and to the name of Jesus in faith, the power of the kingdom is at work.[6]

PERSECUTION AND POWER

Jesus promised his disciples three things—that they would be
completely fearless, absurdly happy and in constant trouble.
William Maltby, quoted in William Barclay, *The Gospel of Luke*

There is a repeated pattern in Acts—the combination of signs and wonders, and the preaching of the gospel that results in new believers and new communities despite persecution.[7] In Acts Luke is showing us what life is like between the coming of the kingdom in Jesus and the coming of the kingdom in fullness at the end of the age. God's people experience the blessing of his victory: forgiveness, eternal life, the Holy Spirit, signs of God's power. They also face persecution and suffering, because God's complete rule over all things awaits Jesus' return in glory.

Shortly after Pentecost, Peter and John came across a crippled beggar as they approached the Temple. They healed him by the power of Jesus. Some people were amazed, and others were infuriated. The authorities had Peter and John arrested and beaten and warned them not to speak about Jesus. They refused.

The disciples in Jerusalem responded with prayer. They were no match for their powerful opponents, yet they didn't pray for safety. They prayed that they would continue to speak the Word with great boldness and power. They prayed that God would stretch out his hand to heal and perform signs and wonders in the name of Jesus. "After they prayed, the place where they were meeting was shaken. And they were all filled with the Holy Spirit and spoke the word of God boldly" (Acts 4:31). Boldness came as the fruit of being filled with the Holy Spirit.

A distinguishing feature of the early disciples' mission was their courage and boldness in the face of persecution. They boldly proclaimed the gospel, and they warned their hearers of the judgment of God. They spoke openly and publicly. Their boldness did not come naturally. It was a work of God that was as much a miracle as the healing of a crippled beggar.

There was a close connection between the advance of the gospel and demonstrations of God's power, but it was the message about Jesus that brought people to faith.[8] Through the miraculous, God became the most important actor in Acts. This is why the Word of God advanced as it did. When the gospel encountered obstacles, God overcame them. This was true even when his messengers faced danger, persecution and death. The gospel can spread through martyrdom or miracle.[9]

ORDINARY PEOPLE

At Pentecost, Peter quoted Joel's prophecy: "In the last days, God says, I will pour out my Spirit on all people. Your sons and daughters will prophesy, your young men will see visions, your old men will dream dreams" (Acts 2:17). He announced to Israel that the Messiah had come; now all of God's people were empowered by the Holy Spirit to proclaim salvation through Jesus Christ.

As the story of Acts unfolds, we see that ordinary people were key players in the spread of the gospel. Through them the good news spread to their families, friends and neighbors. There is no evidence that the gospel first came to Rome through the apostles. It's more likely that Roman Jews who were converted at Pentecost in A.D. 30 established the churches in Rome. Alternatively, it may have been Jewish Christians whose families were from Rome and who returned to their relatives when they were persecuted in Jerusalem.[10]

The Christian movement could not have spread rapidly if it relied solely on a small group of "professionals" to share the gospel. The apostles and other Christian workers set the example and equipped ordinary believers to spread the good news wherever they lived and wherever they went. When the message was met with faith, Christianity quickly became an insider movement as the new converts gossiped the gospel.

OBEDIENCE SCHOOL

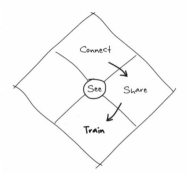

Blessed rather are those who hear the word of God and obey it.

—LUKE 11:28

DISCIPLES IS ONE OF LUKE'S FAVORITE TERMS for describing the followers of Jesus. He uses it thirty times in Acts. Disciples are those who have responded to the gospel with repentance and faith in Jesus Christ. Their sins are forgiven. They have been baptized into the community of his people, and they have received the Holy Spirit. Discipleship, therefore, is a lifestyle of obedience that results from a living relationship with Jesus (Acts 6:7).

Here's what I picture happening the night before Peter and his friends said goodbye to Cornelius. It is past midnight. Peter is exhausted. He will need to be up at dawn to get ready for the three- or four-day journey on foot back to Jerusalem from Caesarea. For these few days, he has spent every moment with Cornelius and many of his household and friends. Peter has nothing left to give to these new believers. Still Cornelius insists, "Come on, Peter, tell us another story about Jesus before you go to bed."

Peter had only a few days to lay a foundation in the lives of these new disciples. Doubtless this would not be the last visit they would receive. Peter or one of his coworkers would be back to teach and encourage Cornelius and the church that was now meeting in his home.

Peter was used to this experience. How long did Peter and the other apostles have to train the new believers at Pentecost? Three thousand were baptized on the same day they were converted. Many of them were pilgrims visiting Jerusalem for Pentecost. Soon they would have returned to their homes in distant lands. Before they left, Peter and the other disciples needed to instruct them in the essentials of following Jesus.

Philip proclaimed Christ with signs and wonders in Samaria. Large numbers believed and were baptized with joy. When the apostles heard that Samaria had accepted the Word of God, they sent Peter and John down. When they arrived, Peter and John prayed for the Holy Spirit to fall upon the Samaritans. They dealt with the corrupting influence of Simon the magician. They would have begun training the Samaritans in what it meant to follow Jesus.

Luke doesn't tell us exactly how long Philip, Peter and John stayed in the Samaritan city, but it wasn't long before they left. On the way back to Jerusalem, Peter and John preached in the Samaritan villages along the way. We don't know how long they stayed in each one. If they were following Jesus' example, it might have been just a few days.

How long did Philip have with the Ethiopian official before they parted and he never saw him again? A day? A few days? Not longer.

DISCIPLESHIP ON THE RUN

The early church was a missionary movement. Movements *move*. The key leaders were mobile. The movement could only expand rapidly if their message and the training of disciples was simple, memorable and readily transferable.

There was no New Testament to give to the new disciples. There was the Old Testament in Hebrew and Greek, but such materials were rare and costly, and most people couldn't read. New believers needed to know the heart of the gospel of salvation through Christ. They needed to know enough to obey Jesus' command to repent and be baptized. They needed to know the presence and power of the Holy Spirit. They needed to learn to follow Jesus with others in community. They needed to be equipped to share their new faith with others. They needed to discover how they could disciple new believers.

The new disciples had to learn a new way of life. Knowledge alone was insufficient. Right from the beginning they had to learn that discipleship meant obeying what Jesus commanded. The immediate goal was not to teach new disciples everything they would ever need to know. It was to teach disciples to obey. Gaps in knowledge would be filled over time as the stories about Jesus circulated and as the apostles' dealt with issues through their personal visits and letters. There was a confidence that the Holy Spirit was present in the life of the disciple to bring out the depth of meaning in the gospel and help them apply it daily.

When Jesus told his disciples to "teach them to obey what I have commanded," he wasn't laying down a new law. Discipleship began with the gospel and the gift of the Holy Spirit, and it continued as the believer learned to live out the faith in every aspect of life. Here are some examples of how the commands of Christ were applied by the early church in the training of disciples.[1]

1. **Repent and believe the good news (Mk 1:15).** At Pentecost, Peter called on the people of Jerusalem to repent and turn to God in faith for the forgiveness of their sins; then they would receive the gift of the Holy Spirit. Not long afterwards, he challenged another Jerusalem crowd to "repent then, and turn to God, so that your sins may be wiped out, that times of refreshing may come from the Lord" (Acts 3:19).

Even Cornelius, a devout and generous person, needed to hear that only faith in Christ for the forgiveness of sin could bring confidence on the day when Christ would judge the living and the dead (Acts 10:42-43).

Simon the sorcerer believed and was baptized, yet his heart was not right with God. Simon followed Philip around and was impressed with the displays of God's power. When Peter and John arrived, he offered them money in exchange for the power to bestow the Holy Spirit on others. Peter's rebuke shook Simon to the core: "May your money perish with you! . . . I see that you are full of bitterness and captive to sin" (Acts 8:14-24).

2. **Baptize them in the name of the Father and of the Son and of the Holy Spirit (Mt 28:19).** Repentance and faith led immediately to baptism— the converts at Pentecost, the new believers in Samaria, the Ethiopian official, Cornelius and his community, Saul of Tarsus, Lydia and her household, the Philippian jailor and his household, and Paul's converts in Corinth.

In the New Testament, conversion has five aspects, all of which took place at the same time, usually on the same day: repentance, faith, confession by the individual, the giving of the Holy Spirit and baptism by another disciple.[2] Luke showed little interest in who did the baptizing. On only a few occasions did Luke clearly identify the person who performed a baptism. Ananias who baptized Paul was simply a "disciple." Peter's command to baptize Cornelius, his relatives and friends was presumably carried out by his companions, whom Luke described as Jewish believers.[3]

3. **As I have loved you, so you must love one another (Jn 13:34).** Jesus had taught his disciples what love looked like. It meant generosity, costly service, forgiveness of wrongs, courage to confront sin, and purity in sexual relationships. Discipleship meant community. Following Pentecost, those who were saved were "added to their number." The disciples in Jerusalem were devoted to sharing their lives with each other. They learned, ate and prayed together; they shared their resources with the needy, and they worshiped together (Acts 2:42-47).

4. **Do this in remembrance of me (Lk 22:19-20).** The disciples met in homes for "the breaking of bread." The term normally refers to an ordinary meal. The disciples celebrated the Lord's Supper in the context of a meal shared in homes. For the early disciples, the breaking of bread was when they were especially aware of Jesus' presence.

5. **Always pray and do not give up (Lk 18:1).** The disciples were together constantly in prayer as they waited for the Spirit to come. Following Pentecost, they continued to gather constantly in prayer. The apostles set the example as leaders and devoted themselves to prayer and the ministry of the Word. At many turning points in the advance of the gospel, we find the disciples praying. They prayed together, continually and earnestly. In their life of constant prayer, they were following the example and teaching of Jesus.

6. **Give, and it will be given to you (Lk 6:38).** Luke records that "all the believers were one in heart and mind. No one claimed that any of their possessions was their own, but they shared everything they had" (Acts 4:32). Luke puts names and faces on the generosity of these first disciples of Jesus. One of them was Joseph, who was originally from Cyprus. The apostles called him Barnabas, which meant *son of encouragement.* He was a wealthy man. When the need arose, he sold his land and took the proceeds to the apostles to distribute to the poor in the community. There was a disciple in the coastal city of Joppa whose Jewish name was Tabitha; her Greek name was Dorcas. She was "always doing good and helping the poor" (Acts 9:36). There were many others like her. Generosity characterized the life of Tabitha and the church in Jerusalem.

There was no compulsion. The church did not abolish private property. Instead, disciples learned to use the resources they had to demonstrate love to those in need.

7. **Go and make disciples of all nations** (Mt 28:19). Every day in the Temple courts of Jerusalem and from house to house, the good news of Jesus was proclaimed—and every day the Lord was adding to those who were being saved (Acts 2:42; 5:42).

The gospel spread through the apostles and leaders such as Philip, Stephen and Barnabas. Unnamed believers led the way in making disciples in Cyprus, Phoenicia, and Antioch. The task of making disciples was the responsibility of the whole movement.

As the movement spread, new disciples were taught both the gospel message and the life that flowed from it. They were equipped to form communities of disciples in their locations and to continue to make disciples of others.

DISCIPLESHIP FOR LIFE

New disciples were taught to obey what Jesus had commanded. The movement was spreading rapidly. New regions were opening up. Thousands were becoming disciples. The apostles and other workers could not settle down and oversee every new initiative. If they had, the movement would have stalled. They had to find ways of making disciples that were simple and transferable.

The apostles and other workers did not control every aspect of the mission. They had confidence that God was at work through his dynamic Word and the Holy Spirit. They trained new believers in the gospel and its implications for how they should live. By necessity, and sometimes by design, they often moved on soon after people came to faith. Long-term discipleship took place as leaders circled back to visit the disciples and churches in a given location. If the leaders couldn't go in person, they sent a team member to speak on their behalf or a letter to be read out in the churches. Peter traveled throughout Judea, Galilee and Samaria, engaging in pioneer evangelism. He also strengthened and encouraged groups of existing disciples in cities such as Joppa and Lydda on the coastal plain. These places had first heard the gospel through Philip (Acts 8:40; 9:31-35).

Believers heard, memorized and retold the Gospel stories and sayings before the New Testament was written down. At first, there were no Epistles; as the letters were written to deal with issues, they were read out to the church and circulated to other churches. Eventually these documents were collected and, with the Gospels, became the New Testament we have today.

For the first decade after Pentecost, the apostles were based in Jerusalem

and provided a unified witness to the truth of the gospel and the accuracy of
the accounts of Jesus' teaching and saving work. The teachings of Jesus and
the apostles circulated from person to person and church to church. Along
with the Old Testament, this body of teaching provided the material for
long-term growth in discipleship.

Intertwined with this process was the activity of the Holy Spirit who was
present in the conversion of individuals, their transformation as they learned
to follow Jesus, and their participation with other disciples in community.[4]
The Spirit and God's Word gave the movement its life and shaped its direction.

LIFE IN THE FIRST CHURCH

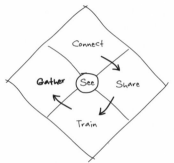

The history of the rise of the movement is the history of the proliferation of the churches, first in Palestine and from there throughout the Roman provinces that ringed the Mediterranean.

—PAUL BARNETT,
*MESSIAH: JESUS—
THE EVIDENCE
OF HISTORY*

YOU HAVE TO FEEL SORRY for the apostle Matthias. He gets one mention in the New Testament and is never heard of again. One popular view of this account is that the apostles made a mistake in choosing Matthias to replace the traitor Judas. Some think they should have waited and chosen Paul as the twelfth apostle. Instead they chose Matthias, who subsequently vanished from the pages of New Testament history.

Matthias was not the only apostle to disappear from Luke's account; nine of the eleven remaining apostles are not mentioned again after the first chapter of Acts. Peter is the only one Luke follows in detail, but even Peter disappears soon after Luke picks up the story of Paul. Later, when the apostle James was executed, he was not replaced. Nor were any of the others.

The apostles knew what they were doing when they filled the position vacated by Judas. Judas alone had to be replaced because he had forfeited his position by apostasy. Why was it so important that the original group of the Twelve be restored? Jesus chose the Twelve to represent the twelve tribes of Israel. The Twelve are the link that unites God's dealings with Israel as a nation and the emergence of the Christian movement, which will include both Jews and Gentiles.

There must be twelve apostles who witness to the resurrection. There must be twelve on whom the Spirit falls. There must be twelve because Jesus always intended that following his death and resurrection, a restored people of God would be formed out of Israel and the Gentiles would be added to them. The goal of Jesus' mission was not just to save individuals but to call out a people for God's name.[1] Jesus called the Twelve to be both the link with Israel and the beginning of the new people of God.

WHAT'S IN A NAME?

For Luke, the story of Jesus of Nazareth was incomplete without the story of the spread of the early church.

The word *church* is just one term that Luke used to describe the communities of Jesus' followers. Luke also refers to them as *saints, disciples, Christians*, the *people, believers*, the *brothers* (the term includes both male and female), and *those who belong to the Way*. The most common terms he used were the *church*, the *brothers* and the *disciples*.

The word *church* doesn't occur until the fifth chapter of Acts. The word we translate as *church* can mean a gathering of people for any purpose. Using the word *church* enabled Jesus' followers to distinguish their gatherings from those in the Jewish synagogues and those in the pagan temples. It also enabled Jesus' followers to retain their link with God's people in the Old Testament, because this same word was used in the Greek Old Testament for the gatherings of God's people.[2] Just as God had set apart Israel as his people, now his church was the restored people of God to whom the Gentiles were added. For Luke, *church* could refer to one local community of believers[3] or all of God's people (Acts 20:28).

Another term used to describe Jesus' followers was *Christians* (belonging to, or followers of Christ). This term was coined for the first time in Antioch. Previously, Jesus' followers were regarded as a faction of Judaism. In Antioch, for the first time large numbers of Gentiles were converting without becoming Jews. The term *Christian* set them apart as being neither pagan

Gentiles nor a Jewish sect but a separate movement founded by Jesus.[4]

The terms we use to describe the communities of Jesus' disciples are important, but not nearly as important as the reality they describe.

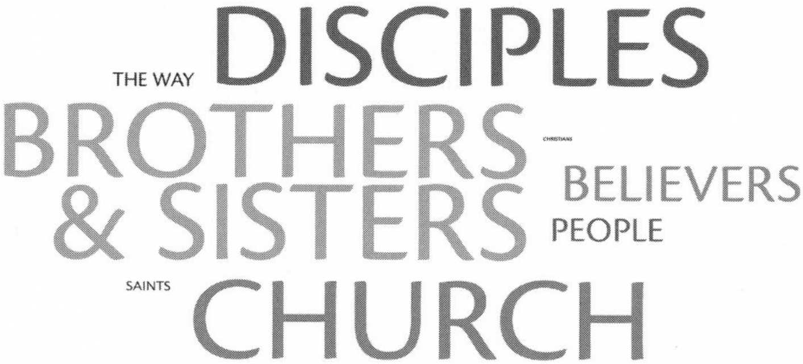

THE WAY **DISCIPLES**
BROTHERS CHRISTIANS **BELIEVERS**
& SISTERS PEOPLE
SAINTS **CHURCH**

Figure 11.1. A word cloud of Luke's language for Jesus' followers in Acts. The more often Luke uses a word, the larger it appears here. The least common term is Christians.

SIMPLY CHURCH

From the beginning the church in Jerusalem was a network of many churches meeting in homes.[5] Jerusalem was a large city, and there were thousands of Jesus' followers. The church also met on the Temple mount. The outer courts and the covered porticoes outside the inner Temple were large enough for thousands of people to gather. They were busy places where pilgrims came and locals met socially and for business.

Luke described the life of the first church in five summary statements.[6] The first statement (Acts 2:42-47) reveals how new disciples were added to the community by the Lord and how they devoted themselves to the apostles' teaching, to fellowship, to the breaking of bread and to prayer.

1. The believers devoted themselves to the apostles' teaching. The apostles' teaching and preaching was based on what they had seen and heard. It included Jesus' teaching and the events of his life, death and resurrection. It also included texts from the Old Testament that pointed forward to Jesus as the Messiah. The apostles' teaching was not actually their teaching; it was the Word of God about Jesus Christ. Peter's messages in Acts are the best examples we have of the apostles' teaching.

- Peter called people to repent and turn back to God in light of the death and resurrection of Jesus and the coming of the Holy Spirit.

- He proclaimed God's offer of salvation through the Messiah, Jesus. Salvation could only be found through faith in him. God was offering this salvation to Jews and to Gentiles.

- Salvation meant forgiveness of sins, reception of the Holy Spirit and membership in the community of God's people. Salvation also included rescue from persecution, healing from sickness and freedom from demonic oppression and greed.

- Peter proclaimed Jesus as Lord and Messiah, son of David and God's Servant. Jesus is holy and righteous, Leader and Savior. He gives repentance and forgiveness of sins. God has confirmed his authority through signs and wonders. According to God's plan, he was handed over to evil men so that we might have salvation through his death. On the third day God vindicated Jesus by raising him from the dead.

Luke used *the word* to describe the apostolic message about Jesus. It is the dynamic Word of God that brings salvation and adds disciples to the life of the church. It is this gospel of salvation through Jesus Christ that creates the church.

2. They devoted themselves to the fellowship, to the breaking of bread and to prayer. The first followers formed communities of disciples. They shared their new life in the Spirit with each other. Most synagogues in the countryside and outside of Israel met in converted houses, so it was natural for Jesus' followers to meet in private houses. The followers of Jesus, excluded from Jewish synagogues, often met in the homes of prominent converts whose houses could accommodate up to fifty people. When Peter was freed from prison, he went to Mary's house where the believers were praying. It was a large house with a gateway that led to a courtyard and rooms. James and the brothers were meeting in other locations.[7]

Luke records that all the believers were together and they were of one heart and soul (Acts 4:32). They expressed their love for God in corporate worship. Their love for each other was expressed in action. Wealthier members freely sold their possessions and shared the proceeds with those in need. They shared the Lord's Supper as they broke bread together in homes.

The believers prayed together regularly. Prayer and the ministry of the Word were the first priorities of the apostles (Acts 6:4). When the church was under the threat of persecution, they gathered for prayer, calling on God for boldness in proclamation and power in signs and wonders (Acts 4:24-31). At almost every important turning point in the mission of the early church, Luke mentioned prayer.[8]

3. And the Lord added to their number daily those who were being saved. The life of the Jerusalem church bore fruit. Jesus' followers proclaimed the gospel publicly in and around the Temple. They proclaimed the gospel in the synagogues of Jerusalem. They proclaimed the gospel as they met in homes throughout the city.

Every day they courageously proclaimed the good news despite threats and persecution from the authorities. When opposition came, the believers did not pray for safety, they prayed for boldness. Signs of God's power accompanied the gospel. People came into Jerusalem from the towns and villages of Judea bringing the sick and those afflicted with unclean spirits for healing.

The number of Jesus' followers in Jerusalem grew dramatically—from 120 to three thousand, then to five thousand, among them many Pharisees and priests. Luke recorded that outsiders were afraid to join them, yet they held the believers in high esteem (Acts 5:13-16). Every day, men and women came to faith in Jesus and were added to the church.[9]

LEADERSHIP

Luke showed very little interest in establishing the exact nature of the organization of the early church—a reluctance he shared with Paul.[10] Luke identified a number of leadership roles but seemed more preoccupied with the spread of the gospel than with the need to describe a system for church government.

The Twelve. In the early years the Twelve exercised leadership over the church in Jerusalem. They prayed and preached and taught. They played a role in church discipline. They engaged in evangelism in Jerusalem, Judea, Samaria and beyond. They led in the resolution of disputes and the appointment of coworkers. They consolidated the churches in new regions. They were engaged in important decisions regarding the Gentile mission.[11]

The apostles themselves described the heart of their responsibility as *"prayer and the ministry of the word"* (Acts 6:2). Today the phrase "prayer and the ministry of the word" conjures up impressions of a quiet monastic existence. In Acts this phrase could mean nothing less than pioneering evangelism, the instruction of new disciples, and the planting and strengthening of new churches. *The word* in Acts is a dynamic, unstoppable force that grows and multiplies and results in the creation of new communities of disciples. *Prayer* is offered up in the midst of the challenges and opportunities of a dynamic missionary movement. *Prayer* precedes the coming of the Spirit in power for mission. After their release from custody, Peter and John join the believers in *prayer* for boldness in proclaiming the gospel. Peter is in *prayer* when God intervenes to lead him to the house of Cornelius. "*Prayer and the ministry of the word*" were activities of the leaders of a dynamic, expanding missionary movement.

Around A.D. 41, the role of the Twelve as leaders of the church in Jerusalem changed. Herod Agrippa executed the apostle James, and Peter fled Jerusalem. Leadership of the church in Jerusalem appears to have transferred from the Twelve to a council of elders, with James the Lord's brother becoming the "first among equals."

The city had become too dangerous for Peter and the other apostles. Increasingly Peter was engaged as a mobile missionary beyond Jerusalem. There is some evidence that the remaining apostles followed Peter's example and also took up outreach beyond Jerusalem.[12]

The Seven. As the church grew rapidly, there was a conflict over the distribution of food to the church's Hebrew and Greek-speaking widows. The Greek-speaking widows were being neglected. The apostles resolved the issues by appointing seven leaders to fix the problem. These leaders were chosen because of the strength of their faith and the quality of their character. They all had Greek names. Their appointment left the Twelve free to focus on prayer and the ministry of the word (Acts 6:1-6). At least two of the Seven, Stephen and Philip, were also actively engaged in evangelism, however. Philip appears to have preferred evangelism and church planting to "waiting on tables."

The Seven were never called "deacons" in the sense that Paul used the word. The word *service* from which the term "deacon" originates is used of both the Twelve and the Seven. The Seven had a ministry (service) of waiting on tables, just as the Twelve had a ministry (service) of preaching the word and prayer.

The appointment of the Seven showed the Jerusalem church's willingness to adapt leadership structures and roles to meet new needs.

James and the elders. Elders played a growing leadership role in the Jerusalem church, alongside the apostles. When the Christians in Antioch sent relief for the poor believers in Jerusalem, the elders were the ones who received their gifts (Acts 11:30). At the Jerusalem council, the elders were listed together with the apostles. When Paul visited Jerusalem for the last time in about A.D. 57, there was no mention of the apostles; only the Jerusalem elders remained, with James the clear leader.

By A.D. 41/42 James and the elders appear to have taken up the leadership of the Jerusalem church after the apostles fled the city. James, the Lord's brother, was leader of the Jerusalem church from A.D. 41 to 62, when the Jewish historian Josephus records that the high priest had him stoned to death.

Luke did not tell us how or when these elders were appointed. Nor did he tell us how James became leader in Jerusalem, or how he was replaced after his death. Luke's interest lay elsewhere. According to Acts, the driving force in the Jerusalem church was not a particular office of leadership or form of organization, but the dynamic Word of God and the presence of the Holy Spirit.

The story of Jesus of Nazareth would have been incomplete without the story of the spread of the early church. Intertwined with Luke's reports of the progress of God's Word are the accounts of the life and growth of communities of disciples.

The early church was remarkably free in forming its life as the people of God. Neither the apostles, nor James the Lord's brother, nor Paul controlled the churches. The church, led by the Holy Spirit, spread and multiplied through the dynamic Word of God.

FROM JERUSALEM
TO THE WORLD

*Sacrifice and courage were all that the apostles needed to travel
to Germania or Spain, to Ethiopia or Scythia or to India.*

—ECKHARD SCHNABEL,
EARLY CHRISTIAN MISSION

*If readers of Acts find themselves in a journey, the major
sights are not those created by human hands;
they result from the actions of God alone.*

—BEVERLY GAVENTA,
THE ACTS OF THE APOSTLES

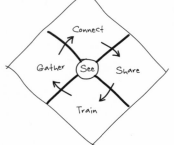

THE BIRTH OF THE CHURCH IN JERUSALEM was also the birth of an international missionary movement. Jerusalem had 100,000 inhabitants. Since the rebuilding of the temple by Herod the Great, Jerusalem was the most visited city in the entire Roman Empire. On the day of Pentecost, there could have been up to a million pilgrims camped in and around Jerusalem.[1]

The Diaspora—the majority of Jews who lived outside of Palestine in the cities of the ancient world—had left their homeland over many centuries through conquest and deportation, or by choice for commercial reasons. Many of the crowd at Pentecost who joined in this new movement took their faith in Jesus back home with them, which explains the beginnings of Christian communities in places such as Damascus, Rome, and Alexandria.[2]

Meanwhile, the disciples of Jesus carried the gospel to Judea, Samaria, Syria and Rome. They engaged in missionary work among Jews, Samaritans, Gentile God-fearers and pagans. As the movement spread, the apostles and other missionaries multiplied workers, training new believers to reach their friends and family, to host and lead communities of disciples in their homes, and to join in the spread of the message into unreached regions. There was nothing automatic about the spread of the gospel from Jerusalem to the world.

JERUSALEM

A group of powerful and dangerous men, representing the same religious aristocracy that had orchestrated Jesus' arrest and surrender to the Romans, rose up in opposition to the Jesus movement in Jerusalem.[3] Among this group were Annas the high priest and his family, the Temple guard, experts in the law and members of the Jewish ruling council.

The flashpoint that ignited the opposition was Peter and John's healing of a lame man and their preaching in the Temple precincts. The apostles were brought before a formidable group; Luke describes them as the rulers, elders and teachers of the law (Acts 4:5-6).

Predictably, these men were concerned about power and reputation. They could not accept the message about Jesus nor could they accept the messengers. They were incensed by the openness and authority with which these Galilean fishermen spoke—shocked that Peter and John were ordinary men who were untrained in theology and without proper credentials. Here were two nobodies, challenging the teaching of scholars and the authority of the leaders of God's people.[4] Their one distinguishing characteristic was that they had been with Jesus.

After threatening them, the authorities released the apostles unharmed. Many of the people who heard Peter's message believed the good news about Jesus the Messiah, and the church grew to five thousand (Acts 4:4). The believers met regularly in private homes, creating the need for hundreds of local leaders.

The information that Luke provides shows how comprehensively the early church fulfilled Jesus' command in Jerusalem. God added daily to their numbers as the movement spread through

- the preaching of the Word

- the healing of the sick

- the witness of ordinary believers to family, neighbors and friends

- the quality of their love for one another

- the courage they demonstrated in the face of violent persecution

- the forgiveness they willingly extended to their persecutors

Through the witness of these disciples, the whole of Jerusalem heard the gospel and saw it demonstrated in acts of power and deeds of love. Their opponents complained they had "filled Jerusalem" with their teaching. When Paul visited Jerusalem in A.D. 57, there were tens of thousands of Jesus' followers throughout Jerusalem and the surrounding region (Acts 21:20).

JUDEA, GALILEE AND SAMARIA

Jerusalem was the birthplace and center of the movement in its early years, but it was not the institutional center, nor did it coordinate the mission. Jerusalem did not exercise control over the new churches. Instead, the churches in Syria, Cilicia, Galatia, the province of Asia, Greece, Rome and Alexandria were all established and developed independently of central control.[5]

Disciples would probably have carried the good news from Jerusalem to the nearby towns of Bethany and Emmaus soon after Pentecost and formed communities of disciples who would have continued to attend the local synagogue. Mary, Martha and Lazarus lived in Bethany, and Luke records Jesus' encounter with two disciples who were walking on the road to Emmaus. Luke tells us that people were also coming in from the towns around Jerusalem to be healed.

The apostles, led by Jesus, had already taken part in campaigns to reach the rural towns and villages of Galilee and Judea. After Pentecost they could have easily followed Jesus' example and led teams on mission to the eighty towns and villages of Judea with the message of the crucified and risen Messiah. Paul's early letters indicate that he knew of the "churches in Christ in Judea" (Gal 1:22; 1 Thess 2:14).

Jesus was from Galilee, and he had relatives and many followers in the region. Luke records that the church in Galilee was multiplying along with the church in Judea and Samaria. Paul mentions that Jesus' brothers were engaged in missionary activity, possibly based in Galilee. Peter and Andrew had families in Capernaum and in Bethsaida, as did the apostle Philip.[6]

Peter, John and Philip the evangelist were active in evangelism and church planting throughout Samaria (Acts 8:4-14, 25). Luke reports that the church throughout Samaria continued to grow in numbers and depth. Later he refers to "all the believers in Samaria" being encouraged by reports from Paul and Barnabas (Acts 9:31; 15:3).

CITIES ON THE MEDITERRANEAN COAST

Philip, Peter and others proclaimed the gospel and established churches in Lydda, Joppa, Caesarea, Ptolemais-Acco and probably Azotos. These churches became centers of outreach in the surrounding regions. Peter was based in Joppa "for some time." Caesarea, which had sixteen villages under its control, was probably Philip's base for years (Acts 9:43; 21:8).

The believers who left Jerusalem after Stephen's death went to Antioch in Syria, converting both Jews and Greeks, and starting churches (Acts 11:20-21). Luke mentions Phoenicia and Cyprus in the same context, which could indicate that the believers were engaged in mission along the entire Mediterranean coast from Caesarea to Antioch—in Byblos, Berytus, Dora, Sidon and Tyre.

SYRIA AND CYPRUS

The gospel's arrival in Antioch was one of the most significant events in the spread of the early Christian movement. Antioch was the capital of the Roman province of Syria; it was the third largest city in the empire. Believers from Jerusalem brought the gospel to Damascus and Antioch,[7] continuing the mission among Jews. But some disciples from Cyprus and Cyrene began sharing with Greek-speaking Gentiles. Luke records that "the Lord's hand was with them, and a great number of people believed and turned to the Lord" (Acts 11:21)·

The developments in Antioch were a major step forward in the mission to the Gentiles. The apostles in Jerusalem did not initiate the breakthrough, but they played an important part by sending Barnabas to Antioch to consolidate and extend the work. Barnabas recruited Paul to help.

The church in Antioch grew rapidly, and a great number of people—both Jews and Greek-speaking Gentiles—believed and turned to the Lord. A year later, Antioch was the launching pad for a new phase of missionary outreach to the Gentiles led by Paul and Barnabas.

ROME

The Christian faith was established in Rome as early as A.D. 31. The most likely scenario is that Jewish pilgrims who were converted at Pentecost returned to proclaim that Jesus is the Messiah in the synagogues of Rome. Rome had a population of up to a million people; of them forty thousand to fifty thousand were Jewish—the second largest Jewish community outside of Palestine. The Jews gathered in at least eleven synagogues scattered throughout the city, but they were concentrated in the area known as Trastevere ("across the Tiber").[8] There were many Gentile converts and sympathizers attached to the synagogues of Rome who would have been responsive to the gospel. It's most likely that converted Jews and Gentile God-fearers established the first churches in the Trastevere area. From there the gospel spread to the rest of the city and to the Gentile population.[9]

Once the way was made clear for the gospel to go to the Gentiles, Luke's attention stayed on the apostle Paul until the gospel reached Rome. In A.D. 49 there was a serious disturbance in the Jewish community of Rome that led to their expulsion by the emperor Claudius (Acts 18:2). There is good evidence to suggest that the disturbances were a reaction to the presence of Jewish Christians proclaiming Jesus as the Messiah in the synagogues of Rome. Paul's letter to the Romans identifies multiple churches meeting throughout the city by the mid-50s (Rom 16:3-16).

NORTH AFRICA

Luke didn't report everything he knew about the spread of the early Christian movement in the book of Acts. There is good evidence that Christianity spread to Egypt, particularly Alexandria, in the 30s.

The highest concentration of Jews outside Palestine was in Egypt, especially in Alexandria where the Jewish community dated from the sixth century B.C. The New Testament refers to Jews and Jewish Christians from Cyrene in North Africa, an important Greek city with a large Jewish community. Jews from Cyrene were at Pentecost in A.D. 30 (Acts 2:10). Their synagogue in Jerusalem was a focus of Stephen's ministry. Some of them were converted, and they took the gospel to Antioch in Syria. One of the leading prophets and teachers of the church in Antioch was Lucius from Cyrene. It's likely there was a church established in Cyrene at an early date.[10]

INDIA

Later church sources provide credible evidence that the apostle Thomas reached India. Indian products were readily available in Palestinian markets. The routes for merchant shipping between Egypt, Arabia and south India were well established since the first century B.C. Proof of a Christian presence in India dates to the third century. There is no reason why the gospel could not have reached as far as India within a generation.[11]

MULTIPLYING WORKERS

Luke never intended to tell the whole story of the rise of the Christian movement. He gives us carefully selected snippets rather than detailed histories.

We don't hear what finally happened to Peter or the other apostles. His focus in Acts is equally on Stephen, Philip, Barnabas and the believers who took the gospel to the Jewish Diaspora. The Holy Spirit was at work through all sorts of people. Luke was not writing individual biographies; this is the story of the unstoppable advance of the Word from Jerusalem to the world.

There were no parallels in the ancient world for an international missionary movement. Jesus was the disciples' model. As he had trained his first disciples, they trained and released others. The Twelve were Aramaic-speaking Jews from Galilee. Early on they recognized the need in Jerusalem for leadership to come from the Greek-speaking Jews of the Diaspora.

Among the leaders they appointed, at least two played a pivotal role in the advance of the gospel beyond Jerusalem. Philip led in reaching the Samaritans. Others took the gospel for the first time to the pagan Gentiles in Antioch. These two events were dramatic breakthroughs in the expansion of the movement across racial and religious barriers. Neither of them came at the initiative of the apostles. Yet the apostles in Jerusalem quickly supported and worked with those who had led the way. They recognized that God was at work.

The apostles made their contribution to the spread of the gospel, but Jesus had taught them that the task could never be completed unless they trained and multiplied workers. The Christian movement spread through the efforts of countless unidentified believers. No formal schools had to be established. Workers were trained in the field.

There is no evidence that an apostle started the church in Rome. The church in Rome might have been established by Roman Jews who were converted at Pentecost or by some of the believers scattered by persecution following Stephen's martyrdom. Many other churches were established in this "haphazard" way. New churches were springing up and growing in so many locations that the apostles in Jerusalem had no hope of controlling the movement.

The early Christian mission went far beyond any precedents set by the missionary outreach of Jewish Diaspora. The Jewish Diaspora brought Gentiles into the synagogue through attraction. Gentiles were drawn to the faith of Israel in one true God who was holy, just, and loving. The early Christian missionaries went even further. Not waiting for the world to come to them, they traveled to unreached cities and regions to proclaim the gospel of Jesus Christ and establish communities of his disciples.[12]

In every city, town and village where the gospel gained a foothold, believers shared their faith with family, friends and neighbors. This is how most people heard the good news. Pioneering missionaries did not settle down to pastor the new churches. Instead, they trained local leaders to take over that responsibility and moved on to new territory, occasionally returning or sending envoys or letters.

Within forty years the Christian missionaries had planted churches in Syria-Cilicia, Cyprus, Galatia, Asia, Mysia, Macedonia, Achaia, Cappadocia and Pontus-Bithynia. There were also groups in Italy and Rome, in Dalmatia, on Crete, and possibly in Illyricum and Egypt. Churches were planted in the major cities of the Roman Empire—Jerusalem, Damascus, Caesarea, Antioch, Rome, Corinth, Alexandria and Ephesus.[13] Those churches served as bases for outreach into the surrounding regions. The early Christians were following the example set by Jesus to reach *all* the people in a region, whether they lived in cities or small settlements and despite their social status or religious background.

We know that Jesus called some to the life of a full-time mobile missionary. Their commission was to fish for people, to lead them to faith in Jesus and to bring them to join the community of his disciples. We can identify at least forty such workers in the New Testament.[14] Their primary task was to take the gospel to new, unreached locations. They were to gather the first disciples into a community or communities and then establish them in the faith before moving on.

Instead of centering leadership in Jerusalem, the apostles dispersed around A.D. 41/42 to proclaim the good news in Judea, Samaria, and among the nations. Peter became a mobile missionary among both Jews and Gentiles. Paul was not the only active missionary among the Gentiles (Rom 15:20; 1 Cor 9:5).

Paul's leadership took the movement to a whole new level, but the mission to the Gentiles was underway before he appeared on the scene. That's because the mission did not begin with Paul, or Peter, or any of the apostles. Jesus of Nazareth laid the foundation. Following Pentecost, the risen Lord continued to move the early church forward in its worldwide mission.

Jesus founded a missionary movement. His methods of training workers had been simple and reproducible. These workers in turn trained others as he trained them—head, heart and hands. Large amounts of money and complex structures were not required for this movement to expand. All the disciples needed were faith and obedience.

Jesus of Nazareth laid the foundations for a worldwide missionary movement through his example and the training of his disciples. Jesus' resurrection and the sending of the Holy Spirit transformed his despairing and defeated disciples into a missionary force that boldly proclaimed the gospel and gathered disciples into worshiping communities wherever they went.

The movement advanced beyond the control of the original apostles as God multiplied workers who took the gospel into uncharted waters. The apostles could barely keep up with what God was doing on the fringes. Paul's leadership took the mission to a new level, but God had already worked through others to prepare the way.

Before moving onto Paul, we'll pause for our next contemporary case study.

Ying Kai and the Power of Multiplication

Still other seed fell on good soil.
It came up, grew and produced a crop,
some multiplying thirty, some sixty, some a hundred times.

—MARK 4:8

Ying and Grace Kai are from Taiwan. For a number of years they served as missionaries in Hong Kong. Every year they started a new church and led about thirty people to Christ.[1] In 2000 a Hong Kong businessman challenged Ying with the needs of an unreached region in Asia that for security reasons we'll call "Nandong."

Ying was reluctant. He knew about the reputation of Nandong's authoritarian government. So the businessman took Ying and Grace on a tour of the region. Later Ying recalled his reactions:

As we rode the train, we passed many factories. The man told us about every factory we passed. He would say, "This factory has 3,000 workers. I know the owner. He hopes that someone will come to share the gospel, but we cannot find anyone who will come."

The biggest factory we passed has 70,000 people. When we saw all of the lost people of these factories, God opened our eyes and our minds. I realized, "These people need the gospel."[2]

Ying was called by God to reach the twenty million people in this rapidly growing urban center where each day thousands of new migrant workers arrive looking for work and a better life.

Ying knew that he would have to do things differently to reach Nandong. He knew that merely adding disciples and churches would not be enough; he had to tap into the power of multiplication. As Ying prayed, God gave him three insights for those who are called to make disciples:

- **Go, not come.** The Great Commission does not say we are to invite people to come to us. It says we are to *go*. We must go to where the lost are and train new believers to also go to the lost—into factories, homes, shops, and neighborhoods.

- **Everyone, not some.** We must make disciples of *all*, not just a few. We typically choose whom we want to share the gospel with, trying to pre-judge who might accept it. But God said to share with everyone. We cannot predict who will believe and whom God will use to birth a movement.

- **Make disciples and trainers, not passive church members.** Jesus wants true *disciples* who obey his commands—including the commands to witness to others and train new believers to do the same. Every disciple must be a trainer.

Ying the church planter and pastor became Ying the trainer and catalyst for church planting movements. He called his process of making disciples "Training for Trainers" (T4T). "Trainer" conveys the idea of someone who both grows in his loving obedience of Jesus and passes on what he learns to others through witness and training.

The T4T process trains believers to share the gospel and make disciples in a reproducible way. The discipleship training process includes new group and church formation along with leadership development.

Ying and Grace began by training one class of thirty believers. They taught the trainees that each of them had a unique story to tell of how they met Jesus. They trained them to tell their story and helped them identify five people they would share with in the following week.

The next week seventeen of the thirty trainees reported sharing their story, and one farmer had shared with eleven people. The following week Ying raised the level of accountability and allowed only those who were sharing their story to continue with the training. Two months later, the trainees had started twenty small groups. After six months there were 327 small groups and 4,000 newly baptized believers scattered across seventeen towns. Within twelve months, there were 908 house churches with more than 12,000 new Christians.

One old farmer who had never before planted a church started twelve house churches in two months and 110 in the first year. He began every day reading his Bible from 5 a.m. to 7 a.m. Then he worked in the fields until 5 p.m., at which point he went home for dinner and family time. At 7 p.m. he went back out again, and he worked in "God's fields" until midnight.

In another town a sixty-seven-year-old woman became a Christian and in one year led more than sixty families to become believers.

In another example, Ying lost touch with a Christian factory worker he had trained. After six months, he learned that the worker had been transferred to another large factory with ten thousand workers. During those six months, the worker had started seventy small groups and seen ten generations of reproduction (churches planting churches).

By the year 2003, Ying and Grace were training 300 to 400 believers each month. As the Kais trained them to be trainers of trainers, they found that many would witness, some would start new groups, and a smaller number would go on to train their new group members to repeat the process. Hundreds and then thousands began to come to faith.

Immediately after coming to faith, new believers were equipped and held accountable to witness to relatives, neighbors and close friends. These new believers were taught to train and follow up with those they led to Christ. The trainers learned simple, reproducible Bible lessons and taught them to new believers who were encouraged to form into new churches.

Urban streams of new converts jumped from neighborhood to neighborhood and from factory to factory as believers changed jobs. The T4T training prepares new believers to be seeds so that when the church is scattered, whether by dangers or opportunities, new churches are planted.

In the most recent survey of the Kais' ministry, more than 1.7 million people have come to faith and been baptized. Every month trained workers start two thousand house churches and small groups in villages, urban highrise apartments and factories. Over 140,000 churches have been started in what is currently the world's fastest growing church planting movement.

In other parts of the world, T4T has birthed new church planting movements within Hindu, Muslim and animist contexts among both literate and nonliterate peoples. T4T has also begun to bear fruit in the United States and Australia.

Ying Kai's strategy has been to aggressively train every willing local Christian in how to be more obedient in their spiritual life, how to effectively share their faith person to person, how to immediately follow up with new believers, and how to initiate reproducing groups which often become churches. Training, encouraging, and holding existing and new Christians accountable to become trainers of trainers has characterized this church planting movement. Ying's story demonstrates the power of multiplication at work.

At the heart of this amazing movement is a simple process for training disciples.[3] When trainees meet, their time is divided roughly into thirds. They spend time focusing on each of these three areas.

1. LOOK BACK

Pastoral care. Trainees ask each other, "How are you doing?" and take time to minister to one another's needs in prayer, biblical counsel and encouragement.

Informal worship. Trainees praise God in a culturally appropriate and reproducible way. It could be prayer or singing, with or without an instrument or mp3 player. Some groups read the Psalms out loud.

Accountability. Trainees share in mutual loving accountability about how they have been followers of Jesus (obeying the previous meeting's Bible lesson) and fishers of men (witnessing to and training others) since the last meeting.

Vision casting. Trainees are reminded what God has designed them to become and what he plans to do through them.

2. LOOK UP

Trainees receive enough biblical content to obey and pass on to others. After a series of six basic discipleship lessons, participants learn how to do inductive Bible study by asking the following questions: *What does it say? What can I obey? What will I share with others?*

3. LOOK FORWARD

Practice. Trainees spend time practicing what they have learned to gain confidence and competence to pass it on to others.

Goals and prayer. Trainees set goals for how to obey the lesson and to take the next steps in witnessing and training others; then they recommission each other through prayer.

PART THREE

What Jesus Continued to Do

PAUL AND HIS TEAM

FINALLY HE GETS IT!

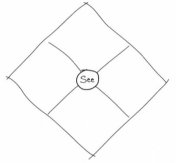

*Paul's mission was an unprecedented happening in
terms both of the history of religion in antiquity
and of later church history. . . . With Paul,
for the first time we find the specific aim
of engaging in missionary activity
throughout the world.*

—MARTIN HENGEL,
*BETWEEN JESUS
AND PAUL*

THE APOSTLE PAUL WAS FROM TARSUS, the capital of the Roman province of Cilicia on the southeastern coast of what is now Turkey. Tarsus was a wealthy city of half a million people; it was also an important center of Greek learning.

Paul (known by his Jewish name "Saul" until he begins missionary work among Gentiles)[1] grew up in a world of devout Judaism, surrounded by gross paganism. The high god of Tarsus was Baal Tars (lord of Tarsus). The secondary god, Sandan, figured in fertility rites. Every year the people paraded Sandan through the streets of Tarsus on a decorated float before burning him on a funeral pyre. Then the city celebrated the resurrection of the god in a feast that led to all kinds of excess.[2]

Paul belonged to a prominent Jewish family with links to the Pharisaic movement. Despite being Jewish, they were part of Tarsus's social elite. To become a citizen of Tarsus required substantial wealth, and Paul inherited citizenship of both Tarsus and Rome from his father.

Roman citizenship brought status and privileges. An accused citizen was guaranteed a fair public trial. A local official could not have him executed, beaten, chained or tortured without a proper process, which included the right to appeal for a trial in Rome. A Roman citizen convicted of a capital offense was spared the shameful death of crucifixion. On at least three occasions, Paul used his citizenship to his advantage (Acts 16:37; 22:25-29; 24:27; 25:11).

Growing up in a Jewish family, Paul could speak Aramaic and Hebrew. Because he lived in a Gentile city, Paul could also speak and read Greek fluently. He probably knew some Latin. When he was young, Paul's family moved to Jerusalem where he eventually studied in the rabbinical school of Gamaliel, the most respected scholar of his age. This was an opportunity only the wealthy could afford. Like all rabbis, Paul learned a trade to support himself, and he chose to be a tentmaker. The term *tentmaker* may have a broader meaning of "leatherworker," as most tents were made of leather.

Paul arrived in Jerusalem to begin his studies up to ten years before Jesus began his public ministry. Paul was there during the time of Jesus' ministry, trial and execution. There is no reason to believe he met Jesus, but he must have heard reports from those who had.

SAUL BITES THE DUST

The forward advance of the Christian movement was not the sole responsibility of the twelve apostles. Luke draws our attention to others who made a significant contribution, including Stephen, a leader among the Greek-speaking Jews of the Jerusalem church. Stephen was a man of grace and power who performed miracles and proclaimed the gospel to other Diaspora Jews who had settled in Jerusalem. Stephen was opposed by Jews who had settled in Jerusalem from Cyrene and Alexandria in northern Africa and by others who were from Cilicia and the Roman province of Asia (modern Turkey). These Jews attended the Synagogue of the Freedmen.

Among Stephen's opponents was Paul of Tarsus. Paul was enraged that this sect was placing Jesus above the traditions of the Temple and the Law of Moses—the very pillars of the Jewish faith. He was offended by the message of a crucified Messiah whose death atoned for sin.

Paul was in the mob that dragged Stephen before the Jewish ruling body. During his trial Stephen was accused of preaching against the Temple and the Law. Stephen argued that the age of salvation had dawned and the good news must go out from Jerusalem to the nations. Jerusalem and its Temple were no longer the center of God's mission. The Messiah Jesus had fulfilled the Law and removed the need for the Temple, and the Gentiles could now be included in God's people.

Stephen was mobbed and stoned to death while Paul looked on with approval. Afterward Paul emerged as the leader of the campaign against Jesus' followers. Not content with Stephen's death and the expulsion of many of Jesus' followers from Jerusalem, Paul sought to "destroy" the church (Gal 1:23). In his rage, Paul may have even carried out his threats to murder Jesus' followers (Acts 22:4; 26:10).

Paul's campaign of persecution was counterproductive. As the disciples fled to friends and relatives who lived among the Jewish Diaspora, they took the gospel with them. So Paul sought authority to hunt them down as far away as Damascus, in the Roman province of Syria, 150 miles northeast of Jerusalem.

Damascus was a prominent and wealthy city on one of the great crossroads of the ancient world. It had a large Jewish community, but it was a pagan city; its coins bore the images of Greek gods, and the dominant building was the temple of Jupiter. The journey from Jerusalem to Damascus took a few days by horseback and over a week by foot. As Paul traveled on the road to Damascus, Jesus confronted this enemy of the Christian movement and transformed him into its greatest missionary.

On the road to Damascus Paul was blinded by a light and fell to the ground. He heard the voice of Jesus saying, "Saul, Saul, why do you persecute me? It is hard for you to kick against the goads" (Acts 26:14). A goad was a wooden stick with metal spikes used to prod and drive livestock. Kicking against it would only cause the animal harm. Like a stubborn animal, Paul was resisting God and doing harm to himself.

In an instant, Paul's world was shattered. He was humbled, blinded and confused. The raging persecutor was led by the hand into Damascus as a captive of Christ.

On the Damascus road, Paul discovered that Jesus was the crucified and exalted Messiah, the Son of God, the Lord of all, the Savior of the world (Gal 3:13-14). Paul's zeal for the Law had led him to oppose God and his Messiah.

Paul, the worst of sinners, was forgiven and reconciled to God through Christ on the Damascus road. Stephen's dying prayer, "Lord, do not hold this sin against them," had been answered.

Paul's companions took him to a house in Damascus where he stayed and waited in darkness for what God would do next. The Lord appeared to a disciple in the city named Ananias and told him to go and pray for Paul's sight to be restored. Ananias argued with the Lord, just like Peter had done when he received a command he did not understand. The discussion was cut short with God's command: "Go!"

Ananias arrived at the house and acknowledged Paul as a "brother." He prayed for Paul's sight to be restored and for Paul to be filled with the Holy Spirit. Then Ananias baptized him and brought Paul into fellowship with the other disciples in Damascus. Paul began preaching immediately in the synagogues of Damascus. Opposition grew, and Paul grew increasingly powerful.

Paul traveled to nearby Arabia to continue his missionary work (Gal 1:15-17). There is no evidence for the popular belief that Paul spent three years in quiet contemplation in the Arabian desert; Arabia was not all sand. It included the area of the modern country of Jordan and was home to the Nabatean kingdom, a flourishing civilization with cities, seaports and farming land. In cities such as Petra there were synagogues where Paul could meet fellow Jews and local Gentiles who were attracted to the God of Israel. Through these Gentiles the gospel could have spread to the surrounding community.[3]

When he had completed his mission in Arabia, Paul returned to Damascus where the representative of King Aretas of the Nabateans tried to have Paul arrested (2 Cor 11:32-33). Paul's mission in the cities of Arabia had stirred up trouble.[4]

Paul related his Arabian mission closely with his call to preach Christ among the Gentiles. He told the Galatians he began to discharge this call before he went up to Jerusalem to see the apostles. Therefore none could say that any human authority, including the Twelve, commissioned him as an apostle to the Gentiles.

THE CALL

The story of Paul's conversion and call is so important that Luke tells it three times in the book of Acts (Acts 9:1-22; 22:2-21; 26:1-23). In each account we see that it is God, through the Lord Jesus, who is the initiator. Paul was chosen to know God's will and to see the risen Lord and hear his voice. Jesus appeared to Paul to appoint him as a servant and a witness.

Paul's mission was not his idea. He wrote that on the Damascus road he was "captured" by Christ (Phil 3:12). The apostles in Jerusalem did not commission him; he didn't need their authorization. The call to take the gospel to the Gentiles came directly from Jesus. Paul's mission was an extension of the mission of Jesus.

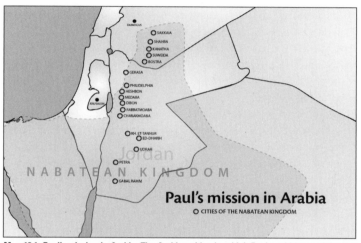

Map 13.1. Paul's mission in Arabia. The Arabian cities in which Paul could have ministered, beginning with the Jews and Gentiles he found in the local synagogues. See Eckhard Schnabel, *Paul the Missionary.*

Paul had very little instruction in his new faith (Gal 1:12). What he lacked in information, he made up for in obedience to his Lord's command (Acts 9:15-16).

He was to be a witness to what he had seen and heard, and to what he would see. He was to open eyes and turn people from darkness to light and from the power of Satan to God, so that they could receive forgiveness of sins and a place among those who are made holy by faith in Christ.

The scope of Paul's mission could not have been broader. He was to be a witness to Jews, Gentiles and their kings—to "all people." He was called to spread the gospel throughout the whole world. He was told that he must suffer for the name of Jesus. He would experience the same fate he had inflicted on others. The persecutor would become the persecuted. Paul would fulfill his calling in weakness, depending on God who would rescue him from all his enemies and ensure the completion of his mission.

THE STRATEGY

By the time of Paul's conversion, the Jesus movement was already spreading across the empire and was established in Rome. The mission to the Jews in Palestine and the Diaspora was well underway. Paul was not even the initiator of the mission to the Gentiles; Philip and later Peter had unlocked the door of faith to the Gentiles. Anonymous believers in Antioch had opened it ajar, and now it was flung wide open by Paul.[5]

Paul wanted to reach as many people as possible, and the quickest way to reach them was to reach the cities. His travels stretched in an arc from Jerusalem through Syria, to Asia Minor, into Europe, to Rome and possibly to Spain (Rom 15:19-24).

The known world was larger than just the Roman Empire, but Paul limited his mission to mostly Greek-speaking provinces within the Empire. Paul was not a "foreign missionary" in the modern sense of the word. His ministry was conducted in cultural and language settings with which he was familiar. The vast majority of Jews outside of Palestine lived in the major cities of the Roman Empire. The population density in these cities could be up to two hundred people per acre—equivalent to the industrial slums of a Western city. Living quarters were cramped, and privacy was rare. Life was lived on the streets, in the marketplaces and in the public squares.[6] The cities were also home to large populations of Gentiles who spoke Greek.

Since the conquests of Alexander the Great, the cities had become the source of political and social change in the Mediterranean world. The cities were where the power was concentrated and where new ideas emerged. The Roman Empire was a federation of self-governing cities. A common Greco-Roman culture and a common language (Greek) linked them. They were centers of communication and education. There was a constant flow of people, goods and ideas on the extensive system of roads and shipping lanes connecting the cities.

Under Roman rule, sea routes and roads were relatively safe from pirates and bandits. Travel was easier and more common than it had ever been before, or would be again, until the nineteenth century.[7]

In contrast to the cities, life in the rural villages was hard and focused on survival, so the culture was conservative. Local languages were spoken instead of Greek, making the communication and the flow of ideas more difficult. In the Gentile provinces of the Empire there were no significant Jewish communities beyond the cities.

Paul's strategy was simple; he traveled by land on Roman roads and by sea from city to city sharing the gospel, making disciples and gathering them into Christian communities. His point of contact with an unreached city was normally the Jewish community. This is what he did in Arabia, in Syria, in his home province of Cilicia, on Cyprus, in the provinces of Galatia and Asia, in Macedonia and Achaia (northern and southern Greece), and possibly in Spain and Crete.[8]

Each city had a unique flavor, but a visitor like Paul would immediately recognize the important temples, the government buildings, the market place and city square, the gymnasium, the theater, even the inns, taverns and shops.[9] As he moved around the city, Paul would have no problem communicating with the locals in Greek.

Paul saw himself as a master builder (1 Cor 3:10-15). In the ancient world, a master builder supervised the whole construction project, whether it was a new home or a public building such as a temple, government building, marketplace or theater. Paul's employer was God. Together with his coworkers he had a job to do.

1. Paul saw the end. "From Jerusalem all the way around to Illyricum, I have fully proclaimed the gospel of Christ. It has always been my ambition to preach the gospel where Christ was not known" (Rom 15:19-20). Through God's intervention Paul shared God's heart to take the gospel to the Greco-Roman world. He couldn't reach everybody, but he could reach some and through them gather disciples into communities in the major cities along the trade routes of the Roman Empire.

2. Paul connected with people. "It has always been my ambition to preach the gospel where Christ was not known" (Rom 15:20). When he arrived in a new location, Paul typically sought out responsive people in the synagogue or marketplace. The commitment to preach to unevangelized groups and to move on to new groups when the gospel was rejected meant that the apostle's ministry was mobile. Paul recognized that it would be local believers, not he, who would reach their region in depth. The role of Paul and his team was to find responsive people and leave a body of believers behind who would evangelize the region while the apostolic band moved on to the next frontier.

3. Paul shared the gospel. "I have declared to both Jews and Greeks that they must turn to God in repentance and have faith in our Lord Jesus" (Acts 20:21). Paul wanted to save people from the judgment of God. He wanted to "win" as many as possible.[10] For Jews this meant acknowledging that Jesus, the crucified preacher from Nazareth, was the Messiah; Jesus' death was God's answer to the problem of human sin—the problem that neither the covenant with Abraham nor the Mosaic Law could solve—and God vindicated Jesus by raising him from the dead. For Gentiles this meant turning from pagan gods to the God of Israel—the one true living God—believing in Jesus who rescues sinners from the wrath of God, and accepting the atoning significance of Jesus' death on the cross. Gentiles must have their lives shaped by the Jewish Scriptures and by Jesus' and the apostles' teaching as they waited for Jesus' return (1 Thess 1:9-10; 1 Cor 1:18–2:5).

4. Paul trained disciples. "You know that I have not hesitated to preach anything that would be helpful to you but have taught you publicly and from house to house" (Acts 20:20). The proclamation of the gospel was not enough. Paul wanted people to hear, understand and obey the gospel (Rom 10:14-21).[11] He wanted to bring disciples to full maturity in Christ on the day of the final judgment. Paul hoped his converts would be his joy and crown before God on the final day.[12]

For Paul, the "obedience of faith" is the obedience that flowed from faith in Christ (Rom 1:5; 15:18). It was the disciples' total response to the gospel in every area of life, not just their initial conversion. The Christian life is both created and lived through the gospel.

5. Paul gathered communities. "Be shepherds of the church of God, which he bought with his own blood" (Acts 20:28). Paul was not content with the salvation of individuals. He formed disciples into communities and worked to strengthen those communities. Salvation brought disciples into a relationship with each other. Once formed, the new community of faith became a living witness to the grace of God and a means of continuing the mission once Paul and his team had moved on.

Paul's primary ministry was to establish rather than to sustain churches. Yet his pioneering ministry did not end with the birth of a new church. Paul revisited the churches he had founded; he also wrote to them and sent envoys to check on how they were doing. The goal of Paul's ministry of church strengthening was that each church would mature and begin to participate in the apostolic ministry.

6. Paul multiplied workers. "Now . . . there is no more place for me to work in these regions" (Rom 15:23). Looking back over thirty-five years of ministry in A.D. 56/57, Paul knew that there was still plenty to do. However, he believed the work of an apostle was to preach where the gospel was unknown and to plant churches where there were none. As those churches came to a basic level of maturity and as local leaders were trained, the apostle was ready to move on to the next unreached field. On this occasion, he planned a mission to Spain via Rome.

In the years A.D. 47-57 Paul and his coworkers founded churches in the Roman provinces of Syria-Cilicia, Cyprus, Galatia, Macedonia, Achaia and Asia. It was a staggering achievement. Paul believed it was possible to complete his end vision for a region. When Paul stated, "I have fully proclaimed the gospel of Christ" (Rom 15:19), he was referring to the scope of his mission, which included pioneer evangelism; the training of new disciples; the formation of churches and their establishment in the gospel in both belief and behavior; and the equipping of leaders for the churches and the mission in the region. Once this had occurred, Paul could move on to new regions. These were Paul's key apostolic tasks.

Paul's mission was unprecedented. For the first time, there was a concerted missionary effort throughout the world. What Paul achieved remains unparalleled in two thousand years of the history of the Christian movement. Paul's extraordinary example, along with his theology hammered out in his letters to the churches, laid the foundation for the future expansion of the Christian movement.[13]

ANY WAY HE CAN

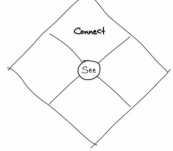

I have become all things to all people so that
by all possible means I might save some.

—PAUL (1 CORINTHIANS 9:22)

IT WAS AROUND MIDNIGHT. Paul and Silas were praying and singing hymns to God; in the surrounding cells, the other prisoners were listening. It had been an eventful day; Paul and Silas had been set upon by a mob, stripped and severely flogged by order of the city's magistrates. Then they were thrown into prison.

Under Roman justice, a prisoner was flogged in preparation for questioning before he was jailed. It was a painful and bloody ordeal that ripped the clothes from his body. The wounds remained untreated as the prisoner was placed in chains. Prisons were cramped, noisy and foul with the stench of unwashed bodies.[1]

Despite their ordeal, Paul and Silas, with their feet in stocks, passed the time in the darkness praying and singing while the other prisoners listened in. This unplanned launch into prison ministry is a reminder of how keen Paul and his coworkers were to make the most of every opportunity—even setbacks—to connect with people and share the gospel.

Paul shared the gospel with anyone who would listen. He spoke to government officials, prominent politicians, Greek philosophers, angry mobs, pagan sailors, occult practitioners, Roman soldiers, businesswomen, wealthy aristocrats, craftsmen and jailors. Paul shared anywhere he could. Paul proclaimed the gospel in marketplaces, in private homes, in prisons, in a public lecture hall, in an outdoor theater, in court, even on a sinking ship. His purpose was always the communication of the gospel to those who were ready to receive it. He was intentional about finding responsive people in strategic locations.

To this end, Paul focused his efforts on cities where there were Jewish communities. By the first century, five to six million Jews lived in cities outside Palestine. In some cities they numbered up to 10-15 percent of the population. There was a substantial Jewish population in virtually every town of any size in the regions around the coast of the Mediterranean Sea.[2] These Jews of the Diaspora were Hellenistic—they spoke Greek and lived in a Greek culture.

Early Christian expansion followed the network of synagogues of the Jewish Diaspora. Paul and other missionaries connected with these social networks. In the first century, if there was a Christian community in your neighborhood, it was most likely that you lived in a large port city that was Greek in language and culture, and that was home to a Jewish community.[3]

The Jews of the Diaspora had been successful in attracting Gentile sympathizers and converts to their faith. These Hellenistic Jews and Gentiles

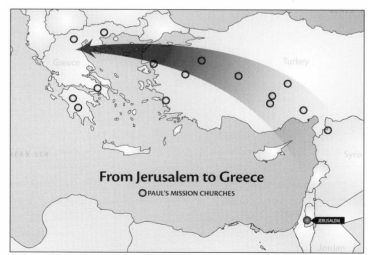

Map 14.1. From Jerusalem all the way around to Illyricum, I have fully proclaimed the gospel of Christ (Romans 15:19). See Paul Barnett, *Paul: Missionary of Jesus*.

who worshiped the God of Israel were the most responsive people in the Roman Empire to the gospel. Jews living outside of Palestine were open to new ideas. The Gentiles who were attracted to the Jewish faith were even more responsive. Once converted, they became the beachhead from which the gospel spread in depth to the wider pagan population.

What was true for Paul was also true of the great mass of rank-and-file Christians who took the gospel to the empire. For missionaries headed out from Jerusalem, the pressing first questions were: *Where should we go? Who will receive us?* The answers seemed obvious. All across the Greco-Roman world were relatively well-to-do communities of the Jewish Diaspora with whom the missionaries had ties—people who were relatives (even if very distant) or friends of friends.

THE WORD TRAVELS TO CORINTH

Corinth was, along with Ephesus, one of the two most important cities that Paul visited as a missionary. He stayed in both places long enough to establish churches that reached out into the surrounding regions. The Romans destroyed ancient Corinth and then rebuilt it as a Roman colony in 44 B.C. By the early A.D. 50s Corinth was becoming the most prosperous city in Greece. It was a commercial port city of 145,000 people, well connected to the cities along the Mediterranean and in the rest of Greece.

The Corinthians worshiped both Greek and Roman gods and goddesses, as well as the emperor. Corinthian religion was infamous for its sexual immorality. The temple of Aphrodite (the goddess of love) overlooked the city from a nearby mountain. A thousand female slaves served there as temple prostitutes.

Paul came to Corinth early in A.D. 50 "in weakness with great fear and trembling" (1 Cor 2:3). Since entering the province of Macedonia, he had been driven out of one city after another, but not before he had left behind small groups of believers in Philippi, Thessalonica and Berea. The Athenians had not expelled him, but for the most part they had responded to the gospel with amused indifference and ridicule.

The time in Corinth was a departure from the normal pattern of Paul's ministry. For the first time since he left Antioch with Barnabas five years before, Paul had a long ministry in one place. The fruit of this ministry was a vibrant but volatile new church.

In Corinth Paul met Aquila and Priscilla, who had recently arrived from Rome. They too were tentmakers (or leatherworkers). Through them Paul secured work and a place to stay. Cutting and stitching leather was long, hard work. Tentmakers belonged to a class of people who were looked down upon by the wealthy and the educated. Paul, who was comfortable in the presence of rulers, philosophers and wealthy aristocrats, willingly returned to working with his hands.

As usual Paul began his mission in the synagogue at Corinth. Some Jews and Gentiles believed. Others ridiculed and rejected his message, and soon opposition boiled over in the synagogue. Paul shook out his clothes in protest and declared that he was going to the Gentiles. Paul and the new believers left the synagogue, and Paul formed this group into the nucleus of a small community of disciples. His ministry base was now in the home of Titius Justus, a newly converted Gentile.

Previously, rejection in the synagogue had meant Paul was forced out of a city. This time things were different. Jesus intervened through a vision and told Paul to stay and continue the mission in Corinth. He promised Paul protection and fruitfulness because he had many people in Corinth (Acts 18:9-10) He urged Paul to keep speaking and not be silent. With this encouragement, Paul stayed another year and a half in Corinth (A.D. 50-52).

Paul shifted to a predominantly Gentile mission in Corinth. Individual Jews still converted, but now Paul ministered in a mission and a community of disciples that were not synagogue-focused. His teaching further shook the Jewish community when Crispus, the ruler of the synagogue, came to believe and was baptized together with his family. Many more followed them, both Jews and Greeks.

Paul would later write to the Corinthians and to all God's "holy people throughout Achaia" (2 Cor 1:1). His pioneering ministry had borne fruit in the great city of Corinth and was spreading throughout the surrounding province of Achaia.

TRAVEL PLANS

Paul pursued a general strategy of taking the gospel to unreached cities. As he went, he was open to God's intervention and guidance regarding particular locations. Often Paul's stay in various cities was cut short by persecution, but God was still at work: even persecution would not disrupt his plan for the spread of the Word and the establishment of new churches.

Paul planned his missionary travels, but he knew that he was dependent on God to carry out his plans. He was guided by obedience to God's call on the Damascus road to preach the gospel to Jews and Gentiles, and the strategy of reaching major cities with Jewish communities along the trade routes of the Roman Empire. He was guided by visions, he prayed and sought prayer for guidance, and he made rational decisions in the light of circumstances. He was guided by the rejection of his message and by his call to be a pioneer missionary in fields that were unreached by others. At times he had no direct control over where he would go and to whom he would speak.

There are two constants in Paul's decision making: his tenacity in obeying God's call and God's intervention to direct him through common sense, revelations and circumstances. Other than these two elements, there is no formula for how Paul chose the fields he worked in or the people he spoke to.

In Acts 16 we find Paul and his companions traveling throughout what is now modern Turkey around Phrygia and Galatia because they had been "kept by the Holy Spirit from preaching the word in the province of Asia." They tried to enter Bithynia, but the Spirit of Jesus would not allow them, so they went down to the Aegean port city of Troas. Now Paul must have been confused about what to do next. Where was he to go?

Finally in Troas Paul had a vision of a man begging him to come to Macedonia to help. The messenger from Macedonia was a responsive person. When God wanted to communicate to Paul where he should go next, it was in the form of a responsive person. Human receptivity played an important part in how Paul made decisions about where to go and how long to stay. Paul sought out those who welcomed the gospel; when he met with resistance, he moved on to find responsive people.

WHEN PAUL CAME TO TOWN

When Paul and his team (Silas, Timothy, Titus and others) arrived in a new location, they came uninvited. There was no one to prepare the way for them or their message. Where and how did they begin? How did they make initial contact with people?

Paul did not expect people to come to him. He went to where they were. He sought them out in places where they were open to listen to his message and engage in conversations. For Jews and Gentiles sympathetic to Judaism, the synagogue was the natural place for discussion concerning religious matters. For pagan Gentiles, the city square was the setting for hearing and discussing matters of philosophy and religion. In Greek cities that was the marketplace; in Roman cities, the city square was the forum. Other times Paul would meet with people in lecture halls, workshops and private homes.

Synagogues. "As his custom was, Paul went into the synagogue, and on three Sabbath days he reasoned with them from the Scriptures" (Acts 17:2). Immediately after his conversion Paul went to the synagogue in Damascus and began preaching about Jesus and debating with his fellow Jews that Jesus is the Messiah (Acts 9:20-22). This pattern continued throughout the rest of Paul's ministry. Paul sought out cities that had Jewish communities, bypassing major cities such as Neapolis, Amphipolis and Apollonia that had no Jewish community.[4] He would have had relational connections, directly and through others, to members of the Jewish community in the cities he visited. He typically began his mission in the local synagogue. The synagogue was also the place where Paul could meet with Gentiles who worshiped Israel's God. Some were full converts (proselytes), and others attended services but had not formally converted (God-fearers). These Gentiles had rejected paganism for belief in the one true God and the high moral standards that flowed from that belief. They were the people most likely to become followers of Christ. They were seeking the God of Israel, but to convert to Judaism they had to accept the social stigma of circumcision. When the requirement to submit to the Jewish law was removed, these Gentile God-fearers became the bridge across which the gospel spread to pagan Gentiles.

Paul came to the synagogue as a rabbi trained by Gamaliel and was often given the opportunity to teach from the Law and the Prophets on the Sabbath. On every occasion, Paul and his message were eventually rejected but not before some of his audience, both Jews and Gentiles, had responded with faith. Despite violent and potentially deadly opposition, Paul continued to visit the synagogues of the cities he entered. If he was forced out of the synagogue but able to remain in the city, he moved to other venues such as the home of a wealthy sympathizer (in Corinth) or a lecture hall (in Ephesus). In Philippi there was no synagogue (to form a synagogue required ten Jewish males), so Paul and his companions went outside the city gate to the river where they assumed Jews and Gentile God-fearers would gather for prayer (Acts 16:13, 16). Paul found a number of women there, including Lydia, a God-fearing Gentile who believed his message and was baptized with her whole household.

Homes. "Believe in the Lord Jesus, and you will be saved—you and your household" (Acts 16:31). On a number of occasions Paul's ministry led to the conversion of whole households—for the Philippian jailer, the merchant Lydia, Jason in Thessalonica, the household of Crispus the synagogue leader in Corinth, and the household of Stephanas, also in Corinth.[5] Private homes were a place where social distinctions—between rich and poor, slave and free, male and female—could be more relaxed than in the public gaze. The household (or *oikos*) was the building block of Greco-Roman society. Under Roman law the father of the household had authority over his immediate family and other dependents such as relatives, slaves, hired workers and even business associates. Household members were connected to each other through formal and informal ties—family, friendship and work relationships.

Paul described Stephanas and his family as the "first" converts in the province of Achaia. They were "first fruits"—not just the first converts but a pledge from God of more to come. They became the nucleus of a growing community in Corinth and throughout Achaia. Their work and witness resulted in others being added to the faith.[6]

Reaching households of people who became new believers was an important part of Paul's practice. Through households the gospel traveled from person to person across the ties of existing relationships. Private homes also provided a natural center of life for the formation of a new church.

The workshop. "Because [Paul] was a tentmaker as they were, he stayed and worked with them" (Acts 18:3). Paul worked as a maker and repairer of tents and other leather products. He did this because he needed to earn a living and did not want to be regarded as someone peddling the gospel for money.

Paul's work was not primarily a method for connecting with people. In many locations Paul would not have had enough time to set up shop before he was forced to leave. In some locations his trade gave him the chance to meet a range of people, including others involved in the trade.[7] The people who practiced different crafts and trades clustered in the same streets and neighborhoods. He would also have met both Jewish and Gentile customers.

The vast number of people in the large cities of the Roman Empire lived in multi-story buildings. The ground floors had shops that faced the street; the owners would live above the shops or at the rear. There might also be room for a workshop and accommodation for employees and slaves. These households formed around a small enterprise represented a good cross-section of society and were linked to other households through family, friendship and commercial ties.[8]

City squares. "[Paul] reasoned . . . in the marketplace day by day with those who happened to be there" (Acts 17:17). Paul spoke to individuals and crowds in public places. The cities of the Roman Empire were densely populated, and homes were small and crowded. Life was lived on the streets and in the public squares. The city square was a prime location to meet a wide range of people.

The marketplace (*agora*) was the political and commercial center of Greek cities. In Roman cities and colonies, marketplaces were spread throughout the city, and the forum was the political and religious center. Corinth was a Roman city with an enormous central plaza that served as its forum. It was there that Paul would have preached.

In Athens, Paul went every day to the marketplace and talked to those who happened to be there. Paul was able to meet large numbers of people in the marketplaces, including the city's leading citizens and officials.

A lecture hall. "Paul . . . had discussions daily in the lecture hall of Tyrannus" (Acts 19:9). In Ephesus Paul set up a base outside the synagogue in the lecture hall of Tyrannus. There he taught, debated and persuaded every day for two years.

In the Greco-Roman world, business (including formal lectures for fee-paying clients) was done in the cooler part of the day, starting at dawn and ending at 11 a.m. A meal and an afternoon rest followed the morning's work. More people were asleep at 1 p.m. than at 1 a.m. Work would begin again at 4 p.m. Paul's daily sessions were probably conducted outside working hours, between 11 a.m. and 4 p.m. Both the hall and his audience would have been available then. This would have left the mornings free for Paul to earn his living as a leatherworker.[9]

Interactions with prominent people. "When the proconsul saw what had happened, he believed, for he was amazed at the teaching about the Lord" (Acts 13:12). On some occasions, the entry point into a community was through a prominent person such as Sergius Paulus, the governor of Cyprus (Acts 13:6-12) or the "leading women" of Thessalonica and Berea (Acts 17:4, 12). In Ephesus Paul had friends among the "Asiarchs," the leading officials of the city (Acts 19:31), and in Philippi the businesswoman Lydia was one of the first to believe (Acts 16:31).[10] She dealt in purple cloth, which was a luxury item, and she had a household that could accommodate Paul and his coworkers.[11]

Sergius Paulus was the person of highest social status converted through

Paul. After Paul and Barnabas left him, they headed north for Pisidian Antioch. Paul and Barnabas climbed the steep roads that led from the coast into
the rugged Taurus Mountains. The city lay a great distance away on the
other side of the mountains—3,600 feet above sea level! The journey was
arduous and dangerous.

Why did Paul go to all this effort? Sergius Paulus may have been the
reason. His family, the Sergii, were important landowners in the area. The
governor could have provided Paul with letters of introduction to aid his
journey and to connect him with family members and friends. Pisidian Antioch had fifty villages under its control in the surrounding countryside,
with a total population of over 50,000 people.[12] Luke recorded the conversion of both Jews and Gentiles as the word of the Lord spread throughout
the region (Acts 13:49).

During trials and imprisonments. "Then Agrippa said to Paul, 'Do you
think that in such a short time you can persuade me to be a Christian?'"
(Acts 26:28).

Paul also used his trials before two different Roman governors (Antonius
Felix and Porcius Festus) and a Jewish king (Herod Agrippa II) to explain the
gospel. He did the same at his trial before the Emperor in Rome (2 Tim 4:17).

Paul spent years in prison—two years in Caesarea, another two years in
Rome and a brief time in Philippi. Paul wrote that he had faced far more
imprisonments than his opponents, suggesting there were periods in jail we
know nothing about.

Paul made use of his two-year imprisonment in Rome to proclaim the gospel
to the Praetorian Guard and to many others (Phil 1:13). The soldiers of the
Praetorian Guard—the emperor's personal bodyguards—had sixteen cohorts of
a thousand men. Their role was to protect the emperor and his family, and to
discourage and suppress plots and disturbances. They were at the very heart of
the Roman Empire. Over the two years, many of these legionnaires would have
heard the gospel from Paul, and some passed it on to their comrades.

Paul mentions there were believers in "the emperor's household" (Phil
4:22).[13] The household of a Roman aristocrat included his family, servants,
slaves and freedmen. Often their duties were specialized, such as domestic
servants and professionals providing medical, commercial and secretarial
help. Caesar's household was equivalent to a modern civil service based in
Rome but also in households scattered throughout the provinces. Members
of Caesar's household were powerful and socially mobile, despite being

slaves and former slaves.[14] Many of them also had heard the gospel and come to faith in Jesus Christ through Paul's imprisonment.

Paul used every situation—including setbacks, persecution, and imprisonment—for the advance of the gospel into new fields. When he was driven out of city after city, the gospel spread. When he settled in Ephesus for three years, the gospel spread throughout the whole province of Asia. When he was on trial, the gospel continued to spread. When he was imprisoned in Rome, the gospel spread and reached the emperor's personal bodyguard and the imperial civil service. Paul took advantage of every circumstance, planned and unplanned, to connect with people and advance the spread of the gospel because he was confident that God was already at work.

15

ONE GOSPEL

I [Jesus] will rescue you [Paul] from your own people and from the Gentiles.
I am sending you to them to open their eyes and turn them from darkness to light,
and from the power of Satan to God, so that they may receive forgiveness
of sins and a place among those who are sanctified by faith in me.

—ACTS 26:17-18

I consider my life worth nothing to me; my only aim is to finish the race and
complete the task the Lord Jesus has given me—the task of
testifying to the good news of God's grace.

—PAUL, SPEAKING TO THE
EPHESIAN ELDERS (ACTS 20:24)

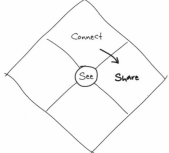

AT THE HEART OF PAUL'S MISSION was the proclamation of the good news of Jesus Christ—the same gospel preached by James, Peter and John (Gal 1:1; 1:11–2:10). Paul does not have his own gospel. There is only one gospel.

THE GOSPEL TO THE JEWS

Paul and Barnabas arrived in Pisidian Antioch (in modern Turkey) in the summer of A.D. 46. The city was a Roman colony and home to thousands of

Roman veterans and civilian settlers. It had a strong Jewish community. As usual, Paul and Barnabas went to the synagogue on the sabbath and were invited to speak to the Israelites and Gentiles gathered there.

Paul's actions at Pisidian Antioch provide an example of how he communicated the gospel to the Jewish people who lived in the major cities of the empire. There are many parallels with Peter's Pentecost speech. Paul's message that day came in three parts: he explained that the coming of Jesus of Nazareth was the climax of God's dealing with Israel throughout its history; he told them that God had fulfilled his promises in the life, death and resurrection of Jesus; finally, he called his audience to put their faith in Jesus for the forgiveness of their sins, and he warned them of the danger of rejecting God's gift.

In his message, Paul quoted extensively from the Jewish Scriptures. He presented Jesus as the Messiah; through him comes the forgiveness of sins to all who believe. This included both Jews and Gentiles gathered in the synagogue, but Paul shaped his message for a predominantly Jewish audience. Pious Jews knew they needed God's grace for the forgiveness of sin, and such Jews looked to the coming of the Messiah for salvation. Paul was speaking with them in terms they would understand. Jesus' resurrection from the dead was evidence that Jesus was the Messiah, whose death on the cross brought final salvation.

Some people welcomed the message, and others rejected it. Understanding was no guarantee of acceptance.

Paul and Barnabas were invited back to speak again at the synagogue on the following sabbath. When the synagogue leaders saw almost the whole city—a crowd of thousands—turn out to hear God's Word, they rejected Paul and his message. So Paul and Barnabas took the gospel to the Gentiles who welcomed it.

The Word of the Lord spread to the Gentiles throughout the city and the whole region, which included fifty villages (Acts 13:48-49). Eventually the missionaries were forced out by a powerful coalition of Jewish leaders, Gentile God-fearing women of high standing, and the leading men of the city, but with the same dramatic gesture that Jesus had taught his disciples, Paul and Barnabas shook the dust off their feet in protest and warning, and then moved on.

Throughout the city and the region, they left behind communities of believers who were filled with joy and the Holy Spirit. Some months later Paul and Barnabas revisited Pisidian Antioch on their way back to Syria. They strengthened the new disciples, encouraged them to remain true to the faith and appointed elders for each church (Acts 14:22-23).

This pattern, with some variations, was repeated in city after city.

THE GOSPEL TO THE GENTILES

Athens. Paul's usual practice was to travel with members of his team, but early in A.D. 50 Paul arrived in Athens alone. Opponents from Thessalonica had interrupted his successful mission in Berea, and Paul left Macedonia in a hurry by sea. The plan was for Paul to wait in Athens until Silas and Timothy caught up.

Athens's glory days were five hundred years in the past, and the city was no longer important politically or militarily. The population had dwindled to around 25,000. Athens retained one claim to fame—its reputation as a great center of learning.

The visit to Athens was not a planned mission trip, but Paul was not the sort of person to wait around. As he wandered the city, he was deeply disturbed by the city's many gods and its ignorance of the one true God (Acts 17:22-31). Athens was renowned for its thousands of statues of the gods and its many pagan temples. Every gateway and porch carried its protecting god. Every street, every square, had its shrine. A Roman poet observed that it was easier to find a god in Athens than a man![1]

Moved by what he saw, Paul took the gospel to the Jews and God-fearers in the synagogue. In addition, every day he went to the marketplace—the hub of community life in a Greek city—and spoke with whomever he met. The philosophers of Athens heard about this and sought Paul out to give an account of this "strange new teaching" about "foreign gods" to the philosophers and council of the Areopagus—the body that approved new altars, temples and additions to the religious calendar.

In this setting Paul focused his message on the nature of God and how he can be known. His speech did not cover the totality of the gospel, just one aspect of it. Paul explained he was not trying to introduce a "new" god; he had come to explain the true nature of the "unknown god" whose altar he had discovered while walking about the city. This god did not require any land for a temple; the God Paul proclaimed does not live in temples made by human hands. Those whom this God had created cannot control him.

Throughout his speech Paul used language and arguments that were shaped for his audience of philosophers.[2] He sought common ground with them, yet Paul was not trying to add to their accumulation of religious knowledge but rather using their own words and ideas to challenge their religious beliefs. He argued that human beings were created to seek God and to know him in a genuine relationship. Sadly, their speculations and idolatry had kept them from a true knowledge of God.

Once he had established this foundation, Paul announced the coming judgment of the world by the One God had raised from the dead. He called those gathered to repent, turning the tables on his investigators so that now they were in the spotlight.

Paul did not begin his message with Old Testament quotes and with the teaching about Christ. With those pagan philosophers, the beginning point was God, the Creator and Lord of all things. Paul declared that Gentiles who know nothing of God's revelation to Israel could not find God in idolatry or philosophical speculation. Humanity has failed to know God as he is. Paul called his pagan audience to abandon their traditional gods and turn to the living God who can only be known through repentance and faith in Jesus Christ.

Most of Paul's audience responded to his message with either cynicism or indecision. Yet even among these philosophers, the Word did its work; some of them believed and were formed into a small community of disciples before Paul left for Corinth.

Thessalonica. The message Paul delivered in Athens was his defense before a court of investigation. Earlier Paul had been in the marketplace daily, sharing the gospel with individuals and small groups. Luke does not tell us how Paul communicated with them, but we get an idea of the gospel he shared with Gentiles from his first letter to the Thessalonians, written around the same time he was in Athens. The letter, written weeks or a few months after the new church was started, helps fill out our understanding of Paul's gospel to the Gentiles.

Thessalonica was the capital of the Roman province of Macedonia and the largest city in the region. In 42 B.C. the Romans had made it a free city with the right to govern itself on a Greek pattern. Most of the new believers there had been pagan Gentiles. In his letter Paul reminded these new disciples how he and his companions came with boldness in the power of the Holy Spirit, speaking the Word of God, not men. Paul proclaimed the God of Israel as the living and true God. He called the Thes-

salonians to turn away from the futility of idol worship and turn in faith
to the living God of Israel.

Table 15.1. First Thessalonians provides insight into the gospel Paul shared with pagan Gentiles. See Roland
Allen, *Missionary Methods: St. Paul's or Ours?* 4th ed. (London: World Dominion Press, 1956), pp. 90-91.

The Gospel in 1 Thessalonians
There is one living and true God (1:9).
Idolatry is sinful and must be forsaken (1:9).
The wrath of God is ready to be revealed against pagan Gentiles for their impurity (4:6) and against the Jews for their rejection of Christ (2:15-16).
The judgment will come suddenly and unexpectedly (5:2-3).
Jesus the Son of God (1:10), given over to death (5:10) and raised from the dead (4:14), is the Savior from the wrath of God (1:10).
The kingdom of Jesus is now established and all are invited to enter it (2:12).
Those who believe and turn to God are now expecting the coming of the Savior who will return from heaven to receive them (1:10, 4:15-17).

Paul explained the story of the life and ministry of Jesus of Nazareth, his
death and resurrection, and the significance of these events. Forgiveness of
sin and deliverance from God's wrath came through Jesus' death on the
cross in the place of sinners. Through faith, the Thessalonians would be set
free from the rule of sin for a new life in the Spirit under the rule of Christ.
Finally, at a time appointed by God, Jesus will return to judge the world and
rescue those who believe in him.

THE GOSPEL ACCORDING TO PAUL

Paul spoke of the gospel as an uncontainable force that advances powerfully
and purposefully.[3] The word of the gospel is not just "words" but God at
work bringing salvation. At the heart of the gospel Paul proclaimed was a
crucified and risen Savior. This was revealed to Paul on the road to Damascus, but it was the same gospel made known to the other apostles.

Paul proclaimed the gospel in both Greek and Jewish settings, adapting
his presentation to his audience: "I have become all things to all people so
that by all possible means I could save some" (1 Cor 9:22). His starting point
with Jews was Jesus Christ as the fulfillment of God's purposes for Israel,
with extensive quotations from the Jewish Scriptures. With pagans, he used
terms and authorities that were familiar to them and began with God who
was the Creator and Lord over all. Whatever his starting point, audience or
context, Paul always returned to the center of the gospel—Jesus Christ, cru-

cified and risen. Paul adapted the delivery of his message to different audiences but not at the expense of the heart of the gospel. Paul did not avoid speaking of God's coming judgment or of Jesus' sacrificial death for the sins of the world. Any other gospel was no gospel (Gal 1:6-10; 1 Cor 3:10-15).

Paul knew that it was not a natural thing for a Jew or a pagan to put their faith in a Savior who was executed on a cross. No matter how culturally appropriate Paul was in his communication, his message was always going to be a scandal to Jews and foolishness to Gentiles. For Jews, it was unthinkable that the eternal God would make himself known through a crucified criminal. Greeks were impressed with human wisdom and lofty ideas. The story of a crucified Savior made no sense to them.

To follow Jesus, both Jews and Gentiles had to abandon important aspects of their culture. The polytheistic Gentiles of Thessalonica had to abandon their faith in many gods and put their trust in a Jewish Savior. They had to abandon their visits to the pagan temples and excuse themselves from the religious festivals and rituals that dominated public and private life. This brought them into conflict with their community. Paul commended the Thessalonians because they received the word with joy inspired by the Holy Spirit, despite the persecution they experienced (1 Thess 1:5-6).

Paul preached with confidence because God himself was powerfully at work to enable both Jews and Gentiles to come to faith in a crucified Savior. God's power was at work in the preaching of the gospel, whether it was done by public proclamation in the synagogues and marketplaces or in private conversations. The proof of the gospel was in its power to save Jews and Gentiles, slaves and free, men and women. The fruit of the gospel was disciples who followed Jesus and were gathered into communities.

Paul rejected attempts to "prove" the gospel through clever arguments. The truth of salvation through Jesus' death and resurrection was found in the power of the Holy Spirit. The sharing of the gospel was effective, but not because of any technique. It was the work of the Holy Spirit. The gospel came not just in words but in power and in the Holy Spirit with full conviction (1 Thess 1:5; 2 Thess 3:1).

16

THE OBEDIENCE OF FAITH

Therefore I urge you to imitate me. For this reason I have sent to you Timothy, my son whom I love, who is faithful in the Lord. He will remind you of my way of life in Christ Jesus, which agrees with what I teach everywhere in every church.

—PAUL (1 CORINTHIANS 4:16-17)

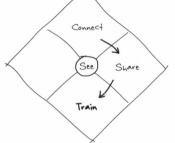

PAUL SPENT ABOUT A QUARTER OF HIS MINISTRY under arrest. On one occasion Paul was under house arrest, probably in Rome awaiting trial, when a runaway slave came looking for him.

Onesimus was a slave in the household of Philemon, a friend of Paul's. Onesimus must have known something of the gospel, as Philemon was a Christian in whose home the church gathered. Onesimus had fled after he wronged his master in some way. Under Roman law a master had the right to hunt down and brutally punish an escaped slave, and anyone harboring an escaped slave was liable to pay the owner for compensation. Onesimus may have hoped Paul would mediate between him and his master.

Through Paul, Onesimus became a believer. Paul loved him as a father loves his son and came to rely on his help during his imprisonment. Paul wanted to reconcile Philemon and Onesimus, so Paul wrote a short note for Onesimus to take back to Philemon.

The letter to Philemon gives us an idea of how Paul trained disciples to follow Christ in a world corrupted by sin. Paul wanted Philemon to see how Christ could transform his social relationships. Onesimus was still a slave under the law, but he should no longer be treated as one because he was now a brother in Christ. Paul reminded Philemon that both slaves and masters are servants of Christ and members of the one household of faith. Philemon, Onesimus's master, himself had a master in heaven. Paul could have ordered Philemon to act in a particular way; instead he appealed to the truth of the gospel and its implications for how Philemon should treat a brother in Christ who happened to be a slave.

Paul offered to repay any wrong Onesimus had done, but because Philemon had found Christ through Paul, he owed Paul a greater debt than Onesimus owed him.

The shortest letter Paul wrote, Philemon is a window into how Paul trained disciples. Both Philemon and Onesimus came to know Christ through Paul. Having shared the gospel of God's grace with them, Paul was now, from prison, teaching them how to live out the gospel's implications. He was not laying down a new law; he was teaching disciples to follow Christ.

PLEASING GOD

Paul didn't just convert people and move on. He taught new believers how to live a life modeled on Jesus—a life that is only possible through the power of the Holy Spirit.

This was not easy. Paul had to deal with sexual immorality in the church that even pagans would not tolerate. He had to deal with believers who took each other to court to settle their differences. Both Jewish and Gentile converts were in constant danger of mixing their former beliefs with their new faith in Christ.

Paul wrote to the Galatians, "You were running a good race. Who cut in on you to keep you from obeying the truth?" (Gal 5:7). The gospel is not just something we believe; it's something we obey. The obedience of faith begins with conversion but must go on to include an ongoing change of life. Paul told the Galatians that he continued to suffer like a woman in labor "until Christ is formed in you" (Gal 4:19). Bringing them to the obedience of faith was an important part of Paul's mission.

Paul's letters typically focused on two themes: (1) the truth of the gospel and (2) how believers should live in response to that truth. His priority was to establish believers in the obedience of faith—a way of life that was consistent with the character of God as revealed in Jesus Christ. Paul's letters followed a similar pattern: starting with the grace of God in Jesus Christ, he would remind believers of who they were in Christ and what God had done for them. This focus on the reality of their salvation and all its benefits dominated Paul's letters. Once he had laid this foundation, he moved on to show how these truths must transform the lives of God's people.

Gentile conversion to faith in Christ involved a radical break with their culture. Gentiles had to abandon their belief in the gods and turn to the one true and living God of the Jewish Scriptures. They had to put their faith in a Savior who had been executed as a criminal on a Roman cross and raised physically from the dead.

Imagine the changes in the life of a new believer who lived in Ephesus, for example. He would no longer visit the temple of Artemis or participate in the rituals and festivals in her honor. He would not bow before the statue of the goddess when he visited the public baths, and he would remove the idols from his home. He would no longer worship the Roman emperor as a god. His break with paganism could not have been more obvious to his community.

In addition, this new believer would leave behind all kinds of sexual immorality—adultery, visiting prostitutes and homosexual behavior—as well as forsaking greed and drunkenness. All of these were acceptable in Ephesian society, as long as they were carried out discreetly and within limits.

A Jewish believer would need to accept that Jesus of Nazareth was the promised Messiah. Jews could no longer rely on obedience to the law of Moses for salvation. They had to approach God in faith and humble dependence, on equal footing with the Gentiles. Their ancestry was of no advantage when it came to being right with God. They had to face the threat of expulsion from the synagogue and of rejection from friends and family who did not share their faith in Christ. Jewish believers also had to accept the influx of uncircumcised Gentiles to the community of God's people.

In Paul's first letter to the Thessalonians, written soon after the church was started, Paul reminded them of the truth of the gospel and urged them to respond to God's grace with obedience. Paul likened his ministry among the Thessalonians to that of both a father and a nursing mother. Paul and his companions lived blamelessly among these new believers and challenged them to follow their example. After Paul was "torn away" from them, he sent Timothy back from Athens to strengthen and encourage them as they faced persecution.

Paul could challenge the Thessalonians to imitate Christ because they were learning and passing on the stories of Jesus' life and the content of his teaching. Paul also reminded them that the God who called them to imitate Christ had also given them the Holy Spirit (1 Thess 4:8). He commended their progress and challenged them to live holy lives by avoiding the sexual immorality typical of pagan society. Paul encouraged them to grow in love for one another, work hard with their hands so that they would not be dependent on anyone, and live a life that would win the respect of unbelievers.

For Paul, discipleship was about grasping the full implications of what God has done in Christ and then living them out in every aspect of life. It was the obedience that springs from faith in Christ and is made possible by the Holy Spirit. Paul was confident that even though he had left these new disciples prematurely, the Holy Spirit was present and would enable them to come through their suffering with joy.

Paul had good grounds for his confidence that these new disciples could go on to maturity despite their separation. Already they had become imitators of Paul and his coworkers, and of the Lord. Already they were a model of faith to all the believers in Macedonia and Achaia. Already their faith in God was known everywhere (1 Thess 1:6-8).

Paul was not a moralist introducing a new law for Jesus' disciples. He never tired of explaining the good news about Jesus and teaching believers how the reality of their salvation changes everything. Following Jesus was more than a profession of faith. It was a path to be walked, a way of life. They were to no longer live for themselves but for Jesus who died and was raised for them.[1]

WHEN YOU COME TOGETHER

*It was through the household and the house church
that Christianity and its otherworldly "assembly"
first put down its roots, then grew to
undermine the old civic values and
the very shape of the pagan city.*

—ROBIN LANE FOX,
*PAGANS AND
CHRISTIANS*

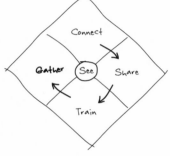

BEFORE HE MET CHRIST, SAUL HAD A MISSION—to destroy the church
(Acts 8:3). That meant going from house to house and dragging men and
women off to prison to await trial, punishment and sometimes death. On
the road to Damascus, Saul learned that Jesus identified with his people
(the church) so closely that to persecute his followers was to persecute
him (Acts 8:3; 9:4-5).

Saul's surrender to Jesus meant his inclusion into the people of God. This
began with God sending a disciple named Ananias to pray for the restoration of Saul's sight and the filling of the Holy Spirit. Ananias baptized Saul
immediately and introduced him to the disciples at Damascus.

From the time of his conversion and call, Saul (who eventually adopted
his Greek name Paul) proclaimed the gospel and formed disciples into

churches wherever he went. But Paul didn't just start churches. He founded and shaped communities of disciples.

Paul's mobility enabled him to form many churches. He was often forced to leave them after a short time. The new disciples had limited instruction in their new faith and faced extreme pressure from their local community to revert to their former way of life. The churches were shaken by conflict. Paul's daily concern for all the churches was one of the greatest challenges he faced. In his absence he wrote letters and sent workers to strengthen the churches. When he could, he returned personally.

Saul the persecutor had gone from house to house dragging off Christians. He wanted to destroy the church. Paul the apostle went from house to house teaching the disciples with humility and tears. He wanted to strengthen the church. Paul reminded the Ephesian elders that the church is not just another gathering but "the church of God" bought with Jesus' blood (Acts 20:28).

Corinth and Ephesus were the only two cities we know of where Paul enjoyed an extended stay. In many locations Paul had just weeks or months to form a church before he was driven out, but he always found a way of staying in touch. He would often circle back and visit, or leave behind a team member, or send a team member or letter—all for the purpose of strengthening the churches. Although Paul was a pioneer evangelist and church planter, he also conducted an extensive ministry in bringing the churches to maturity. Paul was anxious to see that the churches would remain faithful and obedient to the gospel. His goal with every church was to bring it to maturity—where it no longer depended on him but could become a full partner in the spread of the gospel.

IN SPIRIT AND TRUTH

The successful establishment of new communities of disciples was closely connected to the use of private homes.[1] Homes served both as bases for missionary work and meeting places for new believers. They were the place that believers could gather in reasonable security for worship, fellowship and learning.

In the cities of the Roman Empire, most people lived in multi-story apartment buildings. Many families lived in one small room—too small for a meeting of any more than a few people. So most Christians who lived in the cities met in small groups of up to fifteen people in tenement buildings. Large public facilities for meeting and sharing meals were not available. Gentiles met in pagan temples or private homes for community meals and gatherings. Jews met in private homes or in synagogues, many of which were converted homes. Christians from both Jewish and pagan backgrounds were familiar with meeting in homes for fellowship meals. Larger gatherings required the use of private homes that only the wealthy could afford. The largest room in the home of a prominent person could hold thirty to fifty people. More could be accommodated if hallways and other rooms were used.[2]

The conversion of whole households would have provided space for gathering disciples. Examples in Paul's ministry include Lydia the merchant, the jailor in Philippi, and Crispus the synagogue ruler and Stephanas in Corinth.[3] If the church in a city or town was too large to meet in one place, like the church in Rome, it met in a network of homes (Rom 16). Paul's letter to the Romans was not addressed to a single gathering of believers.[4] Phoebe probably took Paul's letter to the Romans from one gathering to another throughout the city.

So "church" could refer to a network of fellowships scattered throughout a city, or it could refer to one of the fellowships—"the church that meets in your home." Small gatherings based around an individual household were the basic unit of the Christian movement.

Paul gathered new believers into communities of disciples. Through Paul's example and instruction, these new churches learned what it meant to be the people of God together. Each local church had a minimal formal organization. Leadership was determined by the leading of the Holy Spirit, who gave gifts to each one for the building up of the community. Every ministry, including leadership, was a gift of the Holy Spirit. There are only incidental references to the details of organization and leadership structure of the churches in Acts and Paul's epistles. This was no oversight; Paul's churches were structured loosely, not systematically. The church throughout the world was one, but that unity was "in Christ." The one church was expressed in individual communities, united by their confession of the one Lord Jesus Christ and by their faithfulness to the gospel.

Despite this reluctance to formalize church life, there was a definite shape to that life that was common to all.

1. **Hearing and obeying God's Word.** As churches were formed, followers of Jesus met to hear, learn and obey God's Word; this Word came to them through the Old Testament Scriptures and the teachings of Jesus and the apostles, including Paul.

The churches continued the synagogue practice of reading and teaching the Scriptures, both the Old Testament and the accounts of Jesus' life and teaching. Those accounts spread from person to person as stories and memorable sayings before they were written down in the form of the Gospels that we have today. Letters from the apostles were also read and studied. In an era when few people could read, the public reading of these writings was essential.

As followers of Jesus read and learned the Word of God together and as they worshiped God in song, "the word of Christ" dwelled among them (Col 3:16; Eph 5:18-20).[5] Disciples learned together how to obey the teachings of the Jewish Scriptures and the teachings of Jesus and the apostles.

2. Life in the Spirit. Paul believed that the Holy Spirit brought the new community into existence. He knew that the Lord Jesus was present with his people through the Spirit. Paul had a deep confidence in the Spirit to guide and strengthen the church in his absence.[6]

There were visible demonstrations of the Holy Spirit's power—both signs and wonders, and joy in suffering. Spirit-inspired prophecy was an important part of church, and both men and women prophesied. Paul encouraged prophecy for the purpose of building up the church and even the conversion of visiting unbelievers.[7]

Paul reminded the Galatians that their life in the Spirit, including the miracles God was doing among them, came from the gospel and not by obeying the Law.

The Corinthians had an abundance of spiritual gifts that Paul affirmed. Some of these disciples also had an unhealthy obsession with charismatic gifts, especially speaking in tongues. Paul did not put this fire out but taught them to regulate their spiritual experiences. He reminded the church in Ephesus that Christ had gifted some as apostles, prophets, evangelists, pastors and teachers in order to equip them for ministry. As each member played their part, the community would grow up into the fullness of Christ (Eph 4:11-13).

When believers gathered, they were to expect that the living Word of Christ was among them as they taught and admonished each other and as they worshiped God with songs of all kinds. All of this was possible because they were filled with the Holy Spirit. Likewise, God through the Holy Spirit inspired their prayer.[8]

3. Baptism and the Lord's Supper. Ananias, a disciple in Damascus, baptized Paul immediately after Paul's sight was restored, and he was filled with the Holy Spirit. Paul, in keeping with early church practice, required new believers to join the community of Jesus' followers through repentance, faith and baptism in Jesus' name. They were baptized immediately when they put their faith in Christ, as a sign of cleansing from sin and reconciliation with God through Christ. It was a sign that the believer was now alive to God and under the rule of the Holy Spirit. In pioneering contexts Paul baptized some new converts. He soon passed that task on to his coworkers and to the recently baptized believers (1 Cor 1:13-17). Paul provided no restrictions on who could baptize a new disciple.

Paul passed on to his churches what he "received" regarding the meal Jesus instituted before his death. During the meal Jesus identified the bread and the wine as symbols of his body and blood, soon to be given over to death on the cross. Paul passed on the Lord's command to celebrate the meal in remembrance of him as the new covenant people who were awaiting his return (1 Cor 11:17-22). He taught the new believers to celebrate the Lord's Supper in a manner that expresses their unity, not their differences. Paul did not place any restrictions on who could lead the church in the celebration of the Lord's Supper.

4. Love for one another. Just as the message of a crucified Jewish Savior of the world was absurd to the ears of a pagan Greek or Roman, so was the idea of the community of his followers. The Greeks looked back to their golden age when a community of equals ruled the city. Yet that community of equals had excluded slaves, women and foreigners—the majority of the population. Roman society was no better; it was structured as a hierarchy under the emperor, who was considered a god. The idea of a community in which differences in wealth, power and ethnicity should play no part was bizarre to both the Greeks and the Romans.[9] But Paul worked hard to establish communities that reflected the character of God as revealed in Jesus.

Paul's "one another" sayings scattered throughout his letters reveal the quality of relationships that Paul expected in the churches: they were to be devoted to one another in love; they were to live in harmony with one another and accept one another as Christ had accepted them; they should bear one another's burdens, serve one another and patiently bear with one another in love. Paul charged them to be kind and compassionate to one another, forgiving each other just as in Christ God forgave them. They were to encourage and build up one another.[10]

5. Local leadership. The churches Paul started were not ruled over by the churches in Jerusalem, Antioch or anywhere else. From the beginning they were churches in their own right. Each new group of believers met together as equal and complete parts of the Christian movement.[11] Not even Paul ruled over these new churches. He urged them to "grow up" in Christ and become adults in the faith (1 Cor 14:20; Eph 4:14).[12]

There was no leadership elite; Christ alone was Lord. Believers were to follow the example of Christ in how they related to each other. Paul presented himself as a model because he modeled himself on Christ. He encouraged believers to honor and follow the leadership of people like Epaphroditus and Stephanas, who laid down their lives and devoted themselves to serving God's people (Phil 2:28; 1 Cor 16:15-16).

Authority in the church was not based on position or power but on relationship and function. Paul never used the term *priest* to describe local leaders; there were no ordained clergy in the churches he planted. The whole body of Christ participated in a variety of ministry functions, such as evangelism, teaching, showing mercy, healing and prophecy. The functions people performed mattered more than the positions they occupied.

Paul made it a priority to appoint local leaders rather than to govern and control the church himself. He could do this because of his trust in the gospel and in the Holy Spirit. He intervened only when the church was in danger of denying Christ through false teaching and sinful behavior. He didn't abandon the churches he formed but returned to strengthen them whenever possible.[13]

Paul appointed elders and overseers in the churches he planted, regarding them as appointed by the Holy Spirit. He appears to equate the two roles to each other, telling the Ephesian *elders* to "keep watch over yourselves and all the flock of which the Holy Spirit has made you overseers" (Acts 20:28).[14] The elders emerged from each newly formed church and would exercise responsibility for a cluster of churches in a city or region. Their qualifications had to do with the character of their Christian walk and their faithfulness to the gospel.

Paul urged the churches to submit to these elders and overseers, and everyone who joined in the work of the gospel. Paul reminded the church at Corinth how Stephanas and his household had served them, and reminded the Ephesians that the gifts of leadership (apostles, prophets, evangelists, pastors and teachers) were given to equip the church for ministry and maturity in Christ. Paul gave both Timothy and Titus responsibility for appointing overseers and deacons in the churches on his behalf.[15]

Paul's letters and the accounts in Acts don't provide a lot of detail about the relationship between overseers, elders and deacons. That relationship may have even varied from place to place. We should, therefore, hold the models of church leadership and governance that we build from Paul's example lightly. Church leadership can come in a variety of forms: apostles, prophets, pastor-teachers and evangelists. Whatever form it takes, the purpose is the same—to equip God's people for ministry, for building up the body of Christ so that believers "reach unity in the faith and in the knowledge of the Son of God and become mature, attaining to the whole measure of the fullness of Christ" (Eph 4:11-13). Ultimately Paul's focus was not on the position and status of church leaders but on faithfulness to the gospel in what they taught and how they lived.

6. **Partners in the gospel.** The churches Paul planted were communities that regularly added new converts as the believers talked about their faith—with their families, in the workshop, on the street in the neighborhood or with outsiders who visited their meetings.[16] Paul praised the church in Thessalonica because the word of the Lord "rang out from you not only in Macedonia and Achaia—your faith in God has become known everywhere" (1 Thess 1:8). Paul expected believers to conduct themselves in such a way that they could win others, including unbelieving husbands and wives (1 Cor 7:16; 10:31–11:1).

The church in Antioch provided a base that Paul and Barnabas returned to between missionary journeys. The Christians at Philippi actively participated in Paul's missionary work through financial support, prayer and sharing the gospel. For at least two years the church at Ephesus provided a base for Paul from which the gospel could go out to the whole of the Roman province of Asia (Acts 19:10). During his time in Ephesus, Paul's coworker Epaphras planted churches in the neighboring cities of Laodicea, Hierapolis and Colossae. Later Paul wrote to challenge the Ephesians to remain faithful in the spiritual battle and to continue to take the offensive in proclaiming the gospel (Col 1:3-8; 2:1; 4:13; Eph 6:10-20).

Paul was glad that his example in prison (possibly in Rome) had inspired the local believers to speak the Word of God more courageously and fearlessly. Later he wrote to the church in Rome to seek their support as a base for his mission to Spain in the western half of the Roman Empire (Phil 1:14; Rom 15:23-28). By example and teaching, Paul ensured that his churches were engaged locally in spreading the gospel and more widely in partnership with his mission to reach whole cities and regions.

Individuals shared their new life in Christ with family and friends; new household churches were started locally and wider afield. The work continued long after Paul had moved on to new fields. Then the churches participated in the mission through prayer, financial support and a steady stream of workers going back and forth between Paul and their home churches.

Meanwhile Paul continued to stay focused on taking the gospel into unreached cities and regions.

18

NOTHING LEFT TO DO

Luke is chronicling not the life and times of Paul . . . but rather a phenomenon and movement that was continuing and alive and well in his own day.

—BEN WITHERINGTON,
*THE ACTS OF THE APOSTLES:
A SOCIO-RHETORICAL
COMMENTARY*

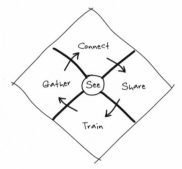

IN THE SPRING OF A.D. 45, five men gathered at Antioch in Syria to fast and to worship the Lord. In the room was Barnabas, a Levite from Cyprus; Simeon called Niger ("black"), possibly an African; Lucius from Cyrene in northern Africa; Manaen, a boyhood friend of Herod Antipas, who had executed John the Baptist and played a part in Jesus' trial; and finally Paul, still known as Saul, a Pharisee born in the city of Tarsus (in modern Turkey) and educated in Jerusalem.

The diversity of this group reflected the city in which they lived. Antioch was located on the Orontes River; it was a wealthy, cosmopolitan city of 250,000 people of diverse religions and ethnic backgrounds. Ten percent of the population was Jewish, having been there since the second century B.C. and having attracted many Gentile converts and God-fearers.[1] Only Rome and Alexandria were larger and more important to the empire, and Antioch became, after Jerusalem, the most significant center of Christianity. It was an ideal base from which the Christian movement could spread beyond Palestine to the wider world.

The gospel arrived in the Syrian capital in A.D. 31/32 with a group of disciples who had fled Jerusalem. It spread to the Jewish community and to Gentiles connected with the synagogue, and from them to their pagan friends and relatives. For the first time, Gentiles were converting to faith in Christ in large numbers. In Antioch the followers of Jesus were first called "Christians" (Acts 11:26),[2] distinguishing them as being neither Jews nor pagans but followers of Christ.

When the apostles in Jerusalem heard about what was happening in Antioch, they gave Barnabas the job of consolidating the work. Around A.D. 43 Barnabas traveled over one hundred miles from Antioch to Tarsus in search of Paul's help. The two had met a decade before, after Paul had returned from his mission in Arabia and Damascus to visit the church in Jerusalem (Acts 9:27). Since he left Jerusalem, Paul appears to have been involved in pioneering work in Syria and Cilicia between A.D. 33-43.[3]

After a year of ministry in Antioch, Barnabas, Paul, Simeon, Lucius, and Manaen were worshiping God when the Holy Spirit interrupted their gathering to reveal that Barnabas and Paul's work at Antioch was completed. The new church was established. It was time for Barnabas and Paul to return to evangelism and church planting in unreached fields. Antioch, the first church with a significant mix of Jews and Gentiles, was now the origin of a band of mobile missionaries intent on taking the gospel to Jews and pagan Gentiles in the major cities of the Roman Empire.

This was not a commissioning service. Paul had already been commissioned over ten years before on the Damascus road, preaching immediately afterward to Jews and Gentiles in Damascus, Arabia and Syria, as well as in Cilicia and its capital, Tarsus. Paul was already a seasoned missionary when Barnabas arrived in Tarsus and recruited him for the work in Antioch. But now that the church in Antioch was established, the Holy Spirit was sending Barnabas and Paul back into pioneering work. The church was to acknowledge this, bless them and release them. It was the Holy Spirit, not the church, who was the primary agent in calling and sending out these experienced missionaries.[4]

Paul and Barnabas would return to Antioch to report back to the church, but the church did not have authority over their mission. Paul went on to form an apostolic band with which the churches partnered by sending workers, giving financial support and praying.

Paul saw his mission field as regions. He focused his efforts on strategic centers as a means to reaching a whole region: Philippi for Macedonia, Thessalonica for Macedonia and Achaia, Corinth for Achaia, Ephesus for Asia. These were the centers for communication, culture, commerce, politics and religion. Paul opened up contact, spread the gospel, made disciples and laid the foundation for an enduring Christian community in these cities, in the hope that the gospel would spread from these centers into the surrounding countryside and towns.

Eventually Paul looked back and concluded that his job was done; he had fully preached the gospel from Jerusalem in Palestine to Illyricum in modern Greece (Rom 15:18-24). He had taken the gospel into unreached regions, formed churches and multiplied workers, some of whom served locally in established congregations, others of whom established new churches in the surrounding areas, and still others of whom became mobile missionaries.

PAUL'S TEAM

Paul rarely worked alone. He surrounded himself with coworkers— mobile missionaries who traveled with him and local workers from among the churches. Luke wrote with authority because he had traveled and ministered with Paul.[5]

There are about one hundred names linked with Paul in the New Testament; thirty-eight of them are coworkers. Most of his team members came from the churches he started. Many of his fellow missionaries were relatively new converts. Timothy was responsible for the church at Thessalonica just three years after his conversion. Paul's missionary band was always changing as workers came and went between Paul and the churches.

Like Jesus, Paul trained his workers as he traveled and served with them. Paul's coworkers traveled hundreds of miles by sea and on foot, sometimes with Paul but sometimes alone. Paul repeatedly described their ministry as "hard labor."[6] The work was difficult—dangerous travel, violent opposition, lack of resources and even prison. They moved constantly while relying on the generosity of others, the work of their own hands and Paul himself for financial support.

Paul involved coworkers when he wrote letters to the churches. Sosthenes, Timothy, "the brothers" and Silas are mentioned in eight of Paul's thirteen letters as co-senders. Paul's letters reveal how much he valued their service and how much he loved them. He uses different terms for his team members: brother, companion, apostle, servant, fellow slave, fellow soldier, fellow prisoner and fellow worker. These fellow missionaries were not under the direct authority of their churches but of Paul, yet while Paul is clearly their leader, these terms describe relationships of equality. They are not Paul's "assistants." They are partners in the spread of the gospel.

The most frequently mentioned associates were Barnabas, Timothy, Luke, Priscilla and Aquila, Silas (also known as Silvanus), Titus and Tychicus. Some, like Timothy, were almost constant members of the team. Others worked with Paul for a time and then worked separately—Barnabas, Silas and Apollos—or returned to their churches. Paul's partners acted independently and courageously. While Paul was based in Ephesus, Epaphras founded churches in the surrounding cities of Colossae, Laodicea and Hierapolis (Col 1:3-8; 4:13). Priscilla and Aquila oversaw the work in Ephesus while Paul was away. Timothy and Erastus checked in on the progress of the churches in Macedonia while Paul remained in Ephesus. Gaius and Aristarchus bravely faced a mob's anger while the disciples restrained Paul from confronting the crowd.

Four generations

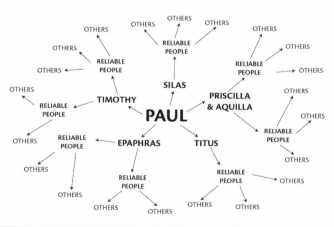

Figure 18.1. "And the things you have heard me say in the presence of many witnesses entrust to reliable people who will also be qualified to teach others" (2 Tim 2:2). Adapted from a diagram first developed by Nathan Shank and Wilson Geisler. See Nathan and Kari Shank, "The Four Fields: A Manual for Church Planting Facilitation," www.churchplantingmovements.com (accessed December 5, 2011), p. 74.

Paul's letters name seventeen women associated with his mission. In Romans 16, Paul identified Phoebe, a "deacon" or servant of the church in Cenchreae (the eastern port town of Corinth) and a financial supporter of many, including Paul. He also greeted Mary, who had worked hard for the church. Pioneering missionaries Junia and her husband, Andronicus, were in prison with him; Paul described this couple as "outstanding among the apostles" (Rom 16:7).[7] Tryphena and Tryphosa were two women who "work hard in the Lord." Paul's dear friend Peris is another woman who worked "very hard in the Lord." Elsewhere Paul referred to Euodia and Syntyche, two women who "have contended at my side in the cause of the gospel" (Phil 4:2-3).

The husband and wife team of Priscilla and Aquila were close partners with Paul. Like him, they were tentmakers or leatherworkers. They made a significant contribution to the work in Ephesus, Corinth and Rome. Relatively wealthy, they moved from city to city, establishing households that provided a meeting place for a church.[8] In A.D. 49 they were among the Jews expelled from Rome by Emperor Claudius's edict. They moved to Corinth where they worked with Paul in preaching and teaching. Two years later they went with Paul to Ephesus, where a church met in their home (Acts 18:18-19; 1 Cor 16:19). They invited Apollos, an itinerant Christian teacher, into their home and helped complete his understanding of the gospel (Acts 18:26). After Paul left Ephesus, they stayed behind to continue the work there. By A.D. 56 they were back in Rome with a church meeting in their home (Rom 16:3-5). Wherever they went they hosted, and probably led, churches in their home. They risked their lives for Paul, and like Paul, they worked with their hands to support themselves—two examples of the complex and fluid network of local and missionary leaders that Paul called "coworkers."

EPHESUS, WHERE IT CAME TOGETHER

For most of his ministry, Paul was given just enough time to preach the gospel and gather a group of disciples before he was forced out of a city. Sometimes he had weeks, even months, but never years. In Corinth, however, just when we would expect Paul to be forced out of the city, God intervened through a vision and told Paul not to leave. Paul remained in Corinth for eighteen months, a precedent that would be repeated in Ephesus.

Paul's stay in the city of Ephesus from A.D. 52 to 55 was unlike any other. These three years were Paul's longest recorded ministry in a city. Here Paul was able to complete his work; he left at the time of his own choosing. Ephesus was Paul's last major campaign as a free man. It was not just another stop along the way; it was the climax of his ministry, and it touched the whole Roman province of Asia. For centuries to come, the churches formed throughout Asia were among the most influential in the world.[9]

Ephesus was the capital of the Roman province of Asia in what is today Turkey. With over 200,000 people, it rivaled Antioch in Syria as the third most important city in the empire after Rome and Alexandria. All the roads of Asia converged on Ephesus, making it the cultural, communications and commercial hub of the region.

In the first century A.D., Ephesus experienced a building boom. New temples and impressive buildings were constructed. The Temple of Artemis, one of the "seven wonders of the world," attracted tourists from all over the Roman Empire.

Paul arrived in Ephesus early in the summer of A.D. 52. He was given exceptional freedom to preach and teach boldly in the synagogue for three months (Acts 19:8). Eventually a group within the Jewish community opposed Paul and ridiculed his converts. The Jewish believers in Jesus and the Gentiles attached to the synagogue left with Paul and formed a separate community. This was the last record of Paul ministering in a synagogue.

Paul's mission to Jews and Gentiles continued in the lecture hall of Tyrannus. There he taught, debated and persuaded every day for two years. God also did extraordinary miracles of healing and deliverance from demonic oppression through Paul. Ephesus was home to magicians, sorcerers and adherents to many forms of pagan religion; Paul's miracles showed God's power over sickness and demons. New believers openly confessed their sins and burned their books on sorcery, which were worth a fortune—equal to the wages of a laborer over fifty thousand days.

As usual, Paul was not alone. Aquila, Priscilla and Timothy were with him from the beginning of his mission in Ephesus. Other coworkers included Epaphras, Philemon, Aristarchus from Macedonia, Gaius from Corinth, Tychicus and Trophimus. There was also a visit by Stephanas, Fortunatus and Archaicus from Corinth.[10]

This was a period of unprecedented fruitfulness. God had opened "a great door" for effective ministry (1 Cor 16:8-9). Luke records that "the word of the Lord spread widely and grew in power." Incredibly, "all the Jews and

Greeks who lived in the province of Asia heard the word of the Lord" (Acts 19:10) through Paul and the believers and workers he trained and sent out into Ephesus and the surrounding region.

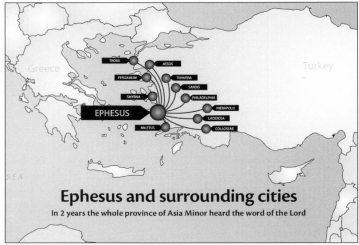

Map 18.2. All the Jews and Greeks who lived in the province of Asia heard the word of the Lord (Acts 19:10). Map adapted from Arther G. Patzia, *The Emergence of the Church* (Downers Grove, Ill.: InterVarsity Press, 2001), p. 128.

Paul did not take the gospel to the whole province of Asia on his own. He was based in Ephesus where he was teaching every day. It was Epaphras who established churches west in the neighboring cities of Laodicea, Hierapolis and Colossae in the Lycos valley (Col 1:3-8; 2:1; 4:13). To the north, the churches in the cities of Smyrna, Pergamon, Thyatira, Sardis and Philadelphia (referred to in Rev 2–3) could also have been started around this time. For centuries following, the region was one of the leading centers of Christianity.

This great advance came at a price. Paul had many enemies. Dealing with them was like "fighting wild animals" (1 Cor 15:32; 16:8). The strength of the opposition is an indicator of just how effective Paul and his workers were in reaching the city and the province. The most important god in Ephesus, Artemis, was believed to be the daughter of the pagan gods Zeus and Leto. The cult of Artemis was one of the most powerful in the ancient world. There were temples of Artemis in the region stretching from Spain to Syria. The temple at Ephesus contained a many-breasted image of the goddess that was supposed to have fallen from heaven. Artemis was believed to be the founder and protector of Ephesus, and her image and name were everywhere. She was lord over supernatural powers and provided health and protection. Her temple was made of marble and was the largest building in the Greek world. It drew many pilgrims to Ephesus, and the whole city prospered because of it. When Paul came preaching about the one true God revealed in Jesus Christ, he was on a collision course with the cult of Artemis and its followers.

The final collision came as a riot in the last months of his stay in Ephesus. Demetrius, a leading silversmith who manufactured miniatures of the temple and its goddess, stood to lose money if the Christian movement continued to turn people away from idolatry. Christianity had spread throughout the whole province and was seriously undermining his trade and that of other craftsmen. Motivated by religious zeal and greed, Demetrius called a meeting of the silversmith guild, which soon turned into a mob gathered in the great outdoor theater of Ephesus, which was carved out of the side of Mount Pion and could hold 25,000 people.

The mob seized Gaius and Aristarchus, two of Paul's coworkers. Paul wanted to enter the theater and face the crowd, but the disciples prevented him. Paul had some friends in high places among the "Asiarchs" who helped protect him—leading men of the province and the wealthy aristocracy. The leading official of the city subdued the crowd by reminding them of what their Roman overlords might do if they heard of the disturbance, and the riot was over.

The Word continued to advance in Ephesus despite forceful opposition from one of the most powerful pagan cults of the time. The gospel penetrated both the Jewish and pagan worlds. The whole province heard the word of the Lord. The workers Paul mobilized planted churches in surrounding cities. Elders were appointed over the many churches that met throughout Ephesus. Paul finished the task he had been given and was ready to move on. All of this was achieved in just three years.

FINISHING THE JOB

At the end of Paul's stay in Ephesus, Luke tells us, he returned to Jerusalem with a contribution from the Gentile churches to the poor believers there. The Gentile believers wanted to show their appreciation to the Jewish believers for the gift of the gospel that came through them. The collection was for Paul a symbol of the unity between Gentile and Jewish believers.

After Jerusalem Paul intended to move on to Rome, hoping it would provide

158 WHAT JESUS STARTED

a platform from which he could launch his push into Spain. He needed the believers' assistance, and he wanted to be a blessing to them. In an astonishing remark, Paul declared that he had fully proclaimed the gospel from Jerusalem all the way to Illyricum. He had "no more room" to work in these regions.

How could this be? There was still plenty of work to be done. The churches established in Thessalonica, Corinth and Ephesus required the leadership of someone like Paul if they were to continue to grow in maturity and reach out to take the gospel to their regions. Paul knew this, but he also knew that his job—the apostolic task of evangelism, establishing new believers in their faith and forming new churches in strategic centers—was done. Paul preached the gospel where it had never been heard. He planted churches where there were none. He brought those churches to sufficient maturity that they could continue the work as he moved into new unreached fields. The disciples in Thessalonica, Corinth, and Ephesus were now responsible to reach the provinces of Macedonia, Achaia and Asia respectively. Paul's eastern Mediterranean mission was coming to an end because he saw his responsibility was to be involved in pioneer evangelism and to establish communities of disciples, which would multiply workers to continue ministry in the region. Like Jesus before him, Paul must move on.

Years later, in A.D. 112, Pliny the Younger, governor of Bithynia, wrote to Emperor Trajan about the spread of the Christian movement: "This contagious superstition is not confined to the cities only, but has spread through the villages and rural districts." Paul and others had done their job.

"AND SO WE CAME TO ROME"

The book of Acts, as a history of the mission of the church,
has no ending as long as Jesus' promise to return remains unfulfilled.
—Eckhard Schnabel, *Early Christian Mission*

The story of Luke and Acts is full of purposeful movement. Jerusalem is the dramatic destination of the Gospel of Luke; Rome is the destination of Acts.[11]

Paul had been trying to visit Rome for two years. Finally he arrived as a prisoner after experiencing riots, accusations, assassination attempts, imprisonment, trials and shipwreck along the way.

Rome had between 600,000 and 1,000,000 inhabitants.[12] As a Roman citizen who had appealed to Caesar, Paul was allowed to stay in his own accommodation, lightly chained to a soldier. He may have rented a third story apartment. Private homes were expensive in Rome; most people lived in high-rise apartments. The ground floors of apartment buildings were reserved for shops. Only the very wealthy could afford the second story. Above the third floor, apartments were smaller and may not have had enough room for Paul, the soldier and Paul's many visitors. Paul paid for the accommodation himself and so must have had access to a fair amount of money to rent space on the second or third floor.

Paul continued to spread the gospel despite being chained to a Praetorian guard. Boldly and freely he preached the kingdom of God and taught about the Lord Jesus Christ to both Jews and Gentiles, including the soldiers who rotated every four hours to guard him. He probably used this time to write his prison letters—Philemon, Colossians, Ephesians, and Philippians. In each of them he anticipated his release.[13]

The final scene in Acts is a reminder of the unstoppable advance of the Word of God. Nothing can stand in the way of God's saving purpose—not beatings, not imprisonment, not shipwreck, not even poisonous snakes and the power of the empire. The gospel reached the capital and found faith even in Caesar's household and among his elite guards.[14]

Paul may have been tried and convicted, even faced the executioner's sword after two years under house arrest in A.D. 62, although it is strange that Luke does not mention this. It is more likely that he was freed and returned to missionary work, possibly in Spain, then arrested again and executed in Rome around A.D. 66.[15] Luke left the story of the early Christian movement unfinished; whatever happened to Paul, the gospel would spread unhindered and bear fruit throughout the inhabited world. By leaving his account unfinished Luke was reminding his generation, and future generations, that they inherit the mission Jesus gave to his first disciples. Their mission has become our mission.[16]

We leave Paul in Rome awaiting trial. Meanwhile the Word continued to advance, as it has ever since. We'll pause to hear the story of Julius Ebwongu and then move on to examine how we can join the movement that Jesus started and play our part in changing our world.

Julius Ebwongu
Shifts the Paradigm

In July 2008 the first of three hundred pastors of the Uganda Assemblies of God (UAOG) left their churches with the aim of starting a reproducing church in every sub-district of Uganda. Each pastor took a trainee with them and left behind a trainee to lead the sending church.[1]

Over the next six months the pastors and their trainees planted more than four hundred churches. By March 2009 they had planted 857 churches; that number increased to 1,300 churches by the middle of the year. By June 2010 the UAOG had planted 2,800 churches in just two years.

The pastors and their families then returned to their home churches, and their trainees took over the leadership of the new churches. The most recent estimates (2011) show that the UAOG now has over five thousand churches in Uganda, up from just 240 in 2004.

PROJECT 300

Uganda is an African nation with a tragic past. Since independence from Britain in 1962, Uganda has experienced civil war, murderous dictators and the AIDS epidemic. The population of 31 million people is young and growing at 3.4 percent a year. Ugandans speak fifty-two different languages.

Since the 1980s Rick Seaward, founding pastor of the Victory Family Centre in Singapore, has been engaged in church strengthening and church planting in Uganda by partnering with the UAOG. In 1986 they planted a Victory Family Centre church in Kampala.

Among the first converts in this new church was a young Ugandan, Julius Ebwongu. With Seaward's encouragement, Ebwongu went on to plant a church in the nation's capital, Kampala; this church grew to 2,500 members. In 2004 Ebwongu became the national leader of the UAOG.

Ebwongu was disturbed that while most Christian ministries focused on the cities, 80 percent of Uganda's 31 million people lived in the countryside. To reach Uganda, he knew, they would have to reach the villages. A new model of ministry was required.

With input from Seaward, the UAOG had grown from twenty-eight churches in 1991 to 240 churches by the time Ebwongu took over the leadership in 2004. The prevailing mindset was one of addition rather than multiplication. Local pastors believed that the ideal church was large rather than reproducing, so that was the type of church they aspired to lead. Most UAOG leaders and pastors assumed that church plants required a long time and large amount of money and resources. They assumed foreigners had the resources and thus the responsibility to reach the nation.

Ugandan Assemblies of God Churches (1991 - 2010)

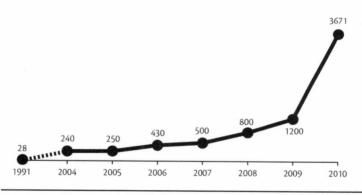

Figure I.0. Growth in the number of UAOG churches (2004-2010).

In 2005 Ebwongu developed a strategy called "Project 300" which challenged the three hundred pastors of the UAOG to each train two lay leaders: one to serve as an interim pastor and the other to plant churches. After two years of training, each of these pastors would leave the church in the hands of their associate and step out with the second trainee to plant a church.

Meanwhile, Seaward brought two people to Ebwongu—Ray Belfield, his eighty-year-old missions pastor, and Bill Smith, a Baptist trainer in church planting movements. Together they challenged Ebwongu to lift his sights higher and move from planting single churches to launching a church planting movement across the nation. Ebwongu invited Bill Smith to train all his pastors in church multiplication. With Smith, Ebwongu helped his pastors shift from their traditional view of church and ministry to a church planting movement mindset.

IT'S ALL IN THE MINDSET

Left to themselves, most of the UAOG pastors would not have voluntarily
moved themselves and their families to new villages to plant churches. Ebwongu's vision and leadership was at the heart.of the transformation of the
UAOG into a church planting movement. When biblical teaching on the
nature of church was coupled with experiential learning, the leaders discovered their assumptions were wrong. Ebwongu helped his leaders embrace a simple model of church that was biblically defined and easily replicated. He helped his pastors shift from a shepherding model to a pioneering
model of leadership.[2]

Table I.1. Two paradigms in church leadership

Old Paradigm	New Paradigm
The best people to plant churches in Uganda are foreign missionaries, not Ugandans.	Ugandans are better suited to reach Uganda than foreigners, despite their superior resources and training.
We can't fund church planting ourselves, and it's not our responsibility anyway.	We are called to plant churches.
The resistance to church planting from outside the church is too strong.	Persistence in the face of persecution results in receptivity to the gospel.
Raising up leaders is a long and formal process.	New converts will do what they are expected and trained to do, including planting new churches.
Raising up leaders quickly will result in false doctrine, moral failure and pride.	Ordinary people—regardless of age, gender, education or time since salvation—can participate and succeed in church planting.
We can't plant churches unless our denomination tells us to and provides funding.	Our church planting efforts will not end in failure. This is the plan of God, not a human invention.
Real churches have buildings that are financed by the sending church, not the local converts.	A group of believers, with or without a building, make up a church.
Only well-established churches can plant new churches.	Prayer, followed by proclamation, must precede all other activities in church planting.
We can't saturate our nation with new churches.	We can plant churches all over Uganda without the help of outside funding.
Fewer large and well-resourced churches will do a better job of reaching our nation than small clusters of believers without all the resources.	Small, simple churches are more reproducible and better able to reach Uganda than larger, more expensive and time-consuming alternatives.

Ebwongu's training challenged the unspoken assumptions of the UAOG's
church leaders regarding the nature of the church and who was qualified to
plant and lead churches. The leaders challenged the belief that Ugandans could
only plant churches if they had access to outside funding and expertise. They
challenged the belief that Ugandans could not overcome the obstacles to

reaching the whole nation through church multiplication. They challenged the assumption that church size was more important than church multiplication. They became convinced that the call to multiply churches was a call from God.

The training challenged and redefined assumptions before equipping the pastors in the basics of evangelism, making disciples and forming simple churches. With a new ministry mindset and the basic skills they required, the pastors of the UAOG were ready.

FROM ADDITION TO MULTIPLICATION

In May 2008 the first of the pastors left their churches under the supervision of one trainee to go plant churches in unreached villages with the second. Each pastor and intern would plant two churches. Each of those new churches would then plant another new church within six months. The goal was to increase the number of UAOG churches from eight hundred to 3,600 within two years.

After two years the pastors returned to their original churches, while each trainee remained behind to oversee, mentor, teach and train twelve new pastors, who would each train and mentor twelve new church planters.

The UAOG provided some financial support to church planters who moved from their villages to faraway districts. The funding ended within two years. The second and third generations of churches were not centrally funded.

In the first two months of 2009 the UAOG planted as many churches as had been started in the previous two decades. Between August 2008 and January 2010 they planted over 2,500 churches. By the end of 2010 the total number of UAOG churches had risen to 4,632.

Ebwongu is not interested in "growth at any price." Everyone in the movement is involved in training and mentoring in biblical knowledge, character development and ministry skills. Ebwongu meets monthly with his regional overseers, who meet monthly with their twelve area overseers. They in turn meet with their twelve sectional leaders, who each meet with twelve pastors, who train and supervise their interns.

Training in multiplication begins once a new church is formed. The church planter identifies the leader who will plant the first daughter church and teaches him on the job. The UAOG continues to plant churches throughout Uganda. It is already sending some of its most effective church planters to other African nations as well as partnering with Brazilian AOG churches to help them move to multiplication.

The story of Julius Ebwongu and the UAOG is a tale of partnership in the gospel that stretched from Singapore to Uganda. It is a reminder of how God works through leaders such as Ebwongu to challenge existing assumptions with biblical principles. The pastors of the UAOG learned that they had to see the world differently and turn fresh vision into obedient action. God added his power to their faith and ignited a movement.

PART FOUR

What Jesus Is Doing Today

SEEING THE END

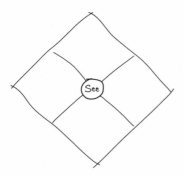

BY THE SECOND YEAR OF MY FIRST CHURCH PLANT, I was confident in my abilities. The new church had survived and grown. Then a painful church fight shook my confidence and prepared me to hear from God. Out of desperation (not discipline), I woke early every morning and spent two hours locked away in my garage praying and reading the Scripture. After three months of seeking God and turning my life and the church back over to him, I heard him speak. My calling was to fuel church planting movements across Australia. Once I had surrendered to God, put aside my plans and lost confidence in my ministry, the vision caught me.

"What *would* Jesus do?" is a helpful question to ask whenever we are faced with an important decision. When it comes to our mission, an even better question is "What *did* Jesus do?" If instead of asking ourselves, "What would Jesus do?" we asked, "What did Jesus do?" our ministries would look very different.

A few years ago I visited friends who had chosen to live and work in the slums of a major South American city. I was deeply impressed with their commitment to serve among the poor as a family, despite high levels of crime and disease. They were a living witness to God's presence in a dark place. I wondered what it would take to reach the whole slum—over 120,000 people—not just one neighborhood. Our vision has to extend beyond one neighborhood to every man, woman and child in such a place.

Jesus would have had a plan to reach every neighborhood. Jesus would have been on the move connecting, looking for households of peace and training workers among the people themselves. Jesus would not be satisfied until the mission moved beyond what he did to a growing movement of ordinary people.

For the most part Jesus limited his mission to the lost sheep of Israel, so that in a few short years he fulfilled his calling. At the same time, his mission to Israel was undertaken with the whole world in mind. As he ministered, Jesus was preparing his followers to take the gospel to the ends of the earth. He was laying the foundation for a missionary movement.

WAKING UP TO A DIFFERENT WORLD

The apostle Peter was at Jesus' side throughout most of his ministry. When it mattered most, Peter failed. He denied Jesus and hid in fear. But Jesus restored him, taught him and sent the Holy Spirit upon him. Peter stood on the day of Pentecost and began the fulfillment of Jesus' command to make disciples of all nations.

Peter had the training, the experience and the authority to lead. Yet ten years after Pentecost, Peter was still struggling with how to fulfill the mission entrusted to him. His vision was limited. He could not see how pagan, uncircumcised Gentiles could be reached, discipled and added to the Christian movement. Then God dragged him to the house of Cornelius.

Peter's story should remind us of two important truths when it comes to vision. First, we shouldn't be surprised if we don't "get it." Our training, knowledge and experience do not guarantee clarity and accuracy of vision. We can assume there are huge gaps in our understanding that by ourselves we cannot bridge. But before we are driven to despair, there is a second reality that Peter's story reveals: God is in charge of his mission. We can expect God to intervene, even shake us to the core, to reveal his purposes.

Between his anointing with the Holy Spirit and release into public ministry, Jesus spent forty days alone in the wilderness learning obedience to the Father's will and ways.[1] Similarly, our end vision won't come from a demographic study or a brainstorming session around the whiteboard. It won't come by consulting the best and brightest. It comes from God and is written on our hearts.

"REACHING THE WHOLE OF MONGOLIA"

In 1990 Augie Joshua planted a traditional Baptist church in his homeland of Mongolia.[2] After thirteen years the church had around one hundred people attending, but it was no longer growing. People were not sharing their faith. They just attended Sunday church services.

Augie was troubled; he turned his discouragement into prayer, asking God to speak through his Word. God told Augie, "I want you to plant more churches." God challenged Augie to leave the old wineskins behind and use new wineskins that God would fill with his new wine (Mk 2:22; Lk 5:37-38). This word from God gripped his heart. The question that dominated his thoughts was, "How can we reach the whole of Mongolia?"

So Augie handed leadership of his church over to another pastor and left to plant new churches.

The next church Augie planted was in a Muslim area about a mile away in the western region of Mongolia. Augie visited a town in the area to prayer-walk and look for a man of peace. He didn't find one, but later he sent a short-term mission team to the same town, and they found a Muslim Kazakh who accepted Christ and became a bridge for the gospel to spread to his friends and relatives.

These Mongolian Kazakh believers formed simple churches that met in traditional Mongolian homes called *gers*. These *ger* churches were easy to start and adaptable to the local culture. Some of the churches are nomadic. When the people move with the seasons, so does the church.

The book of Acts is Augie's guide for what church should look like in Mongolia. Believers eat together, share together, read the Bible and allow God's Word to speak. They worship with Mongolian songs because Augie says Mongolian songs reach the heart.

Today when Augie talks, he rarely goes more than a few sentences without repeating the phrase, "reaching the whole of Mongolia." He says, "That's our vision, our passion, our life, our everything, to plant churches that will reach the whole of Mongolia."[3] At the heart of most church planting movements are key local leaders like Augie with a vision to reach their people.

To see the end, we must approach God's Word with a humble heart and allow his Word and his Spirit to align our lives with his purposes. We must look beyond what we can do and ask, "What needs to be done? What will it look like when our task is finished?" Finally, we must act. Understanding grows with obedience.

CONNECTING WITH PEOPLE

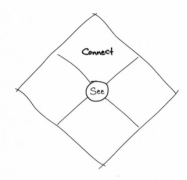

MICHELLE AND I WERE BETWEEN CHURCH PLANTS. I was in England visiting various ministries and learning what I could before we dived back into the next phase of our work. As the London train approached the Leeds station, I looked right at the backpacker about to board it with me. God spoke to my heart, "I want you to share the gospel with him."

I made like Jonah and took off for the other end of the train! I'm not sure why I responded that way. Perhaps I wanted to see if it really was God speaking. Perhaps I was scared. What happened next was amazing. I made it into a carriage at the other end of the train and sat down. A minute later the backpacker entered the same compartment—out of breath—and sat down in the seat in front of me.

At this point I figured God really did want me to share with this guy. So on the way to London, I got to know him. I discovered Mark was a fellow Australian in his late twenties. He had been a political adviser to the state government of Queensland. Following an election defeat, he was out of a job and backpacking around Europe.

Soon we were talking about faith, Jesus and the meaning of life. There was a young woman sitting beside me who listened intently to our conversation. After about thirty minutes, she dived into the discussion and, to my surprise, told Mark the story of how she came to know Jesus. I'm sure he assumed she knew me, but I'd never seen her before in my life.

Mark left the train just before we reached London. I turned to the young woman and said, "Where did you come from?" I discovered that she too was a believer and was involved in church planting in the south of England.

The train journey with Mark prepared me for my next assignment. When I returned to Australia, I spent two years leading an inner city church plant. Three days a week I was out connecting with people and sharing the good news. I'm not a natural evangelist, but every time we went out, God led us to someone just like Mark.

Mission is about people who are far from God. It's about a shepherd searching for one lost sheep. It's about a woman turning her house upside down, looking for a lost silver coin. It's about a father longing for his lost son to return.

Effective disciple makers and church planters spend time—intentional time—connecting with people.

THE CAMEL

The legend says every good Muslim knows ninety-nine names for Allah, but the one hundredth name was only revealed to the camel. The one hundredth name is Jesus, or in Arabic, *Isa.*

Somewhere in the Muslim world, a stranger walks into a mosque and seeks out the imam.[1] He has come with questions about the Qur'an's teaching on various topics. He wants to know what the Qur'an says about the prophet Isa (Jesus) and the Injil (New Testament). He has questions about the prophet Muhammad and what the Qur'an says about salvation.

He hasn't come to dispute or to criticize Islam but to inquire and allow his questions to speak for themselves. The imam is happy to discuss things with the visitor, and a group of worshipers gather around to listen and to join in.

The stranger asks the imam to read a passage in the Qur'an (Sura Al-Imran 3:42-55) so they can discuss it together. From the Qur'an they learn three things about Isa:

1. **Isa is holy.** The passage describes Isa as the Word of Allah (God); he is the Ruhullah (Spirit of God), and he is the Messiah whose name means Savior. He is righteous and born of a virgin.

2. **Isa is powerful.** He gave sight to the blind, healed lepers and raised the dead. It is a Muslim's duty to Allah to obey Isa. To know what Isa has told us to do, we must read the Injil.

3. **Isa knows the way to heaven**. Allah raised Jesus to himself. Isa is in heaven and knows the way to heaven. Those who follow Isa are above those who disbelieve.

Eventually the stranger leaves, but he invites anyone who would like to talk more to join him in the local tea shop.

He leaves the mosque, walks to the tea shop, orders some tea, and waits. Anyone who follows him to the tea shop to talk more may be a person of peace—someone who is responsive and who could be a doorway into a community of relationships.

One of the men who listened intently to the discussion leaves the mosque, crosses the road, and sits down to talk with the stranger in the tea shop. They talk about Isa as they drink their tea. Finally the stranger needs to go, but he would like to talk more later. He asks if he can visit his new Muslim friend in his home, meet his family and his friends, and talk more about Isa and what the Injil says about him.

Defeating a Muslim in a theological argument rarely produces a new follower of Jesus. But an effective connect approach puts us in touch with a wide range of people quickly and enables us to identify possible *people of peace* who welcome the messenger and the message and are bridges into a community.

Notice how in this case the stranger moves quickly from the crowd to the responsive person and then from that person to their relational world. If the gospel is received with faith, it will be a natural next step to form disciple making groups in the local community along relational ties.

The role of the messenger is not to relocate these new believers into an existing Christian environment. That will only alienate them from their community and stifle the spread of the gospel. The messenger must help these new disciples learn how to follow Jesus and form communities of disciples in their world.

CONNECTING STRATEGIES

Tim Scheuer visits homes in Airds, a disadvantaged suburb of Sydney. He and his coworkers do a simple survey to identify responsive people.[2] Ninety-five percent of people they meet are happy to do the survey. The last question asks, "If it was possible to know God personally, would you be interested?" In this region of Sydney where there is very little Christian presence, a staggering 25 percent of people answer, "Yes." Tim then briefly shares the story of how he came to know Christ and asks if he can come back and talk more.

If the person is interested, Tim asks if they would be willing to invite friends, family and neighbors to listen to him.

My wife, Michelle, leads a ministry to international students and immigrants. The connect point is English conversation classes that include a discovery Bible study. English classes that include a discovery Bible study are a simple way of connecting with people who are in a major life transition and identifying those who are responsive. We follow up with people who show interest and invite them to learn more. We have people from Thailand, Vietnam, China, Iran, Venezuela, Korea and Tibet.

Connecting strategies vary, but there are some common characteristics of the most effective ones. The best connect strategies get you face to face with a large number of people and enable you to identify the few who are ready now to learn more about the gospel and following Jesus. These strategies need to be low-cost, flexible, and easily transferable to other workers.

Effective connecting strategies do not require large amounts of funding, time or personnel. What did it cost for Jesus to reach the Samaritan woman's village? What did it cost Peter to reach the household of Cornelius?

Effective connecting strategies are up front with the gospel. The purpose is not to win over disinterested or antagonistic people. It is to identify responsive people who are the doorway into their community. Normally to find the few who are responsive, you must connect broadly. That's the pattern that Jesus set. He visited every town and village. He had a plan to connect with as many people as he could. He was also open to unplanned encounters. Jesus encouraged his disciples to move on when their message was rejected. Paul did the same. The priority is to find the people God has already prepared.

How do you identify responsive people? You must ask and invite. Ask them if you can pray for a need. Ask them about their religious beliefs. Invite them to do a discovery Bible study. Ask them if they would like to know more about a relationship with God.

In the New Testament, methods of connecting with people varied. Jesus systematically visited all the towns and villages of Galilee. Philip was fleeing persecution when he found himself among Samaritans who needed to hear the gospel. Peter and John were going about their normal routine of visiting the Temple for prayer when they met a beggar. The disciples who took the gospel to the Gentiles in Antioch were also fleeing persecution. Paul typically targeted cities with Jewish communities.

Often there is intentionality in strategies for connecting. Sometimes it is God's direct intervention that opens the door to a responsive person. Still other times the messenger happens to be in the right place at the right time.

I have a friend serving in a communist country in Asia. "Barney" had been in the field for a year and was frustrated with a lack of progress. One night he woke with a strong sense that he should travel to a specific region that was eight hours away by bus. Off he went the next day with a local worker for an eight-hour bus ride, wondering if the trip was a wild goose chase.

Barney and his friend arrived at the end of the line. The bus was empty except for one person who walked to the back and asked them if they were Christians. The night before he too had woken with a strong sense that there would be two people on the bus whom God had sent to his village.

The three of them traveled to the village. Barney and his coworker prayed for people and shared the gospel. Some of the villagers were healed of sickness. One skeptical young man watched them the whole time and then gave his life to Christ, becoming the leader of a movement that spread throughout the region. Ten years later there are over ten thousand believers meeting in hundreds of churches.

Waiting to be awakened in the middle of the night is not Barney's normal mode of operation. Nor was it how Jesus or Peter or Paul usually operated. They worked hard to connect with people in their mission field. They expected God to go before them. They expected God to lead and redirect them. They worked systematically.

Early on, a connecting strategy must move from relying on *outsiders* to do the connecting to the *insiders* who reach out to their friends and family. Barney has lived in Asia for over a decade. He knows the language and culture. He is still an outsider and always will be. His job is to ensure the gospel quickly spreads from the outsider to the insiders. Connecting is what an outsider does to spark a movement among insiders. Insiders don't need a connecting strategy; they are already connected. Their job is to take the gospel to their relational world. When they are ready to go into unreached fields, they too will need a connecting strategy.

Barney is now somewhere in Asia sparking church planting movements among Muslims. He prays for miracles, and he's out every day of the week visiting mosques and connecting with people, looking for those people God has prepared.

Most Christian workers focus on their own effectiveness and don't think about what their disciples are doing. The workers who spark church planting movements look beyond what they do and work with insiders to see the gospel spread.

SHARING THE GOSPEL

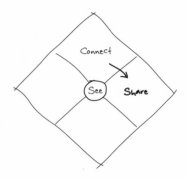

IT WAS THE FLIGHT FROM DELHI TO BANGALORE. The plane was just about to take off when I spotted three empty seats—my ticket to happiness and a peaceful, quiet flight. All I needed to do was jump across the aisle once the aircraft was ready for takeoff, and those seats were *mine*.

I looked left to the guy sitting next to me. He was Indian. The thought crossed my mind that I should stay and strike up a conversation. But what was more important—my need for sleep or his need to know about Jesus? Then I remembered what happened to Jonah. I decided I would stay put and get to know him.

The man's name was Yousuf, and he worked in marketing for a top clothing company. His name told me he was a Muslim, so I struck up a conversation with him about his faith. We agreed that Islam and Christianity have concepts in common such as our belief in one God who expects us to live righteously. He told me of the respect and reverence he had for Jesus as a prophet of God.

I shared with him that there was an important difference between our faiths. Through Jesus, God came looking for us on a rescue mission. Our best efforts will never be enough. We need God's forgiveness through Jesus' death on the cross. I shared the Parable of the Lost Son and how the father forgave his son before the son had done anything to repay him. Through Jesus we are sons, not slaves.

Then I asked him that old preacher's question: "If you stood before God today, would you know that your sins are forgiven?"

He answered, "No." For a while he was silent, and then he told me, "I have a Christian friend who was going to get me a copy of the Bible in Hindi, but he keeps forgetting." I told him I'd send him one.

Some people think that loving people and sharing the gospel are somehow unrelated to each other. As we swapped addresses at the end of the flight, I realized Yousuf and I had become friends because I'd shared the gospel with him.

Giving up those three seats was well worth it.

SOMETHING TO SAY

Michelle and I run a simple four-week training to help people get started in making disciples and forming groups. We teach people how to share their personal conversion story, how to share the gospel, and how to disciple people through a discovery Bible study.

In our first group we had someone who had been a pastor for over twenty years. He could have run the training himself. It was like I was taking him back to kindergarten. Finally he spoke up. "Don't you think this is a bit formulaic?" Until that moment I didn't know that *formulaic* was a word, but I understood what he meant.

We talked for a while. This pastor was still not convinced it was important to have a simple method of sharing his story and sharing the gospel. The next week, however, he came back to the training transformed. For the first time, this pastor had shared the story of his conversion with his father, who had never shown interest in his faith (they had never been able to talk about it). His father was now ninety years old, and *he listened*.

It's often said that we must earn the right to speak. That's a noble sentiment if it means that our lives should reflect the message we proclaim. It's a distortion, however, if it means that somehow we must add something to the work of Christ before the gospel can be effective. Jesus has already earned the right. Many of his encounters were with people he did not have deep, long-term relationships with. The same was true for his followers throughout the book of Acts. The idea that we must earn the right to speak must never become an excuse to remain silent.

A friend of mine has a ministry of teaching English as a second language to Afghan refugees. I asked him how he was communicating the gospel with

them. "I couldn't do that," he told me. "I don't know their heart language."
He is one of many examples of Christians in the Western world who lack
confidence and who are reluctant to share the gospel. The movement that
Jesus founded, however, was clear about its message and active in proclaiming it. The disciples had confidence in the gospel, and they took it to
the world. The gospel was not just expounded and defended on Sunday
mornings, it left the building and was found in the marketplace, in people's
homes, on the road and in the prisons.

BASIC TRAINING

I was meeting with some Christian workers in Bangalore, India. They told me
how they trained existing Indian believers to share their story, to share Jesus'
story and to disciple new believers. They train with the expectation that
people will immediately put into practice what they are learning. Recently
they had trained 120 people. After the first week, the trainees were encouraged
to share their story with five people before they returned for the next session.
Every week they put into practice what they were learning. Every week the
class size got smaller. After six weeks there were just fifteen participants.

Before I could ask the workers why they thought this approach was a
good idea, they told me that the fifteen remaining participants had already
started nine new churches. They pointed across the road and said, "There's
a church meeting in that garage for taxi drivers and their families."

Why start with 120 people when only 10-15 percent are ready to act on
what they learn? Because you can't predict who is really open to learn and to
implement unless you train as many people as possible and see who is ready
to lead the way.

EFFECTIVENESS

Here's a test of the effectiveness of how you share the gospel. Can someone
you have just led to Christ go home that same day and share the gospel with
the people they know and love?

There are some simple methods every believer should master, especially
new believers.[1]

1. Sharing your story. People who have witnessed a recent conversion of
a friend or relative are far more likely to be receptive to the gospel. That
means that training new believers to tell their story is essential to the spread
of the gospel across social networks.

There is something disarming about hearing a person's story of coming to faith in Jesus. Luke tells us Paul's conversion story in Acts and then has Paul tell it again on two other occasions. The story has three elements: Paul's life before he met Christ, how he met Christ, and his life since meeting Christ—all told in just a few minutes.

Can you tell your story in three minutes? Do you have a simple method of teaching others, especially new believers, to share their story?

2. Sharing Jesus' story. We can spend the rest of our lives and into eternity plumbing the depths of what God has done for us in Christ, but can we communicate the heart of the gospel in just a few minutes?

There was a pattern to the early church's proclamation of the gospel that could be adapted for different audiences. Unfortunately, the longer someone is a Christian, the more complicated and fuzzier his understanding of the gospel can become. We forget how we started following Christ. The more complicated we are in our methods of communication, the harder it is for new believers to share the gospel with their friends and family. Can we communicate the gospel clearly and succinctly so that new believers can follow our example?

3. Making disciples. Many of us don't know what to do if someone we've shared with wants to learn more about following Jesus. Do we invite them to our church? Do we introduce them to our pastor? Do we give them a book to read or a video to watch?

From a movements perspective, the most effective approach will be easily transferred to new believers. An example of one approach is discovery Bible study. There are different approaches; one model, *Seven Stories of Hope,* looks at the Gospels and Acts; another, *Creation to Christ,* begins in Genesis and ends in the Gospels; another involves working through a Gospel one story at a time. The process is the same: all you need is a passage of Scripture and some basic questions that anyone could ask.

- In your own words, what does this passage or story say?
- What did you like about the story?
- What does this teach us about God?
- What does this teach us about humanity?
- Is there an example to follow or a command to obey?
- What will you do to obey what you have learned?
- Who could you share this passage or story with?

The strength of using discovery Bible study as an evangelistic method is that it integrates learning with obedience. People are not just learning information about Jesus, they are also learning to follow him. The other strength of discovery Bible study is that it's so simple that a new believer can quickly learn to lead friends and family through the Scriptures. (In the next chapter we'll look at how discovery Bible study can become a lifelong method of growing in maturity.)

4. **Reaching family, friends and strangers.** How does the gospel spread into unreached relational worlds? We assume it's our job. The spotlight is on us or on our church or group, when it should be on finding a *person of peace,* a relational insider who is responsive to the gospel and best placed to share their new faith with the people she knows. The gospel spreads most effectively through networks of pre-existing relationships. The friends and family members of new believers quickly become some of the most responsive people. It is vital to help new and existing believers to identify the people in their relational world, to pray for them by name, and to seek an opportunity to share their story and Jesus' story with them.

Only God can change the heart. Our job is to share and invite and allow the gospel to do its work. We all need simple, transferable methods for sharing our story and sharing Jesus' story. We all need to be able to teach new disciples to do the same.

The reason we see so few people coming to know Christ is often due to our unwillingness to share the gospel and invite people to discover more. Most of us aren't evangelists, but we all have a story to tell and something to say about Jesus.

TRAINING DISCIPLES

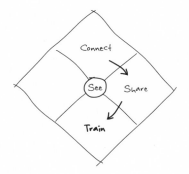

Disciple people to conversion, don't convert people then disciple them.

—DAVID WATSON

THIS WEEK I MET WITH a twenty-something professional. We're working through Matthew's Gospel using a discovery Bible study approach. I had a plan, but my friend is out of control. We are supposed to read one story at a time, but he's devouring great slabs of Matthew and bringing his questions to our times together.

I'm trying not to be the expert; I want him to discover truth for himself. I also want him to begin to obey what he's learning. So after we'd talked for an hour I asked him, "From everything that you've read so far in Matthew, what stands out? What has got your attention?"

He didn't need to think long about the answer. "Forgiveness," he responded. There were tears as he shared a very personal episode in his life and the struggle he had to move on from it.

I was tempted to say, "Hey, don't be so hard on yourself!" Instead I took him seriously and said, "I think God wants to free you from this. You need to talk to God about this issue this week."

We had moved on from abstract ideas to applying God's Word to his life. He hasn't made a commitment to Christ yet, but he is learning what it means to be a disciple, one step at a time.

Discipleship is not a higher order of Christian living that follows con-version. Discipleship begins with the first step of obedience in response to revealed truth. Disciples grow by identifying with Jesus' death and resur-rection through baptism and by learning to obey Jesus' teaching.

Jesus discipled people to conversion; he didn't convert people and then try to disciple them. You don't have to convert anyone. You just need to find someone who is willing to learn more about Jesus and how they can follow him. You begin by doing a discovery Bible study and asking obedience-oriented questions. God does the converting.

The objective of Jesus' ministry to the crowds was to make disciples. Dis-ciples were those who obeyed Jesus' call to follow him and who submitted to his training in making disciples of others. They counted the cost and committed themselves to Jesus and his cause.

The Gospels give a realistic picture of the disciples—both their strengths and their failings. Jesus taught them, corrected them, supported them, forgave them and restored them. Through their relationship with Jesus, his followers grew in their discipleship. The mission Jesus gave to the apostles before he ascended was for them to make disciples of the nations. As new disciples are baptized and learn to obey his commands, Jesus is present. The risen Lord continues to call disciples out of the crowds to follow him.

WHAT DID JESUS COMMAND?

One approach to making disciples is to take one command of Christ at a time and help a new believer learn how to obey it. The goal is not to teach new disciples everything they need to know. It is to teach new believers the habit of *obedience to what they know*. The questions to ask when evaluating any method of making disciples are:

1. Is it obedience-oriented?

2. Is it simple enough that a new believer can begin discipling someone they know?

3. Does it lead to the formation of disciple-making groups and churches?

I was asked to come and preach at a church gathering for people who were recovering from drug and alcohol addiction. The safe thing to do would have been to pull out one of my well-worn messages. Instead I took a risk, breaking people into groups of three to five and telling them to read the story of Jesus and the woman at the well (Jn 4:1-42). Then I asked them to close their Bibles and see how much of the story they could remember.

Over the next thirty minutes I fed the groups a series of questions to help them engage with the Scripture and apply it to their lives. The room was full of energy. Finally we came back together, and I had the groups tell me what the story meant and how they were going to obey what they had learned.

I could have preached a good message on this passage and told them what to do. We would have arrived at the same place with the same essential truths. But now these people had a simple method of learning from the Scripture for themselves that could be easily passed on to others. Now they owned for themselves the insights they had gained. Now they had a group of people who could ask them the following week, "How did you obey what you learned? Who did you tell the story to?"

I enjoy preaching and teaching, and I normally get encouraging responses to my messages. I believe I have a calling to preach and to teach. But no movement can spread in breadth and depth by relying on guys like me with theological degrees. Jesus made sure his message was memorable and would be passed on by ordinary people to others. The Word of God is a dynamic force that changes lives. It cannot be confined to a Sunday morning sermon or a carefully controlled Bible study. Somehow the Word will break out and find its way to where people are in their homes, in the streets, in cafes, in colleges and in workplaces. At the heart of lifelong discipleship must be a simple method, simple enough that a new disciple can quickly pick it up and pass it on. It must be focused on learning to obey what the Scriptures teach.[1] The seven commands of Christ[2] (see table 22.1) are a good place to begin foundational discipleship.

Table 22.1. The Seven Commands of Christ

Commands of Christ	First church	Discovery Bible Study
Repent and believe (Mark 1:15)	Acts 2:38	Jesus and the woman who had lived a sinful life (Luke 7:36-50)
Be baptized (Matthew 28:19)	Acts 2:39	Philip and the Ethiopian (Acts 8:26-39)
Pray (Matthew 6:9-13)	Acts 2:42	Jesus' teaching on prayer (Matthew 6:5-15)
Make disciples (Matthew 28:19-20)	Acts 2:28, 47	The Samaritan woman (John 4:4-42)
Love (Matthew 22: 37-39)	Acts 2:42–47	The Good Samaritan (Luke 10:25-37)
Celebrate Lord's Supper (Luke 22:19-20)	Acts 2:42, 46	Jesus' last meal (Luke 22:7-20)
Give generously (Luke 6:38)	Acts 2:45	The widow who gives (Mark 12:41-44)

There is a world of difference between a command to teach disciples and a command to teach disciples *to obey.* The former focuses on the teacher, the latter on the learner. The first is concerned with transferring information; the second is concerned with life transformation.

Learning to obey Christ is the goal of discipleship. Through the Holy Spirit, Jesus is present as new disciples gather around his Word and learn to follow him one step at a time. Our methods must be simple and transferable so that new disciples can immediately begin teaching others.

Evangelism that aims at decisions rather than disciples will never produce a multiplying movement. Movements spread through new believers who hear, believe and obey!

GATHERING COMMUNITIES

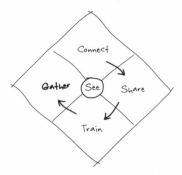

IT'S EARLY SUNDAY MORNING. Lipok and Nathan are traveling down the mighty Brahmaputra River to visit the believers among the Mising people of Assam, a state in northeastern India. They travel by ferry and then on the dirt roads of an island that is home to 300,000 people.

The Mising people live along the fertile riverbeds of the Brahmaputra, which they regard as holy. They live in thatched houses raised on stilts that provide protection from floodwaters during the rainy season and from wild animals during the dry season. When the floodwaters rise, the Mising pack up their few possessions and move across the river or downstream to where stilts have already been erected. The Mising deal with annual floods, malaria and water-borne diseases, yet they continue to live along the banks and tributaries of their beloved Brahmaputra River.

Lipok and Nathan have been working with the Mising people for three years; they teach them to follow Jesus and make disciples up and down the river system that is the Misings' world. One local worker has started three hundred churches in his "stream." He can go where Western personnel and funding can never reach.

The Mising believers' guide for church is Acts 2:38-47. They begin a meeting by confessing their sins and repenting. They baptize new believers outside in the river. They teach the Word of God, celebrate the Lord's Supper and pray for the sick. They share their needs with each other, and if possible those needs are dealt with immediately through a gift or offer of help. Worship flows out of a response to God's Word. They finish by reminding one another of the gospel and by committing to go out and share before the sun sets that day.

FIRST THINGS

A story like that of the Mising believers reminds us that our experience of church is shaped by the world we live in. It also helps us identify what all followers of Jesus share across time and different cultures.

What minimum elements are required to form a community of disciples? To leave anything out that is essential will corrupt what a new community becomes and what it reproduces. To add anything that is not essential will reduce the group's ability to function and spread unhindered.

Movements know what the essentials of church are, and that's what they produce and reproduce. Nothing more—and nothing less. Other things may be desirable but not essential, and nonessentials slow a movement down. On the other hand, some elements are so essential that if they are removed what is left is no longer a church.

The apostle Luke had his list—the bare bones of what a church is. No extra baggage. No essentials neglected.

> With many other words he warned them; and he pleaded with them, "Save yourselves from this corrupt generation." Those who accepted his message were baptized, and about three thousand were added to their number that day.
>
> They devoted themselves to the apostles' teaching and to fellowship, to the breaking of bread and to prayer. Everyone was filled with awe at the many wonders and miraculous signs performed by the apostles. All the believers were together and had everything in common. They sold property and possessions to give to anyone who had need. Every day they continued to meet together in the temple courts. They broke bread in their homes and ate together with glad and sincere hearts, praising God and enjoying the favor of all the people. And the Lord added to their number daily those who were being saved. (Acts 2:40-47)

The more that is added to the list of essentials, the harder it becomes for new believers to form churches in their world. If new believers are not forming churches, a church planting movement is unlikely. Churches may be planted, but they won't multiply.

FROM CHURCH PLANTING TO CHURCH PLANTING MOVEMENTS

When Michelle and I planted our first church, we felt we had to form a church to share the gospel and make disciples. Church first, then gospel, then disciples. Evangelism for us typically meant inviting someone to come to church.

Two decades later we've learned to change the order and priorities to gospel first, then disciples, then churches. When we connect with people, we're not trying to get them to come to our church. We share the good news about Jesus, not the good news about our church. We're looking for responsive people. As people are putting their faith in Jesus, they are also learning to obey what he commanded and become disciples.

Just as the gospel and discipleship must not be separated, so discipleship must always lead to community or church formation.

Adding	Multiplying
Church	Gospel
Gospel	Disciples
Disciples	Church

The shift from the first column to the second column is the difference between planting a church and fueling a church planting movement. The gospel is primary—through it God brings disciples and churches into existence. The gospel creates the church, not the other way around.

THE JOURNEY FROM DEPENDENCY TO PARTNERSHIP

Isn't it curious that Jesus spent no more than three years laying the foundation for the movement he started? At the end of that time his band of disciples was certainly less than perfect in knowledge, maturity, and skills, yet he left them with the challenge. Philip had just a short time with the Samaritans who turned to Christ. Peter had just a few days with Cornelius and his household. Paul had just weeks or months with most of his churches. He had two years at Corinth, but the believers still let him down.

Why didn't these men stay longer and get things "right" from the beginning? Jesus said it was good for his disciples that he went away. He promised to send them the Holy Spirit who would remind them of his teaching and lead them into all truth. Jesus and the apostles had full confidence in the power of God's Word and the Holy Spirit to provide what local churches needed to grow into maturity, even though that journey could be hard.

New Testament churches were expected to take responsibility for themselves: to govern their affairs, fund themselves, remain true to the gospel in belief and behavior, and to participate in spreading the gospel locally and beyond their region.

Paul scolded the Corinthians for their spiritual immaturity (1 Cor 3:1-3) even though they had been following Christ for some time. He praised the Philippians because of their partnership in the gospel. From the first day of their existence as a community, he was confident that God had begun and would continue a good work in them (Phil 1:3).

So what are some of the New Testament essentials that must be in place for any group to form into a healthy church?

1. **Lordship.** Christ is the one head and only foundation of the church. He gives life and leadership to his people through his Word and the Holy Spirit.

2. **Leadership.** Every believer has a role to play in the building up of the community and the spread of the gospel. Leadership of the church is both local and mobile. Paul appointed local leaders in the churches he planted. Paul and his missionary band were responsible for the multiplication and strengthening of the churches.

3. **Five functions.** Local communities of disciples must be engaged in worship, in teaching, in obedience-based discipleship, in a shared life together, and in the spread of the gospel both locally and beyond.

4. **Maturity.** Churches were expected to quickly take responsibility for governance, funding, faithfulness in belief and behavior, and partnership in the spread of the gospel.

Acts uses a range of terms to identify what we refer to as "church"—the believers, the disciples, the brothers and sisters. Whatever terms we use, it is the reality that counts. New disciples must learn to form communities that follow Jesus together. They must know the essentials of what it means to be God's people. They must be given freedom to adapt church forms to their situation. They must take responsibility for themselves and not be dependent on outsiders. They must become partners in spreading the gospel.

MULTIPLYING WORKERS

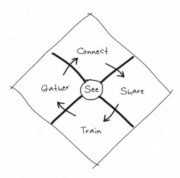

AS THE AYATOLLAH KHOMEINI'S chartered flight touched down at the Tehran airport on February 1, 1979, a crowd of several million Iranians gathered to welcome him home. The Ayatollah was now the undisputed leader of Iran's Islamic revolution.

In 1979 Iran was a nation of 39 million people. The vast majority of these were Muslim. The revolution ushered in a new era of persecution. In 1979 Reverend Arastoo Sayyah, an Anglican priest in Shiraz, had his throat cut. His murder marked the first of a string of assassinations of Christian leaders. Yet by the late 1980s there were many thousands of Persian followers of Jesus in Iran.

A decade before the revolution, God called Haik Hovsepian,[1] a young Armenian Iranian pastor, to go as a missionary to the northern province of Mazandaran to reach Muslims. Few Armenian Christians shared a burden for the salvation of Muslims. If you were born as an Assyrian or Armenian, you were a Christian. If you were born a Persian, you were a Muslim. Ethnicity determined your religion.

Brother Haik found the work hard and slow, but by 1976 he had started five house churches with around twenty Muslim background believers. He believed one day there would be millions of Persian believers, and with that vision in mind, he translated and wrote 150 worship songs in Farsi, the Persian language.

In 1981 the Persian church in Mazandaran had grown to sixty people, and Brother Haik was able to turn the work over to the local leaders he had trained. He returned to Tehran where he challenged the Armenian Christians to open their doors and their hearts to the Persian people and begin using Farsi in their services. New believers began pouring into the churches. In an environment of intimidation, churches met secretly in small groups that soon multiplied. Christian satellite broadcasts helped spread the gospel across Iran as ordinary Iranians smuggled in illegal satellite dishes in defiance of the government. The government demanded to know the names of the Muslim background believers. Brother Haik refused to tell them.

By now the Persian people, especially the young, felt the full weight of the harsh restrictions imposed on them by Islamic law. In 1993 Brother Haik drew international attention to the plight of Mehdi Dibaj, who had been imprisoned by the Islamic courts for over ten years on charges of apostasy. Brother Haik's campaign succeeded, and on January 16, 1994, Dibaj was released. Three days later Brother Haik vanished from the streets. When his body was eventually found, it was covered in multiple stab wounds.

Hundreds of Persian believers came to honor Brother Haik at his funeral despite the presence of government agents who documented those present. These Muslim background believers, inspired by the boldness of Brother Haik and the other Armenian and Persian martyrs, stepped into the leadership of a nationwide church planting movement.

In today's Iran, people have time on their hands—especially the young. The government places many restrictions on what they are allowed to do. The unintended consequence is that believers have time to be together every day. They gather for prayer, Bible study and evangelism. Once a group grows to twenty-five, it forms a second group. New believers are quickly trained to lead new house fellowships and to train others.

The house groups are formed into various networks. In 2008 there were a thousand groups that traced their origin back to Brother Haik's church in Tehran. They are the fruit of Brother Haik's intentional discipleship of just a few dozen Muslim background believers in the late 1980s and early 1990s.

For centuries Persians assumed that if you were a Christian, it was because you were an Armenian. Today Persian believers refer to themselves as *farsimasihi* (Persian followers of the Messiah). The *farsimasihi* are sending and funding missionaries to the surrounding ethnic minorities—the Azeri, the Luri and the Kurds within Iran.

When Brother Haik began his ministry in 1962, he was just seventeen. He pastored his first church in Majidieh, a suburb of Tehran. Imagine if he had remained in Tehran the rest of his life to pastor just one church. No matter how successful that one church became, it would never have had the impact of a movement. Once Brother Haik began to multiply disciples, churches, and leaders, the movement was no longer dependent on him. As tragic as his death was, it became a spark that lit an unstoppable fire that spread across Iran.

1 + 1 = 100

My grandfather Edgar Bashforth fought in World War I in France in the 11th Machine Gun Company. After the war he received government help for returned soldiers and bought land near Brunswick Heads in northern New South Wales. He cleared the land and fenced it. He milled the timber and sold it, and he also raised dairy and beef cattle.

In 1923 Edgar married Lydia Vaughan, a local girl from nearby Mullumbimby. They married at 7:30 a.m. so that they could dash to board the train for their honeymoon! They had seven children, one of whom was my mother, Joan. I am one of their twenty-four grandchildren. Today, Edgar and Lydia Bashforth have one hundred descendants—children, grandchildren, great-grandchildren, and great-great-grandchildren.

How could one couple be the cause of so many people coming into the world? They started things rolling, and they raised a family. Beyond that, they had no direct control. They did not fund, manage, or control the lives of future generations. As good parents they raised their children to a maturity that is defined as healthy self-reliance.

My grandparents' story is not unusual. It's the law of multiplication that God has written into the world he made. Where there is life and health, there is multiplication.

Church planting movements function in the same way. The size and influence of a single church is not what ultimately matters. Far more significant are the multiple generations of disciples and churches that one church of any size can produce.

Directly managed systems can only add churches, never multiply them. Multiplication can only occur when offspring are given the freedom to produce future generations. Church size is not the point. It's healthy multiplication that counts. There is no other way to reach every corner of the planet with the gospel.

VISION TO LEGACY

A vision without action is a fantasy. Action without a vision is drudgery.
A vision with action will change the world.
—Fortune cookie

It's fine to say we have to multiply disciples and churches. Nobody would argue with that. But who wakes up in the morning and says, "I'm going to start myself a church planting movement"? It may be something we want to see happen, but wishful thinking won't make it happen.

Disciple-making movements are a work of God; he invites us to participate in his work as partners. Our contribution is real. We plant and we water, but only God can give the growth.

Here are three questions we need to answer to join in with what God is doing.

1. Do we see the end? What is our end vision? What does it look like for our task to be complete? Jesus knew the answer to that question—he went to every town and village. Paul knew the answer—he planted reproducing churches in the major cities between Jerusalem and Illyricum. Try this exercise: How many people are there in your area of focus? Don't ask, "What can we do?" Ask, "What needs to be done?"

In 1991 Australia had around 11,000 churches, or one for every 1,500 people. By 2006 we had around 10,000 churches, or one for every 2,000 people.[2] The gap is widening every day. If our end vision is to see one church for every 1,000 people, we'd need 10,000 more churches today and one thousand new churches every three years just to keep up with population growth. Meanwhile, the average Australian church is around seventy people. One church for every thousand people is only a beginning.

The reason we make these calculations is to remind ourselves of how great the task is. If business as usual will not get the job done in a country of 23 million, what hope have we in a world of seven billion? Only a movement strategy has the potential to reach a lost world.

2. What will we do? Vision is fine, but nothing happens unless we know what to do when we get out of bed on a Monday morning to face a new week. That's where discipline comes in.

- *Connect.* How are we connecting with people who are far from God? Are we looking for responsive people who are the bridge for the gospel to cross over into new relational worlds?

- *Share.* How are we sharing the gospel in words and deeds so that people put their faith in Christ? Are new believers who are insiders in the community sharing the gospel? How much?

- *Train.* How are we teaching new disciples to follow Christ in obedience? Are our methods simple and transferable? Are disciples learning how to discover and obey the truth of the Scriptures for themselves? Are they teaching others?

- *Gather.* How are we gathering new believers into disciple-making groups? Are the groups forming into new churches that are growing in maturity and reproducing disciples and churches?

Each of the above points can be measured by concrete activities. A worker can look at the calendar at the beginning of a week or a year and ask, "How will I pursue these activities and train others to do the same?"

3. How will we multiply workers? Jesus spent much of his ministry training workers. He taught them to pray for more workers. Paul followed his example. Our own efforts will never be enough. Practitioners must also become master trainers. Jesus' example has never been surpassed. This is how he multiplied workers for a missionary movement:

- *Model:* He modeled effective ministry to his disciples.

- *Assist:* He recruited them to work with him.

- *Watch:* He watched what they did and provided instruction.

- *Leave:* Finally, he left them to get on with the job and to train others.

It is not easy, but it should be simple. The task is immense, but Jesus of Nazareth has led the way, and as the risen Lord he continues to work through his Word and his Spirit and even through us, his people.

STARTING SOMEWHERE

A journey of a thousand miles begins with a single step.

—LAO TZU

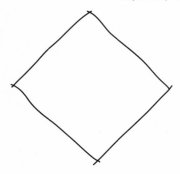

WE'VE COME A LONG WAY since the start of this book, but the journey has only just begun. What happens next will determine whether reading this book has been an intellectual exercise or an experience that will change your life. If God has spoken to you through the message of this book, what matters now is obedience—but where do you begin?

Here's one last story of how God led one leader, his church, and a growing team of workers to a whole new way of seeing the world, one step of obedience at a time.

BACK TO ANTIOCH

Dave Lawton pulled into my driveway around 5:20 a.m. on a cold, dark winter morning. I was traveling with him across town for a 6:00 a.m. prayer meeting. This is not my usual start to the day, but I wanted to learn more about Dave's journey and what he and his team were up to.

God had put the western suburbs of Melbourne on Dave's heart. "The West" is the most socially deprived and unreached region of our city. Dave and his wife, Colleen, had spent their days off over the last twelve months prayer-walking the streets and meeting people.

One day the Lawtons met Davinda and Mandip, a Sikh couple from northern India. As they talked, they discovered that Mandip was out of work and the bills were piling up. Dave and Colleen prayed for them on the spot and asked Jesus to help them through this difficult time. The next day Davinda was in tears. She told them, "You prayed, and God answered." Mandip was back at work.

Davinda and Mandip were part of a group of up to thirteen Sikhs living in a small two-bedroom apartment. Dave decided to follow Jesus' instructions to his disciples on mission and go into their house and eat their food, heal them and tell them the kingdom of God is here.

So with a tablecloth of newspaper spread on the floor and piled high with curries and chapatis, Dave began walking this group of Sikhs through the gospel of Mark and teaching them how to follow Jesus.

Dave says, "It's not about bringing people into our space. We must make disciples in their world." God opened doors and led Dave to different people of peace who welcomed him and connected him with their relational networks. The strategy is simple; Dave and his coworkers pray, they connect, they share the gospel and pray for needs, and they look for persons of peace. They don't focus on individuals but relational networks.

Dave takes seriously Jesus' command to go into people's homes and eat their food. He has no intention of taking responsive people out of their community and placing them in his church. He takes the gospel and the church to them. Through persons of peace he connects with relational communities and gathers them to read the Scriptures, to pray and to learn to obey Jesus. His strategy for leading people to Christ is discipleship. He wants them in the Scriptures, learning to obey so that the Holy Spirit can begin working in their hearts. Dave and Colleen's example has inspired others. Around Australia there are now sixty people who have volunteered to pray, connect with people, share the gospel, make disciples and gather into simple churches.

After a forty-minute drive we arrived at the prayer meeting. There were about a dozen people in the room, all volunteers. This is one of five groups that meet across the city.

I asked Dave, "Where do you get these people?"

He told me, "I pray. I go out onto the streets and into communities and start sharing the gospel. I get out and meet people who need Jesus. That's the best recruitment strategy I have. Engaging with the harvest attracts the right people." Dave has learned to follow Jesus' example by calling and training workers in the harvest.

Before we prayed, Dave pulled out a whiteboard and drew on it all the "households" he and his workers are connected with—Sudanese, Sikhs, "Aussie battlers," Mainland Chinese, Iranian Muslims, Vietnamese, and Australian college students. Dave and the team are not trying to just plant one church. They want to multiply churches across the city.

Team members report in on how they are connecting, sharing the gospel and praying for people in the households. As they connect, they invite people into a discovery Bible study.[1] As people come to faith, they begin to form a church in their world.

Dave's advice to people who want to get started is: "Begin with prayer, but you must pray with the intention of engaging with people. You must be transparent that you are there to share Jesus. Look for responsive people and gather them and their friends and family to do simple discovery Bible studies, and let the Holy Spirit do his work."

Dave has about sixty volunteers throughout Melbourne—north, south, east and west. Over twenty churches have been planted. The vision doesn't stop with Australia. An Australian-Hungarian couple has become the movement's first overseas missionaries. They returned to Hungary to make disciples and plant churches among the Gypsies of Europe.

There is an unusual twist to this story of an emerging missionary movement. When Dave and Colleen began their journey of discovery, Dave was an executive pastor for Crossway, a church of four thousand people. Large churches have demanding schedules, so the ministry to the western part of Melbourne was pioneered on the Lawtons' day off each week.

As Dave's ministry to the western suburbs gained momentum, the leadership released him to devote more time to mobilizing others. Eventually Dave told the church, "You've got to stop paying my salary!" The church's leadership wouldn't hear of it. They just wanted to know that the gospel was spreading, disciples were being made and groups were forming. There wasn't even an expectation that the emerging churches would become "Crossway" churches.

Crossway is a church in the tradition of Antioch, which released Barnabas and Paul to return to pioneering work.

Dave's team keeps growing. Workers are fanning out across Australia. With Crossway's blessing Dave is moving from a salaried staff position to being a missionary supported by Crossway. Dave is setting up a mission entity that is in partnership with Crossway but organizationally separate from it.

When people hear this story, they comment that a church as big as Crossway can afford to support and release workers like Dave. But there is another way to interpret this story: one of the reasons why Crossway is a thriving church is because it has always been willing to give sacrificially of its money and people to local and world missions. A church with a vision like that, regardless of its size, attracts good people and, even more important, attracts God's blessing.[2]

LAST WORDS

What, after all, is Apollos? And what is Paul? Only servants,
through whom you came to believe—as the Lord has assigned to each his task.
I planted the seed, Apollos watered it, but God has been making it grow.

So neither the one who plants nor the one who waters is anything, but only
God, who makes things grow. The one who plants and the one who waters have
one purpose, and they will each be rewarded according to their own labor. For
we are co-workers in God's service; you are God's field, God's building.

1 Corinthians 3:5-9

Dave Lawton, Jeff Sundell, Julius Ebwongu, Ying Kai, Augie Joshua, Tim Scheuer—they all remind us that the risen Lord Jesus continues his mission through his people. The mission he began in Galilee continues to be pursued by his people, who have the dynamic word of the gospel and the power of the Holy Spirit.

Australia, Nepal, the United States, Uganda, China, Mongolia—the settings change, but there is one Lord, one faith, one baptism and one mission that Jesus invites us into.

For every prominent movement leader, there are thousands of others who will go unnoticed by history—but not by God. It's natural that we focus on the leaders who embody a work that God does. But they are only effective because they mobilize, inspire and equip ordinary people to share the gospel, make disciples and form communities. There is a job for everyone to do.

The movement Jesus founded advances because we are all called to connect with people who are far from God. We are all called to share our story and share Jesus' story, the gospel. We can all open the Scriptures and begin learning together how to follow Jesus in loving obedience. We can all form simple groups that gather to worship, to learn, to love and to witness.

We can all play our part in the multiplication of disciples and churches locally and throughout the world.

It's not about our success or failure. It's about God's mission in Jesus
Christ to redeem a lost world. We are his servants. He invites us to share in
the struggle, in the cost, and in the joy of reaching a lost world.

IMPLEMENTATION GUIDE

Don't be afraid; from now on you will fish for people.

—JESUS (LUKE 5:10)

Without Jesus, there would have been no Christian movement.

Many theories have sought to explain the astonishing rise of this new faith. Only one will do. Jesus of Nazareth founded a missionary movement, and as the risen Lord, he continues to lead the way.

There is an inner dynamic in the Christian faith that keeps drawing it back to renewal and expansion. Whenever Christianity puts it feet up and settles down, somewhere out there on the fringe God does something new. As followers of Jesus, we cannot move forward until we return to his example as founder and living Lord.

This guide was written for those who want to follow Jesus and to have him teach them to catch people, make disciples and multiply communities of his followers.

There is a job for everyone to do. The movement Jesus founded advances because we are all called to connect with people who are far from God. We are all called to share our story and Jesus' story—the gospel. We can all open the Scriptures and begin learning together how to follow Jesus in loving obedience. We can all form simple groups that gather to worship, to learn, to love and to witness. We can all play our part in the multiplication of disciples and churches both locally and throughout the world.

WHAT JESUS STARTED

There are six elements that characterize the movement that Jesus founded and still leads today.

1. **Jesus saw the end.** He was moved with compassion. He looked out over Israel and saw sheep, lost without a shepherd. He prepared his disciples to take the gospel to the whole world.

2. **Jesus connected with people.** Jesus crossed whatever boundaries stood in the way and connected with people. No group was beyond his care.

Jesus spent a lot of his time ministering to people—looking for the "sick" not the "healthy," "sinners" not the "righteous." He sought out people who knew they needed God's mercy.

3. **Jesus shared the gospel.** Jesus proclaimed the good news of salvation in words and deeds. In him, God's rule had become a present reality. He preached, taught, rebuked and invited everyone he met to repent and believe. He gave his life as a ransom for many.

4. **Jesus trained disciples.** Jesus led people to put their trust in him and to learn to obey his commands. He modeled and taught them a new way of life.

5. **Jesus gathered communities.** Jesus formed his disciples into communities characterized by faith in him, love for one another, and witness in words and deeds.

6. **Jesus multiplied workers.** Jesus equipped his followers to make disciples of all nations. He sent the Holy Spirit upon them so that they would continue his ministry in his power.

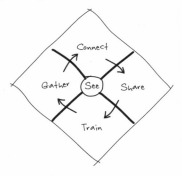

HOW TO USE THIS GUIDE

Throughout the course of these lessons, we'll work our way around the six elements to apply the learning. The studies are designed for ninety-minute sessions every other week (twice a month). They can be adapted to a different format as long as there is enough time between sessions to act on what you've learned and report back.

Stay focused on your progress in applying the learning in the field rather than on rushing through the lessons.

Visit www.movements.net to download additional training resources such as *Following Jesus* and *Fishing for People*.

1. SEE THE END, PART ONE

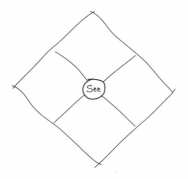

Let us go somewhere else—to the nearby villages—so I can preach there also. That is why I have come.

—JESUS (MARK 1:38)

1.1 As We Begin . . .

Get into a group of no more than three people. Share one highlight or low-light from the previous week.

Share your hopes for this series of studies.

Pray for people you know who are far from God. Don't discuss them. Just pray for them by name.

1.2 Discovery Bible Study

Read Matthew 9:35-38. Without looking at the text, retell the passage in your own words.

What do you like about this story?

What does the passage teach us about God?

What does it teach us about people?

Is there a command to obey or an example to follow?

What do you need to do this week to obey what you've learned?

Who could you share this story with?

Pray for each other.

1.3 What Jesus Did

Come back together as one large group. From memory, and by referring to the Gospels, list as many of Jesus' activities as you can under each heading below.

- Jesus saw the end (his end vision).
- Jesus connected with people who were far from God.
- Jesus shared the gospel.
- Jesus trained disciples.
- Jesus gathered disciples into communities.
- Jesus multiplied workers.

What have you learned about Jesus as the leader of a missionary movement?

1.4 Wrap-Up

Get into groups of two or three and discuss the following items.

Share a significant insight from this study.

How will you obey what you have learned in the next week?

Pray for people you know who are far from God. Don't discuss them. Just pray for them by name.

1.5 Before Our Next Session

Share the story of Matthew 9:35-38 with someone outside the group.

Read the Gospel of Mark, and answer the following questions.

1. How did Jesus see the end? What was his end vision?

2. How did Jesus connect with people who were far from God?

3. How did Jesus share the gospel?

4. How did Jesus train disciples?

5. How did Jesus gather disciples into communities?

6. How did Jesus multiply workers?

2. SEE THE END, PART TWO

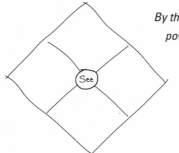

By the power of signs and wonders, through the power of the Spirit of God. So from Jerusalem all the way around to Illyricum, I have fully proclaimed the gospel of Christ.

—PAUL (ROMANS 15:19)

2.1 As We Begin . . .

Get into a group of no more than three people.

Pray for people you know who are far from God. Don't discuss them. Just pray for them by name.

How did you obey what you learned last session?

Who did you share the Matthew 9:35-38 passage with? How did it go?

Share any new insights from reading the Gospel of Mark.

2.2 Discovery Bible Study

Read Acts 14:1-28. Without looking at the text, retell the passage in your own words.

What do you like about this story?

What does the passage teach us about God?

What does it teach us about people?

Is there a command to obey or an example to follow?

What do you need to do this week to obey what you've learned?

Who could you share this story with?

Pray for each other.

2.3 Kingdom Life

Jesus often drew on his experience of agricultural life to describe the nature of the kingdom of God.

Come back together as one group and talk about your firsthand knowledge of how living things grow and reproduce. What do these experiences teach us about how the gospel spreads?

The spread of the kingdom of God is like a farmer who enters an empty field to scatter seed on the ground. The seed sprouts and grows, but he doesn't know how. When the crop has grown, he reaps a harvest (Mk 4:26-29). Like the farmer we must begin by seeing the need to transform an uncultivated field into a fruitful one.

There are four stages in the cultivation of a field. We enter a field where there are people unreached by the gospel and connect with them. We must share the gospel (scatter the seed), train disciples (allow the seed to take root and grow) and gather them into communities of disciples (bring in a harvest).

When workers are multiplied in each of these fields, a church planting movement is the fruit. The "X" in the diagram reflects this reality.

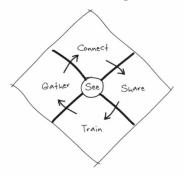

Individually, take a few minutes to reflect on the following questions.

1. **What end has God shown me?**

What end vision has God given you? An end vision does not just ask "What can I do?" but "What needs to be done?" What will it look like for the task to be completed?

.2. **How do I connect with people?**

Who are the people God has called you to reach?

How do you connect with them?

How do you quickly find responsive people?

How do you move from an outsider-driven approach to one that sees insiders spread the gospel through their relational networks?

3. **How do I share the gospel?**

How do you share the unchanging gospel in a simple, relevant way that is easily replicated by new believers?

4. **How do I train disciples?**

Do you have a simple method of teaching new disciples to obey Christ?

Can your new disciples immediately begin sharing the gospel and making disciples?

Do you have a long-term discipleship strategy that enables believers to learn and obey the Scriptures?

5. **How do I help disciples gather into communities?**

Do you teach new disciples what it means to follow Jesus together?

How do you ensure that the communities you form remain true to the New Testament, relevant to the context and simple enough to reproduce multiple generations?

6. How do I grow and multiply workers?

Are you ensuring the ministry multiplies at every level: connecting, sharing, training and gathering?

Does responsibility quickly move from you to the new believers?

2.4 Review

Pair up and take turns drawing the movements diagram and explain the six parts of the multiplication plan, in your own words, without referring to your notes.

2.5 Farmer Paul

What, after all, is Apollos? And what is Paul? Only servants, through whom you came to believe—as the Lord has assigned to each his task. I planted the seed, Apollos watered it, but God has been making it grow. So neither the one who plants nor the one who waters is anything, but only God, who makes things grow. The one who plants and the one who waters have one purpose, and they will each be rewarded according to their own labor. For we are co-workers in God's service; you are God's field. (1 Corinthians 3:5-9)

As one group, review the account of Paul and Barnabas in Acts 14:1-28. What examples of ministry in each of the four activities can you identify?

Implementation 2, chart 1

Stage	Ministry activity
Connect	
Share	
Train	
Gather	

2.6 Your Farm

Individually, identify what you are currently doing in each of the four activities. Include the names of people you are involved with and activities you are engaged in.

Implementation 2, chart 2

Stage	Current ministry activities
Connect	
Share	
Train	
Gather	

What can you learn from Paul's example?

What needs to be different?

2.7 Wrap-Up

In groups of two or three, share a significant insight from this study.
How will you obey what you have learned in the next week?

Pray for people you know who are far from God. Don't discuss them. Just pray for them by name.

2.8 Before Our Next Session

Take some time to connect with people who are far from God.
Identify an area or people group that God has placed on your heart.

Recruit a partner and take an hour to prayer-walk the area. Look for opportunities that God may open up to meet people, pray for their needs or share the gospel.

Report back at the next session.

Repeat the exercise at least weekly until we meet again.

3. CONNECT WITH PEOPLE, PART ONE

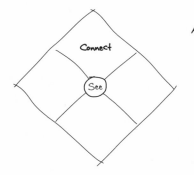

After this the Lord appointed seventy-two others and sent them two by two ahead of him to every town and place where he was about to go.

—LUKE 10:1

3.1 As We Begin . . .

Get into a group of no more than three people.

Share about your experience of entering a new area.

Pray for people you know who are far from God. Don't discuss them. Just pray for them by name.

Without referring to your notes, draw the movements diagram and explain it to one another.

Check in with the other groups to make sure you've got it right.

3.2 Discovery Bible Study

Read Luke 19:1-9. Without looking at the text, retell the passage in your own words.

What do you like about this story?

What does the passage teach us about God?

What does it teach us about people?

Is there a command to obey or an example to follow?

What do you need to do this week to obey what you've learned?

Who could you share this story with?

Pray for each other.

3.3 Connecting

Gather into one group. Think of a time when you moved house, changed schools or began a new job. What was it like connecting with new people in an unfamiliar context?

What made it hard?

What helped?

Who were the key people who connected you with others?

Read Luke 10:1-11. Jesus was always on the move. He was often meeting new people and visiting new places. He also sent his disciples into villages, where they would seek out insiders whom the Spirit had prepared to receive the message. He called them *persons of peace*—key influencers who would welcome believers into their home (a house of peace). The person and the home would become pivotal in the spread of the gospel in their community. The goal of connecting with people is to find houses and people of peace who welcome the gospel. These homes serve as gateways into their communities.

David Watson of CityTeam International explains the person of peace as someone who is receptive to the gospel, is well connected relationally, and has a reputation—either good or bad. The person of peace becomes a doorway for the gospel to enter and spread throughout a community. Meanwhile, Jesus and his disciples moved on to the next town.

When you discover the house of peace, you have discovered the location of your next church plant. New believers within this setting maintain their existing relationships, authority structure and pattern for decision-making. New believers should immediately be mobilized to share the message of Christ with their circle of influence or *oikos* (household).

People of peace are

Prepared. The messengers must take the initiative to find the person of peace. As the messengers step out in faith and obedience, there will be signs that God is powerfully at work as he leads them to the person he has prepared.

Receptive. The person of peace welcomes the messenger and the message. Not every receptive person is a person of peace, but every person of peace is receptive.

Influential. The person of peace's reputation may be good or bad, but it is well known. These are people who, when they respond to Christ, will refer others to him. Because of their influence, many will come along with them.

Oikos (Greek for "household") is the New Testament word for extended household or family. Every new believer has a circle of influence including family, friends, coworkers and neighbors. The person of peace is the doorway into an *oikos*.

Watson observes that dependence on outsiders makes it almost impossible to rapidly replicate new churches. There is no reason to reproduce leaders since the outsider stays in charge. Church planting movements require *insiders,* whom the outsider equips, teaches, trains, coaches and mentors. These insiders then do the same with their people.

Fill in the table below.

Implementation 3, chart 1

What the messenger does	What the person of peace does

What are the advantages of using a person or house of peace strategy for reaching a community?

Find a partner and explain in your own words, without looking at your notes, these terms:

a. Person of peace

b. *Oikos* or household

c. Outsider versus insider

Read your notes again and check that you understand them.

3.4 Wrap-Up

Share a significant insight from this study with your partner.

How will you obey what you have learned in the next week?

Pray for people you know who are far from God. Don't discuss them. Just pray.

3.5 Before Our Next Session

Take some time to connect with people in a new area.

Identify an area or people group that God has placed on your heart.

Recruit a partner and take an hour to prayer-walk the area. Look for opportunities that God may open up to meet people, pray for their needs or share the gospel.

Report back at the next session.

Repeat the exercise at least weekly until we meet again.

4. CONNECT WITH PEOPLE, PART TWO

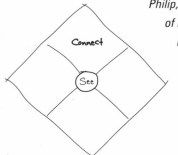

Philip, like Andrew and Peter, was from the town of Bethsaida. Philip found Nathanael and told him, "We have found the one Moses wrote about in the Law, and about whom the prophets also wrote—Jesus of Nazareth, the son of Joseph."

—JOHN 1:44-45

4.1 As We Begin . . .

Get into a group of no more than three people. Share a highlight or lowlight from the last week.

How did you connect with people?

Did you find a person of peace?

What did you learn?

Pray for people you know who are far from God. Don't discuss them. Just pray.

4.2 Discovery Bible Study

Read John 1:35-51. Without looking at the text, retell the passage in your own words.

What do you like about this story?

What does the passage teach us about God?

What does it teach us about people?

Is there a command to obey or an example to follow?

What do you need to do this week to obey what you've learned?

Who could you share this story with?

Pray for each other.

4.3 Your *Oikos*

Stay in your group. Choose one of your relational worlds—family, work colleagues, friends or local community. Take a few minutes to draw a diagram that captures the connections between the people and groups in this relational world. Add in any ties that lead to people and groups outside of your relational networks.

Discuss what your drawing says to you about how the gospel can spread through relationship networks.

4.4 Case Studies

Break into different groups of two to three people. Each group will read a passage from the table below and identify the person of peace, their *oikos*, and the transition from an outsider to an insider strategy.

If you don't have enough people to cover all of the passages, just select two or three of them.

Implementation 4, chart 1

	Group 1 John 4:1-42	Group 2 Mark 5:1-20	Group 3 Acts 10:1-48	Group 4 Acts 16:12-40
Person of peace				
Oikos				
Shift from outsider to insider				

Each group can report back to the main group on their findings.

An effective connecting strategy

- minimizes resistance by focusing on those whom God has already prepared
- identifies insiders who are responsive and connected
- focuses on reaching and discipling groups of people not just individuals
- can be easily taught and passed on to others
- leads to insiders taking responsibility to form new churches and to reach their community

4.5 Finding People of Peace

A person of peace is the doorway to a relational world you are not connected with. They may be someone you have not met before. They may be someone you already know.

Finding people of peace is a partnership between you and God. He is already at work preparing the soil. You must step out in faith and obedience, and meet people.

Read through these simple methods others have used to find people of peace. Then list your own ideas below.

Prayer-walking. Recruit a partner. Pray together and ask God to lead you to an area or a group in your region. As you sense him guide you, go and walk around the area or among the people, praying for them. Be open to how the Holy Spirit is leading you as you go.

Visiting. Visit homes and wherever people gather in their community to look for households and persons of peace. A simple questionnaire can help identify responsive people. Another way to connect with people in their neighborhood is to "adopt a block." See the appendix for adopt-a-block strategies.

Praying for people. A great question to ask when you're out connecting is, "If God would do a miracle in your life, what would it be? Could I pray right now for that miracle for you?"

Teaching English. Begin an English conversation club to help immigrants and international students practice English. Let them know you'll spend some of the time in a discovery Bible study. Follow up with individuals and find out if they want to learn more about Jesus.

Training new believers. Every new believer can be a witness. Some will quickly emerge as people of peace who influence many others. Help new believers make a list of at least twenty-five family members and friends who need Christ. This list represents their circle of influence and therefore their responsibility. Weekly encouragement and accountability to sharing with those on the list can help identify people of peace among new believers.

Your own ideas . . .

Stay as one group and share your ideas for finding a person of peace.

4.6 Wrap-Up

In groups of two to three, share a significant insight from this study.

How will you begin looking for a person of peace this week?

Pray that God would lead each of you to a person of peace this week.

4.7 Before Our Next Meeting

How will you begin looking for persons of peace this week?

Pray for people you know who are far from God. Don't discuss them. Just pray.

5. SHARE THE GOSPEL, PART ONE

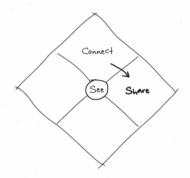

Woe to me if I do not preach the gospel!

—PAUL (1 CORINTHIANS 9:16)

5.1 As We Begin . . .

Get into groups of no more than three people and talk about what happened as you looked for a person of peace.

Pray for any people you met and for anyone else you know who are far from God.

When God leads us to a person of peace, we need to know what to say to them. Two stories are important: our story and Jesus' story. This session we'll look at sharing our story.

5.2 Discovery Bible Study

Read Acts 9:1-22. Without looking at the text, retell the passage in your own words.

What do you like about this story?

What does the passage teach us about God?

What does it teach us about people?

Is there a command to obey or an example to follow?

What do you need to do this week to obey what you've learned?

Who could you share this story with?

Pray for each other.

5.3 Eyewitness News

Think of a time when you had exciting news you couldn't wait to share with others. What was the news?

Who did you tell?

How did you tell them?

What are some reasons that we like to share and listen to stories?

What makes a story *contagious*—something you are eager to share?

Stories touch our emotions; stories help us connect with another person; stories are credible because they are from our own lives. As you connect with responsive people, it is important that you can share your story with them simply and briefly. As you make disciples, you will need to teach them to do the same.

5.4 Paul's Story

Gather back into one group. In Acts, Paul tells his story of conversion three times, beginning with Acts 9:1-22 (see also Acts 22:1-21; 26:1-23). Read Acts 9:1-22. List the main points of Paul's story from the account.

- Paul's life before he met Jesus (vv. 1-2):

- How he met Jesus (vv. 3-19):

- How his life changed (vv. 20-22):

5.5 Your Story

On your own, take ten minutes to write down a few points under each heading.

- Your life before you met Jesus:

- How you met Jesus:

- How your life has changed:

Pair up with someone new and practice telling your story in these three parts. Each person has just three minutes to share his or her story. You may need to appoint a timekeeper!

Repeat the exercise in different pairs.

Return to the large group and discuss the following questions.

- What was it like to share your story with others?

- What was it like to hear other people's stories?

5.6 Wrap-Up

Get in a group of no more than three people. What have you learned this week about sharing the good news?

Who will you share your story with this week?

Pray for each other and for the friends and family members you would like to share your story with before the group meets again.

5.7 Before Our Next Session

Write out and practice your story so you can share it in three minutes.

Ask three different people if you can share your story with them, either people you already know or a possible person of peace. Give each person a chance at the end to provide feedback and ask any questions they want.

Here is one way to start:

a. Contact an old friend who you have never shared your story with—preferably someone who is not yet a believer.

b. Tell him or her you have an assignment as part of a study group.

c. Ask permission to share your story, and ask them to give you feedback about how it went.

Learn the gospel presentation "Share Jesus Without Fear" (below).[1] Come prepared to take someone through it in the next session.

Share Jesus Without Fear
Adapted by Tim Scheuer

The simpler the gospel presentation, the easier it is for new believers to remember and immediately pass it on to their friends and family.

1. Choose a bridging question:
   - A potential person of peace: "If you could know God personally, would you be interested?"
   - Family and friends of a new believer: "I have made a decision to become a follower of Jesus. I would like to tell you about it."
   - Family and friends of an existing believer: "I have never shared with you why I became a follower of Jesus and the difference he makes in my life. I would like to tell you about it."

2. Say: "I would like to briefly share my story with you."

3. Say: "Could I show you from the Bible how you can know God personally?"

4. Let God's Word speak for itself.

Ask your friend to read each of the following verses aloud. (You will find it helpful to mark these verses beforehand in your Bible.) After they have read a verse ask, "What does this say to you?" and listen to their response.
   - John 3:16
   - Romans 3:23
   - Romans 6:23
   - Romans 5:8
   - Romans 10:9

If your friend interprets a passage incorrectly, don't argue or offer your interpretation, but ask him or her to read it again, and then explain your take on it a second time.

5. Check understanding by asking:

- Are you a sinner?
- Do you want forgiveness for your sin?
- Do you believe that Jesus died on the cross for you and rose again?
- Are you willing to surrender your life to Christ?
- Are you ready to invite Jesus into your heart and into your life?

6. If the person says yes, they are ready to invite Jesus into their heart and life . . .

Ask, "Does this prayer say what you want to say in your heart to God?"

Heavenly Father, I have sinned against you. I want forgiveness for all my sins. I believe Jesus died on the cross for me and rose again. Father, I give you my life to do with as you wish. I want Jesus Christ to come into my life and into my heart. I ask this in Jesus' name.

7. When the person accepts Christ . . .

Ask, "Who else needs to hear about Jesus? When will you tell them?"

Make a time to begin discipleship. Take the person through (a) *Sharing Your Story*, (b) *Sharing Jesus' Story* and (c) the *Seven Commands of Christ*.

8. If the person is not ready, but is willing to meet and learn more about Jesus . . .

Ask, "When can we meet next to learn more about Jesus?" Use the *Seven Stories of Hope*.

At any time, if they are ready to put their faith in Christ and follow him, move to the *Seven Commands*.

See the "Share Jesus Without Fear" website: www.allaboutgod.com/share-jesus-without-fear.htm.

6. SHARE THE GOSPEL, PART TWO

> *Now, brothers and sisters, I want to remind you of the gospel I preached*
> *to you, which you received and on which you have taken your stand.*
> *By this gospel you are saved, if you hold firmly to the word*
> *I preached to you. Otherwise, you have believed in vain.*
>
> —PAUL (1 CORINTHIANS 15:1-2)

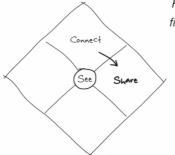

> *For what I received I passed on to you as of*
> *first importance: that Christ died for our sins*
> *according to the Scriptures, that he*
> *was buried, that he was raised on*
> *the third day according*
> *to the Scriptures.*
>
> —PAUL (1 CORINTHIANS 15:3-4)

6.1 As We Begin . . .

Break into pairs. Were you able to share your story with someone? How did it go?

Pray for any people you shared your story with and for others you know who are far from God.

Practice sharing your story with your partner. Allow three minutes for each person.

6.2 Discovery Bible Study

Stay in the same pairs and *read Acts 17:13-32*. Without looking at the text, retell the passage in your own words.

What do you like about this story?

What does the passage teach us about God?

What does it teach us about people?

Is there a command to obey or an example to follow?

What do you need to do this week to obey what you've learned?

Who could you share this story with?

Pray for each other.

6.3 Sharing Jesus' Story

Gather back into one group. Together with your own story, you need to be able to tell others the message of the gospel simply and briefly. This next section is to help you find a consistent way to tell the gospel.

Acts provides us with a number of different presentations of the one gospel. Compare Paul's presentation to a Jewish audience in Acts 14 with his presentation to pagan philosophers in Acts 17. List his main points.

Implementation 6, chart 1

Gospel to the Jews: Acts 14:13-43	Gospel to the Gentiles: Acts 17:22-31

Gospel to the Jews: Acts 14:13-43	Gospel to the Gentiles: Acts 17:22-31

What is the same about the two presentations?

What is different?

Certain themes recur in the various gospel presentations in Acts:

1. God (the nature and character of the God we proclaim)

2. Sin (which every person is guilty of and which results in death and a broken relationship with God)

3. Jesus (the only way and the returning judge; his life, death, and resurrection brings forgiveness of sins)

4. Response (repentance and belief)

5. Salvation (forgiveness of sin and the gift of the Holy Spirit)

Have a volunteer take someone through "Share Jesus Without Fear" in front of the whole group. Take a few minutes to discuss how the presentation went.

Break into pairs. Take each other through "Share Jesus Without Fear." If there is time, repeat the exercise with a different partner.

6.4 Wrap-Up

List the names of three people you could share your story and Jesus' story with before the next session.

Who could you train to share their story and Jesus' story?

In your pairs, pray for the people you would like to share with and for others who are far from God.

6.5 Before Our Next Session

Master a simple gospel presentation. It can be "Share Jesus Without Fear" or an equivalent. Come prepared next time to take someone through your presentation.

Share your story and Jesus' story with three people.

Train someone to share their story and Jesus' story.

7. TRAIN DISCIPLES, PART ONE

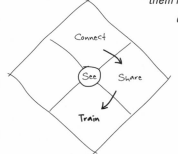

Therefore go and make disciples of all nations, baptizing them in the name of the Father and of the Son and of the Holy Spirit, and teaching them to obey everything I have commanded you. And surely I am with you always, to the very end of the age.

—JESUS (MATTHEW 28:19-20)

7.1 As We Begin . . .

Break into pairs and share a highlight or lowlight from the last week.

Were you able to share your story and Jesus' story since the last meeting? How did it go?

In pairs, practice your gospel presentation.

Pray for the people you shared with and any others who are far from God.

7.2 Discovery Bible Study

Read Luke 5:1-11. Without looking at the text, retell the passage in your own words.

What do you like about this story?

What does the passage teach us about God?

What does it teach us about people?

Is there a command to obey or an example to follow?

What do you need to do this week to obey what you've learned?

Who could you share this story with?

Pray for each other.

7.3 Training Disciples in the First Church

We see the first church obeying what we will refer to as "seven commands of Christ."

Return to the large group. Acts 2:28-47 tells the story of the first community of Jesus' disciples following the outpouring of the Holy Spirit at Pentecost. Study the passage and list the disciples' activities next to the related commands of Jesus.

Implementation 7, chart 1

Seven Commands of Christ	Reference	Examples in Acts 2
1. Repent and believe	"The time has come," he said. "The kingdom of God is near. Repent and believe the good news!" Mk 1:15	
2. Be baptized	Therefore go and make disciples of all nations, baptizing them in the name of the Father and of the Son and of the Holy Spirit. Mt 28:19	

Seven Commands of Christ	Reference	Examples in Acts 2
3. Love	Jesus replied: "'Love the Lord your God with all your heart and with all your soul and with all your mind.' This is the first and greatest commandment. And the second is like it: 'Love your neighbor as yourself.'" Mt 22:37-39	
4. Celebrate the Lord's supper	And he took bread, gave thanks and broke it, and gave it to them, saying, "This is my body given for you; do this in remembrance of me." In the same way, after the supper he took the cup, saying, "This cup is the new covenant in my blood, which is poured out for you." Lk 22:19-20	
5. Pray	This, then, is how you should pray: "Our Father in heaven, hallowed be your name, your kingdom come, your will be done on earth as it is in heaven. Give us today our daily bread. Forgive us our debts, as we also have forgiven our debtors. And lead us not into temptation, but deliver us from the evil one." Mt 6:9-13	
6. Give generously	Give, and it will be given to you. A good measure, pressed down, shaken together and running over, will be poured into your lap. For with the measure you use, it will be measured to you. Lk 6:38	
7. Make disciples	Therefore go and make disciples of all nations, baptizing them in the name of the Father and of the Son and of the Holy Spirit, and teaching them to obey everything I have commanded you. And surely I am with you always, to the very end of the age. Mt 28:19-20	

7.4 Training Disciples Today

The gospel spreads rapidly when there is plenty of "mouth to ear" evangelism going on. A good place to start is to provide simple training in sharing your story and sharing the gospel. Training will be fruitless, however, unless the believers are in groups for regular support and accountability.

Use the table below to evaluate your current ministry in equipping others to share the gospel, with 1 being "not at all" and 5 being "always." What do you need to do next?

Implementation 7, chart 2

Activity	Evaluation (1 = poor, 5 = excellent)					Next steps
You are able to share your story and Jesus' story clearly and concisely.	1	2	3	4	5	
You are regularly sharing Jesus' story and your story with anyone who will listen.	1	2	3	4	5	
You are training others who are willing to learn how to share their story and a simple gospel presentation.	1	2	3	4	5	
Your trainees have listed and are praying for the people in their world who are far from God.	1	2	3	4	5	
You are training believers to search for people of peace who are outside of their existing relationships.	1	2	3	4	5	
You are equipping new believers to immediately share their story and a simple gospel presentation.	1	2	3	4	5	

Identify the people you will approach to train in sharing their story and sharing the gospel.

Implementation 7, chart 3

Name	Name

7.5 Wrap-Up

How will you begin training others to share the gospel and make disciples?

Pray for people who are far from God.

7.6 Before Our Next Session

Share your story and the gospel with three people. If they would like to know more, offer to meet with them again.

Train at least one other person to share their story and the gospel.

8. TRAIN DISCIPLES, PART TWO

As the Father has loved me, so have I loved you. Now remain in my love. If you keep my commands, you will remain in my love, just as I have kept my Father's commands and remain in his love.

—JESUS (JOHN 15:9-10)

8.1 Three-Thirds Training for Disciples

Neil Cole says, "How you disciple the first new believer will determine whether what you are doing becomes a multiplying movement or not." It is important that we train disciples in simple, transferable ways. New believers must be able to quickly reproduce what we model.

In *T4T: A Discipleship Re-Revolution*, Steve Smith and Yin Kai recommend breaking each discipleship training session into three thirds: looking back, looking up and looking ahead. The goal is to reproduce disciples who become trainers of others. You'll notice that we have already been applying this approach in previous sessions.

Get into groups no larger than three and work through the following exercise.

A. First Third: Look Back

1. Care.

   Share any highlights or lowlights since you last met.

   Pray for any needs in the group.

2. Worship.

   Read Psalm 103 and respond to God in prayer.

3. Accountability.

   - Follow:

     How did you obey the lesson from last time?

   - Fish:

     Did you pray with anyone who was in need?

     Did you share your story and/or Jesus' story?

     Did you find a person of peace?

4. Casting vision for reaching lost people and making disciples.

   Have someone in the group share a story of how God has worked through them to share the gospel in recent weeks.

   Pray for people you know who are far from God.

B. Second Third: Look Up

5. New lesson.

   Read Matthew 28:18-20. Without looking at the text, retell the passage in your own words.

   What do you like about this passage?

   What does the passage teach us about God?

   What does it teach us about people?

   Is there a command to obey or an example to follow?

C. Final Third: Look Ahead

6. Practice.

   Have each group prepare and perform a simple mime that acts out the main points of the passage.

7. Set goals and pray.

   What do you need to do this week to obey what you've learned?

   Who could you share this passage with?

   Pray for people who are far from God.

8.2 Unpacking the Three Thirds

Gather as one group. Read over the outline below, close your book, and then see how much of it you can recall from memory.

Implementation 8, chart 1

1. Look back	2. Look up	3. Look ahead
1. Mutual care: How are you doing? 2. Worship: Praising God in a simple, relevant way. 3. Accountability* • Follow: How did you obey the lesson from last time? • Fish: Did you pray with anyone who was in need? • Did you share your story and/or Jesus' story? • Did you find a person of peace? 4. Casting vision* for reaching lost people and making disciples.	5. New lesson: Enough biblical content to obey and pass it on. • Short-term discipleship: e.g., *Seven Commands of Christ*. • Lifelong discipleship: e.g., discovery Bible study.	6. Practice* the lesson until everyone is confident and competent to apply the learning— e.g., retell your story, Jesus' story or this week's story. 7. Set goals and pray:* Goals for personal growth, sharing the gospel and training others.

Steve Smith and Yin Kai recommend that if time is short, make it a priority to cover the sections with an asterisk.

Go over the three thirds until you understand each component and feel confident to lead someone else through it. If there are gaps in your understanding you can learn more by reading Steve Smith and Yin Kai, *T4T: A Discipleship Re-Revolution* (Monument, Colo.: WIGTake Resources, 2011), pages 125-55.

8.3 Wrap-Up

Who could you invite to do a three-thirds discipleship study?

Who could you share the gospel and your story with before the next meeting?

Pray together.

8.4 Before Our Next Session

Share your story and Jesus' story with three people.

Facilitate a three-thirds discipleship group with at least one other person who wants to learn how to follow Jesus.

9. GATHER COMMUNITIES, PART ONE

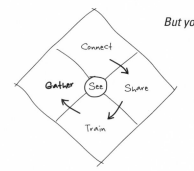

*But you are a chosen people, a royal priesthood,
a holy nation, God's special possession,
that you may declare the praises of him
who called you out of darkness
into his wonderful light.*

—1 PETER 2:9

9.1 As We Begin . . .

What can you thank God for?

Pray for people who are far from God.

9.2 Reporting In

Did you find someone to do a three-thirds group with? How did it go?

Get into groups no larger than three. Review how you are doing in each of these activities. Share your review.

Implementation 9, chart 1

Activity	Progress so far	Next steps
Looking for persons of peace		
Sharing the gospel and/or your story		
Training and mobilizing others to make disciples		
Discipling new believers		
Forming groups and churches of new disciples		

9.3 Discovery Bible Study

Read Acts 2:38-47. Without looking at the text, retell the passage in your own words.

What do you like about this story?

What does the passage teach us about God?

What does it teach us about people?

Is there a command to obey or an example to follow?

What do you need to do this week to obey what you've learned?

Who could you share this story with?

Pray for each other.

9.4 Simply Church

Gather in one group. Luke structured the book of Acts around a number of statements about the growth and spread of the dynamic Word of God. As the Word grows and multiplies, the number of disciples and churches grows and multiplies.

Implementation 9, chart 2

Acts	Text
6:7	And the word of God continued to increase, and the number of the disciples multiplied greatly in Jerusalem, and a great many of the priests became obedient to the faith.
9:31	So the church throughout all Judea and Galilee and Samaria had peace and was being built up. And walking in the fear of the Lord and in the comfort of the Holy Spirit, it multiplied.
12:24	But the word of God increased and multiplied.
16:5	So the churches were strengthened in the faith, and they increased in numbers daily.
19:20	So the word of the Lord continued to increase and prevail mightily.
28:30-31	He lived there two whole years at his own expense, and welcomed all who came to him, proclaiming the kingdom of God and teaching about the Lord Jesus Christ with all boldness and without hindrance.

On a single large piece of paper, list as many activities of churches that you can think of.

Which activities can be removed without a church ceasing to be a church? Identify them and cross them off the list.

What are the essential elements of a church?

When does a group become a church?

Note: The simplest way for a group of new disciples to become a church is to live as a church from the very first gathering.

9.5 The Church That Jesus Started

In the table below, list the activities of the first church in the right-hand column.

Implementation 9, chart 3

Acts 2:38-47	What does the church do?
Peter replied, "Repent and be baptized, every one of you, in the name of Jesus Christ for the forgiveness of your sins. And you will receive the gift of the Holy Spirit. The promise is for you and your children and for all who are far off—for all whom the Lord our God will call."	
With many other words he warned them; and he pleaded with them, "Save yourselves from this corrupt generation." Those who accepted his message were baptized, and about three thousand were added to their number that day.	
They devoted themselves to the apostles' teaching and to the fellowship, to the breaking of bread and to prayer.	
Everyone was filled with awe, and many wonders and miraculous signs were done by the apostles.	

Acts 2:38-47	What does the church do?
All the believers were together and had everything in common. Selling their possessions and goods, they gave to anyone as he had need.	
Every day they continued to meet together in the temple courts.	
They broke bread in their homes and ate together with glad and sincere hearts, praising God and enjoying the favor of all the people.	
And the Lord added to their number daily those who were being saved	

9.6 Church at Cornelius's Place

Acts 10 tells the story of how the Gentiles received the gospel through Peter. After the Holy Spirit fell on Cornelius, his household and close friends, Peter had them baptized immediately, stayed another few days and then left.

As a group, plan the next session together to reflect what a gathering of Jesus' disciples at Cornelius's house might have looked like in the first century. Refer to the characteristics of church in Acts 2:38-47.

Even better, if you have any new disciples, meet with them as church.

Use the outline of the three thirds as a guide. Choose a passage of Scripture to study.

Implementation 9, chart 4

1. Look back	2. Look up	3. Look ahead
1. Mutual care: How are you doing? 2. Worship: Praising God in a simple, relevant way. 3. Accountability* • Follow: How did you obey the lesson from last time? • Fish: Did you pray with anyone who was in need? • Did you share your story and/or Jesus' story? • Did you find a person of peace? 4. Casting vision* for reaching lost people and making disciples.	5. New lesson: Enough biblical content to obey and pass it on. • Short-term discipleship: e.g., *Seven Commands of Christ.* • Lifelong discipleship: e.g., discovery Bible study.	6. Practice* the lesson until everyone is confident and competent to apply the learning— e.g., retell your story, Jesus' story or this week's story. 7. Set goals and pray:* Goals for personal growth, sharing the gospel and training others.

Steve Smith and Yin Kai recommend that if time is short, make it a priority to cover the sections with an asterisk.

9.7 Wrap-Up

Before the next session, how will you connect with people, share the gospel and make disciples?

Pray for people who are far from God.

10. GATHER COMMUNITIES, PART TWO

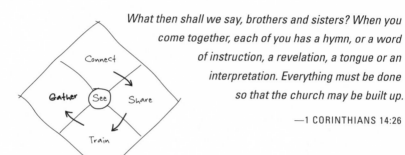

What then shall we say, brothers and sisters? When you come together, each of you has a hymn, or a word of instruction, a revelation, a tongue or an interpretation. Everything must be done so that the church may be built up.

—1 CORINTHIANS 14:26

10.1 When You Come Together . . .

Follow the plan you developed last time and meet as a community of Jesus' disciples.

10.2 Debrief

Discuss what you learned from this gathering of disciples.
How will you help new disciples gather in community that reflect the characteristics of church described in Acts 2:38-47?

10.3 Wrap-Up

In groups of two or three, update each other regarding the people with whom you have been sharing your story and Jesus' story.

Pray for each one by name.

What are your plans this week for connecting with people, sharing the gospel and training disciples?

10.4 Before Our Next Session

Who could you begin training to make disciples? Look for people who want to learn and want to immediately obey what they are learning.

Invite them to join you in working through this implementation guide from the beginning.

List the names of people you could invite.

Implementation 10, chart 1

Name	Name

11. MULTIPLY WORKERS, PART ONE

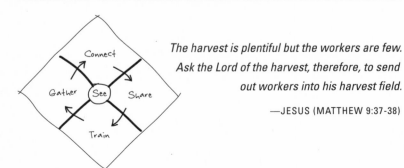

*The harvest is plentiful but the workers are few.
Ask the Lord of the harvest, therefore, to send
out workers into his harvest field.*

—JESUS (MATTHEW 9:37-38)

11.1 As We Begin . . .

Get into a group of no more than three people. Share with one another how you have been sharing Jesus' story and your story.

Pray for people who are far from God.

11.2 Discovery Bible Study

Read Luke 10:1-12. Without looking at the text, retell the passage in your own words.

What do you like about this passage?

What does the passage teach us about God?

What does it teach us about people?

Is there a command to obey or an example to follow?

What do you need to do this week to obey what you've learned?

Who could you share this passage with?

Pray for each other.

11.3 Your Family Tree

Gather in one large group. Go back as far as you can in your family history. Working forward from a couple who were your ancestors—grandparents or great-grandparents or great-great-grandparents—record as many generations as possible. Track as many of their descendants as you can, including your family. Draw this original couple's family tree. Include all of their descendants of whom you are aware.

Who can identify the greatest number of relatives—living and deceased?

What makes such growth possible?

11.4 How Jesus Multiplied Workers

Jesus had compassion on the masses. He knew that to reach them he had to mobilize workers who were faithful and fruitful. He invested his life in the few given to him by the Father. Jesus carefully chose the disciples with two priorities in mind:

- They would be with him.
- He would teach them to catch others.

There were many demands on Jesus' time, but he spent the most time with the leaders who would one day multiply his ministry.

Read Luke 9:35–10:12. What does this passage teach us about how Jesus multiplied workers?

11.5 MAWL: Model, Assist, Watch, Leave

Typically, in training a child to ride a bike, a parent will unconsciously move through four stages:

1. They model how to ride a bike.
2. They assist and hold the bike while the child attempts to ride.
3. They watch while the child rides the bike without help.
4. Finally they leave the child to ride on his own.

Jesus modeled effective ministry to his disciples. He created a safe environment where they could begin to take responsibility. Then he sent them out in pairs and watched their progress. Finally he left the task to them.

In chart one for Implementation Eleven, identify some examples of how you are growing leaders in your ministry. Include the names of the workers/ leaders you are training at each level. List next steps for each level.

Implementation 11, chart 1

MAWL	Examples from your ministry	Next steps
Model		
Assist		
Watch		
Leave		

11.6 Where to Begin

The best way to begin multiplying workers is to provide simple training in sharing their story and the gospel. Training will be fruitless unless they are in a face-to-face group for regular support and accountability.

Use chart two to evaluate your current ministry in equipping others to share the gospel. What do you need to do next to multiply workers?

Implementation 11, chart 2

Activity	Evaluation (1 = poor, 5 = excellent)	Next steps
Have your story and a simple gospel presentation prepared.	1 2 3 4 5	
Begin sharing regularly.	1 2 3 4 5	
Train everyone who is willing to share their story and a simple gospel presentation.	1 2 3 4 5	
Have trainees list and pray for the people in their world who don't know Christ.	1 2 3 4 5	
Send them out each week to share the gospel. Trust God for three people each week.	1 2 3 4 5	
Form accountability groups so workers can report back, pray, and be encouraged.	1 2 3 4 5	
Train people who are ready to act on what they are learning.	1 2 3 4 5	

Activity	Evaluation (1 = poor, 5 = excellent)	Next steps
Look for those who are both faithful and fruitful.	1 2 3 4 5	
Equip new believers to immediately begin sharing their story and a simple gospel presentation.	1 2 3 4 5	

List the names of the people you will approach to train in sharing their story and sharing the gospel.

Implementation 11, chart 3

Name	Name

11.7 Wrap-Up

Break into small groups. Pray for one another and for people who are far from God.

11.8 Before Our Next Session

Review the charts you made during this session. Pick at least two actions from the "next steps" column and do them.

12. MULTIPLY WORKERS, PART TWO

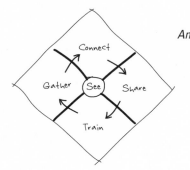

And the things you have heard me say in the presence of many witnesses entrust to reliable people who will also be qualified to teach others.

—PAUL TO TIMOTHY
(2 TIMOTHY 2:2)

12.1 As We Begin . . .

Get in groups of no more than three people. Discuss how you have been sharing Jesus' story and your story.

Pray for people who are far from God.

12.2 Discovery Bible Study

Read 2 Timothy 2:1-10. Without looking at the text, retell the passage in your own words.

What do you like in this passage?

What does the passage teach us about God?

What does it teach us about people?

Is there a command to obey or an example to follow?

What do you need to do this week to obey what you've learned?

Who could you share this passage with?

Pray for each other.

12.3 How Paul Multiplied Workers

Gather as one large group. Paul followed Jesus' example of multiplying workers. Paul's letters and the book of Acts reveal the names of around one hundred men and women who shared in his ministry. Nine of these people were closely associated with his mission.

How many generations of leaders, including himself, does Paul refer to in 2 Timothy 2:1-10?

Why does Paul focus his efforts on equipping leaders who are *reliable* rather than give equal time to everyone?

Four generations

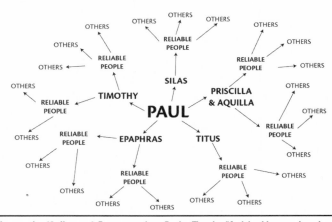

Implementation 12, diagram 1. Four generations. Paul to Timothy: "And the things you have heard me say in the presence of many witnesses entrust to reliable people who will also be qualified to teach others" (2 Tim 2:2).

12.4 How Are You Multiplying Workers?

Draw your own version of the four generations diagram. Place your name in the middle and add the names of the reliable people you are training and any names of the people they are training. Share your four generations diagram with each other.

List the names of up to ten people you could train.

Implementation 12, chart 1

Name	How you will invest in them

Commit before God to dedicate time in your schedule for deep investment in these few.

12.5 Planning to Multiply Workers

On your own, choose one of the people on your list. Take a few minutes and use chart two to assess their stage of development and how you can move them forward.

Name: _____

Implementation 12, chart 2

Activity	Current level of effectiveness	What's next?
See the need		
Connect with people		
Share the gospel		
Train disciples		
Gather communities		
Multiply workers		

With a partner, share your findings; then pray for the person.

Repeat the exercise for the other people on your list in your own time.

12.6 Wrap-Up

How will you connect with people, share the gospel and train disciples?

Pray for people who are far from God.

12.7 Before Our Next Session

Complete your plan to multiply workers for the others on your list (12.5).

Review this series of studies. Complete the chart below by reflecting back on what you have learned from these studies, names of people to whom you have ministered, and what you need to do next to move forward in obedience.

Implementation 12, chart 3

	What have you learned?	What have you done?	What's next?
See the need			
Connect with people			
Share the gospel			
Train disciples			
Gather communities			
Multiply workers			

Bring your completed review sheet to the last session.

13. THE FINAL CHAPTER

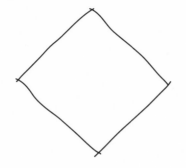

In this way the word of the Lord spread widely and grew in power.

—ACTS 19:20

13.1 As We Begin . . .

How have you shared your story and Jesus' story since you last met?

Who are you training to make disciples?

Pray for people who are far from God.

13.2 Discovery Bible Study

Stay in groups of two or three and *read 2 Timothy 4:1-6*. Without looking at the text, retell the passage in your own words.

What do you like about this passage?

What does the passage teach us about God?

What does it teach us about people?

Is there a command to obey or an example to follow?

What do you need to do this week to obey what you've learned?

Who could you share this passage with?

Pray for each other.

13.3 Your Review

Gather together in one group. Have each person take five minutes to share the highlights from their review sheet. If you want more time to share your plans, break the group up into smaller groups, but do the next exercise as one whole group.

13.4 Your Acts 29

Acts begins with Jesus' command to go to the ends of the earth (Acts 1:8). Acts finishes with Paul in Rome and the final goal unreached. Rome is not the ends of the earth; it is the center of the Roman Empire.

Luke's last progress report (Acts 28:30-31) had Paul in custody in Rome, freely proclaiming the gospel of the kingdom. This open-ended ending shows that the progress of God's Word will continue. We are now living in the era of Acts 29 and beyond. It's our job to write the next chapter of the story.

Write your own twenty-ninth chapter of Acts, describing what your future ministry could look like if you apply the lessons you've learned from these studies.

Have each person share their Acts 29 chapter with the entire group, followed by a prayer of commissioning over the person who shared. If the group is too large, and the time is short, break into smaller groups to share.

Finish by lifting up to God the names of the people you have ministered to over the course of the studies.

Thank God for what he has done.

13.5 What's Next?

How will you check back in with each other as you implement your plans?

How will you pass on what you have learned through this series to reliable people who will train others?

NOTES

In the Beginning Was Jesus

[1]Eckhard J. Schnabel, *Early Christian Mission,* Vol. 1, *Jesus and the Twelve* (Downers Grove, Ill.: IVP Academic, 2004), p. 207.

[2]Rodney Stark, *The Rise of Christianity: A Sociologist Reconsiders History* (Princeton, N.J.: Princeton University Press, 1996), p. 3.

[3]Schnabel, *Early Christian Mission,* 1:880-95.

[4]Ibid., p. 498.

[5]"The missionary work of the first Christians cannot be explained with prototypes in the OT or with models of an early Jewish mission." Ibid., p. 205. See also Scot McKnight, *A Light Among the Gentiles: Jewish Missionary Activity in the Second Temple Period* (Minneapolis: Fortress, 1991), and Martin Goodman, *Mission and Conversion in the Religious History of the Roman Empire* (Oxford: Clarendon Press, 1994).

[6]Following Schnabel, *Early Christian Mission,* 1:11-12.

Chapter 1: Why Jesus Came

[1]Aramaic had been the language of the Persian Empire that included Israel. Jesus was able to read Hebrew in the synagogue of Nazareth (Luke 4:16-20). Later it is likely he used Hebrew to dispute with the Pharisees. Surrounded by Gentiles, Jesus may also have known some Greek. It's doubtful he knew Latin. Even the Romans used Greek in the provinces. Jesus' trial by Pilate would have been conducted in Greek.

[2]Eckhard J. Schnabel, *Early Christian Mission,* Vol. 1, *Jesus and the Twelve* (Downers Grove, Ill.: IVP Academic, 2004), p. 188.

[3]Robert Stein, *Jesus the Messiah* (Downers Grove, Ill.: IVP Academic, 1996), p. 72.

[4]Schnabel, *Early Christian Mission,* 1:214.

[5]Estimates of the population of Palestine in the time of Jesus range from 700,000 to 2.5 million people. See Schnabel, *Early Christian Mission,* 1:122.

[6]Craig L. Blomberg, *Jesus and the Gospels: An Introduction and Survey,* 2nd ed. (Nashville, Tenn.: B&H Academic, 2009), p. 61.

[7]Luke 16:17; Matthew 4:23-25; 8:10-13.

Chapter 2: Let's Go Somewhere Else

[1]See Eckhard J. Schnabel, *Early Christian Mission,* Vol. 1, *Jesus and the Twelve* (Downers Grove, Ill.: IVP Academic, 2004), p. 215.

[2]Mark 6:3; Matthew 13:53-58; Luke 4:1-30.

[3]John 7:2-8; Mark 3:20-21.

[4]Mary gathered with the others for prayer before Pentecost. According to Paul, Jesus' brothers were engaged in missionary work. Jesus' brother James led the church in Jerusalem from A.D. 41 until his death as a martyr in A.D. 62 (1 Corinthians 9:5).

[5]John 4:46-54; Matthew 8:5-13; Luke 7:1-10.

[6]Acts 6:7; 15:5.

[7]John 4:1-42; 7:53—8:11; Luke 7:36-50.

[8]Matthew 27:57-60; Mark 15:42-43.

[9]Matthew 4:25; 5:47; 6:7, 32; 8:5-13; Mark 3:7-8; Mark 5:1-20; 7:24-30; Mark 10:42; Luke 6:17-19; 7:1-10; John 12:20-22. See Scot McKnight, "Gentiles," in *Dictionary of Jesus and the Gospels*, ed. Scot McKnight, Joel B. Green and I. Howard Marshall (Downers Grove, Ill.: IVP Academic, 1992), pp. 259-65.

[10]For insights into the cultural setting of Jesus' encounter with the Samaritan woman see Kenneth E. Bailey, *Jesus Through Middle Eastern Eyes* (Downers Grove, Ill.: IVP Academic, 2008), pp. 200-216.

[11] Schnabel, *Early Christian Mission*, 1:311.

Chapter 3: Jesus' Gospel

[1]See David Jacobus Bosch, *Transforming Mission: Paradigm Shifts in Theology of Mission*, American Society of Missiology Series (Maryknoll, N.Y.: Orbis Books, 1991), pp. 98-104.

[2]See Luke 1:77; 3:3; 24:47; Acts 2:38; 5:31; 10:43; 13:38; 26:18.

[3]See Luke 18:9-43; 19:1-10. Alan J. Thompson, *The Acts of the Risen Lord Jesus: Luke's Account of God's Unfolding Plan*, ed. D. A. Carson, New Studies in Biblical Theology (Downers Grove, Ill.: IVP Academic, 2011), p. 41; and Paul Woodbridge, "Theological Implications of 'Eternal Life' in the Fourth Gospel," in *God's Power to Save: One Gospel for a Complex World?* ed. Chris Green (Leicester, U.K.: Inter-Varsity Press, 2006), p. 92.

[4]Matthew 9:13; Mark 10:45; Luke 19:10; John 9:39; 10:10; 12:46.

[5]For the cultural background to this parable, see Kenneth E. Bailey, *Poet and Peasant* and *Through Peasant Eyes: A Literary-Cultural Approach to the Parables in Luke*, Combined Edition (Grand Rapids: Eerdmans, 1983), pp. 158-206.

[6]See Tim Keller, *The Prodigal God: Recovering the Heart of the Christian Faith* (London: Hodder & Stoughton, 2008), p. 43.

[7]See Bailey, *Poet and Peasant* and *Through Peasant Eyes*, pp. 142-56; and I. Howard Marshall, *The Gospel of Luke: New International Greek Testament Commentary* (Grand Rapids: Eerdmans, 1978), pp. 677-81.

[8]Mark 5:1-20; Luke 19:1-10; John 4:1-42.

Chapter 4: Follow Me and I'll Teach You

[1]For Jesus' calling of his disciples see Kenneth E. Bailey, *Jesus Through Middle Eastern Eyes* (Downers Grove, Ill.: IVP Academic, 2008), pp. 135-46, and Eckhard J. Schnabel, *Early Christian Mission*, Vol. 1, *Jesus and the Twelve* (Downers Grove, Ill.: IVP Academic, 2004), pp. 272-79.

[2]The seven commands of Christ were adapted from George and Richard Scoggins Patterson, *Church Multiplication Guide*, rev. ed. (Pasadena, Calif.: William Carey Library, 2003).

[3]Matthew 26:26-30; Luke 22:19-20; Mark 14:22-25; 1 Corinthians 11:23-26.

[4]The only recorded prayer of Jesus that does not address God as "Father" is when he cried out on the cross— "My God, my God, why have you forsaken me?" (Mark 15:3). Jesus was quoting Psalm 22:1.

Chapter 5: I Will Build My Church

[1]Eckhard J. Schnabel, *Early Christian Mission*, Vol. 1, *Jesus and the Twelve* (Downers Grove, Ill.: IVP Academic, 2004), p. 443.

[2]See Leon Morris, *The Gospel According to Matthew*, Pillar New Testament Commentary (Grand Rapids: Eerdmans, 1992), pp. 424-25.

Chapter 6: Time to Go

[1]See Eckhard J. Schnabel, *Early Christian Mission*, Vol. 1, *Jesus and the Twelve* (Downers Grove, Ill.: IVP Academic, 2004), pp. 348-82.

[2]Matthew 13:47. See ibid., pp. 442-44.

Interlude: Church on the Porch

[1]For a series of interviews and reports see Jeff Sundell, Movements Audio Podcasts, www.movements.net/resources/the-movements-podcast (accessed December 5, 2011).
[2]Jeff Sundell, *Seven Stories of Hope,* www.movements.net/resources/downloads (accessed February 27, 2012).

Chapter 7: Acts of the Risen Lord

[1]See Brian Rosner, "The Progress of the Word," in *Witness to the Gospel: The Theology of Acts,* ed. I. Howard Marshall and David Peterson (Grand Rapids: Eerdmans, 1998), pp. 215-33.
[2]For this section see Eckhard J. Schnabel, *Early Christian Mission,* Vol. 1, *Jesus and the Twelve* (Downers Grove, Ill.: IVP Academic, 2004), pp. 511-17.
[3]See the approach of the Greeks to Philip in John 12:21.

Chapter 8: Missionaries Without Borders

[1]From *hellas,* the Greek word for Greece. Hellenism was the process in which Greek language and culture spread throughout the ancient world following the conquests of Alexander the Great. Hellenism was dominant in the eastern half of the Roman Empire.
[2]F. Scott Spencer, *Journeying Through Acts: A Literary-Cultural Reading* (Grand Rapids: Baker Academic, 2004), p. 119.
[3]Ben Witherington, *The Acts of the Apostles: A Socio-Rhetorical Commentary* (Grand Rapids: Eerdmans, 1997), p. 352.
[4]Acts 9:43; 16:11-15, 25-34; 18:8.

Chapter 9: Eyewitness News

[1]See Eckhard J. Schnabel, *Early Christian Mission,* Vol. 1, *Jesus and the Twelve* (Downers Grove, Ill.: IVP Academic, 2004), pp. 420, 551.
[2]See Schnabel, *Early Christian Mission,* 1:404-5; Eckhard J. Schnabel, *Early Christian Mission,* Vol. 2, *Paul and the Early Church* (Downers Grove, Ill.: IVP Academic, 2004), pp. 1562-64; David G. Peterson, *The Acts of the Apostles,* Pillar New Testament Commentary (Grand Rapids: Eerdmans, 2009), pp. 70-75.
[3]See Peterson, *Acts,* p. 338; and Ben Witherington, *The Acts of the Apostles: A Socio-Rhetorical Commentary* (Grand Rapids: Eerdmans, 1997), p. 100.
[4]The term *witness* in Acts does not refer primarily to what we might describe as personal testimony of what God has done in our lives but with the actual *witness* of the risen Lord. See Alan J. Thompson, *The Acts of the Risen Lord Jesus: Luke's Account of God's Unfolding Plan,* ed. D. A. Carson, New Studies in Biblical Theology (Downers Grove, Ill.: IVP Academic, 2011), p. 77. Cf. Acts 2:32; 3:15; 4:33; 5:32; 10:39-41; 13:31; 22:15; 26:16.
[5]Acts 8:12; 14:22; 19:8; 20:25-27.
[6]See I. Howard Marshall, *New Testament Theology: Many Witnesses, One Gospel* (Downers Grove, Ill.: IVP Academic, 2004), p. 205. Also Robert Maddox, *The Purpose of Luke-Acts,* ed. John Riches (Edinburgh: T & T Clark, 1982), p. 139.
[7]Acts 2:43-47; 4:23-31; 4:32-37; 5:14.
[8]Peterson, *Acts,* p. 85.
[9]See P. H. Davids, "Miracles in Acts," in *Dictionary of the Later New Testament and Its Developments,* ed. Ralph P. Martin and Peter H. Davids (Downers Grove, Ill.: IVP Academic, 1997), pp. 144-52.
[10]Eckhard Schnabel, "Mission, Early Non-Pauline," in *Dictionary of the Later New Testament and Its Developments,* ed. Ralph P. Martin and Peter H. Davids (Downers Grove, Ill.: IVP Academic, 1997), pp. 752-75.

Chapter 10: Obedience School

[1]See George Patterson and Richard Scoggins, *Church Multiplication Guide*, rev. ed. (Pasadena, Calif.: William Carey Library, 2003).
[2]Robert H. Stein, "Baptism and Becoming a Christian in the New Testament," *Southern Baptist Journal of Theology* 2, no. 1 (1998): 6-17.
[3]See Acts 8:12, 38; 9:18; 10:48.
[4]See David G. Peterson, *The Acts of the Apostles,* Pillar New Testament Commentary (Grand Rapids: Eerdmans, 2009), pp. 61-62.

Chapter 11: Life in the First Church

[1]Kevin N. Giles, "Church," in *Dictionary of the Later New Testament and Its Developments,* ed. Peter H. Davids and Ralph P. Martin (Downers Grove, Ill.: IVP Academic, 1997), p. 195.
[2]Deuteronomy 23:1-3; Judges 20:2; 1 Chronicles 28:8; Nehemiah 13:1. In the Greek translation of the Old Testament, the word for the "assembly" (*ekklēsia*) of the Lord is the same word used in the Greek New Testament for "church."
[3]Acts 5:11; 8:1; 11:26; 13:1.
[4]The term "Christians" is only found in the New Testament in three places. The term is always on the lips of others speaking about Christians: Acts 11:26; 26:28; 1 Peter 4:16.
[5]For this section see Eckhard J. Schnabel, *Early Christian Mission,* Vol. 1, *Jesus and the Twelve* (Downers Grove, Ill.: IVP Academic, 2004), pp. 407-16.
[6]Acts 1:14; 2:42-47; 4:31-35; 5:12-16; 5:42. See Schnabel, *Early Christian Mission,* 1:406-16.
[7]Acts 12:11-17. See Bradley Blue, "Acts and the House Church," in *The Book of Acts in Its Graeco-Roman Setting,* ed. David W. Gill and Conrad H. Gempf (Grand Rapids: Eerdmans, 1994), pp. 119-222.
[8]Acts 1:24; 8:14-17; 9:11-12; 10:4, 9, 30; 13:2-3. See David G. Peterson, *The Acts of the Apostles,* Pillar New Testament Commentary (Grand Rapids: Eerdmans, 2009), p. 118.
[9]Acts 2:47; 5:14; 6:7.
[10]Banks draws attention to "the infrequency of terms related to organization and to authority" in Paul's writings. Robert Banks, "Church Order and Government," in *Dictionary of the Later New Testament and Its Developments,* ed. Gerald F. Hawthorne, Ralph P. Martin and Daniel G. Reid (Downers Grove, Ill.: IVP Academic, 1993).
[11]Schnabel, Early Christian Mission, 1:426-28.
[12]Ibid., p. 553.

Chapter 12: From Jerusalem to the World

[1]Eckhard J. Schnabel, *Early Christian Mission,* Vol. 1, *Jesus and the Twelve* (Downers Grove, Ill.: IVP Academic, 2004), pp. 187, 731.
[2]Acts 2:5-13. See Clinton Arnold, "Centers of Christianity," in *Dictionary of the Later New Testament and Its Developments,* ed. Ralph P. Martin and Peter H. Davids (Downers Grove, Ill.: IVP Academic, 1997), pp. 144-52.
[3]For the spread of the gospel from Jerusalem to Rome see Schnabel, *Early Christian Mission,* 1:729-913.
[4]See F. Scott Spencer, *Journeying Through Acts: A Literary-Cultural Reading* (Grand Rapids: Baker Academic, 2004), pp. 59-61.
[5]Schnabel, *Early Christian Mission,* 1:1490. See also Arnold, "Centers of Christianity," pp. 144-52.
[6]Acts 9:31; 1 Corinthians 9:5; John 1:44; 12:21.
[7]Acts 9:2, 10, 19; 11:20-21.

[8]Andrew Clarke, "Rome and Italy," in *The Book of Acts in Its Graeco-Roman Setting*, ed. David W. Gill and Conrad H. Gempf (Grand Rapids: Eerdmans, 1994), p. 466.

[9]See Kevin N. Giles, "Church," in *Dictionary of the Later New Testament and Its Developments*, ed. Peter H. Davids and Ralph P. Martin (Downers Grove, Ill.: IVP Academic, 1997).

[10]Acts 6:9; 11:20; 13:1.

[11]See Schnabel, *Early Christian Mission*, 1:880-97.

[12]See ibid., p. 550.

[13]Eckhard Schnabel, "Mission, Early Non-Pauline," in *Dictionary of the Later New Testament and Its Developments*, ed. Ralph P. Martin and Peter H. Davids (Downers Grove, Ill.: IVP Academic, 1997), p. 757.

[14]Ibid., p. 763.

Interlude: Ying Kai and the Power of Multiplication

[1]See Steve Smith with Ying Kai, *T4T: A Discipleship Re-Revolution* (Monument, Colo.: WIGTake Resources, 2011); and Steve Smith, "Discipleship Revolution: Training for Trainers Process," *Mission Frontiers* 33, no. 1 (January-February 2011): 11-13.

[2]Smith, *T4T*, pp. 46-47.

[3]Adapted from Smith, *T4T*. Used by permission.

Chapter 13: Finally He Gets It!

[1]As a Roman citizen, Paul had three parts to his name. "Paul" may have been his family name. Witherington points out "there was a very good reason for Paul not to go around the Greco-Roman world calling himself Saulos. In Greek Saulos was used for someone who walked in a sexually suggestive manner like a prostitute!" Ben Witherington III, *The Paul Quest: The Renewed Search for the Jew of Tarsus* (Downers Grove, Ill.: IVP Academic, 1998), p. 72.

[2]Dean S. Gilliland, *Pauline Theology and Mission Practice* (Grand Rapids: Baker, 1983), p. 22.

[3]Arabia's major cities were Hellenistic (Greek in language and culture). Other cities Paul could have visited in Arabia included Gerasa, Philadelphia and Bostra.

[4]So Wayne A. Meeks, *The First Urban Christians: The Social World of the Apostle Paul* (New Haven, Conn.: Yale University Press, 1983), pp. 9-11; Martin Hengel, "Paul in Arabia," *Bulletin of Biblical Research* 12 (2002): 47-66; Eckhard J. Schnabel, *Early Christian Mission*, Vol. 1, *Jesus and the Twelve* (Downers Grove, Ill.: IVP Academic, 2004), pp. 1031-45; F. F. Bruce, *Paul: Apostle of the Free Spirit*, rev. ed. (Exeter, U.K.: Paternoster, 1980), pp. 81-82; Paul Barnett, *Paul: Missionary of Jesus* (Grand Rapids: Eerdmans, 2008), pp. 80-82.

[5]F. Scott Spencer, *Journeying Through Acts: A Literary-Cultural Reading* (Grand Rapids: Baker Academic, 2004), p. 140.

[6]See Meeks, *First Urban Christians*, pp. 28-29.

[7]See ibid., pp. 16-18.

[8]Schnabel, *Early Christian Mission*, 1:1299. This focus on cities was not absolute; Paul also ministered in some towns and villages. See Acts 26:19-20.

[9]Schnabel, *Early Christian Mission*, 1:15-16.

[10]1 Thessalonians 2:16; 1 Corinthians 2:2; 9:19-23; 10:33.

[11]Schnabel, *Early Christian Mission*, 1:404-5; Eckhard J. Schnabel, *Early Christian Mission*, Vol. 2, *Paul and the Early Church* (Downers Grove, Ill.: IVP Academic, 2004), p. 978.

[12]2 Corinthians 1:14; Galatians 2:2; Col 1:25-29; Philippians 2:16; 4:1; 1 Thessalonians 2:19.

[13]See Andreas J. Köstenberger and Peter T. O'Brien, *Salvation to the Ends of the Earth: A Biblical Theology of Mission*, ed. D. A. Carson, New Studies in Biblical Theology (Downers Grove, Ill.: IVP Academic, 2001), p. 161.

Chapter 14: Any Way He Can

[1]John McRay, *Paul: His Life and Teaching* (Grand Rapids: Baker, 2007), pp. 146-47; following Brian Rapske, *The Book of Acts and Paul in Roman Custody*, ed. I. Howard Marshall, Bruce W. Winter and David W. J. Gill, The Book of Acts in Its First Century Setting (Grand Rapids: Eerdmans, 2004), pp. 219, 124.

[2]See Wayne A. Meeks, *The First Urban Christians: The Social World of the Apostle Paul* (New Haven, Conn.: Yale University Press, 1983), p. 34.

[3]See Rodney Stark, *Cities of God: The Real Story of How Christianity Became an Urban Movement and Conquered Rome* (New York: HarperCollins, 2006).

[4]Such as Neapolis, Amphipolis and Apollonia. See McRay, *Paul*, p. 141.

[5]Acts 16:14-15, 32-34; 17:5-9; 18:8; 1 Corinthians 1:16; 16:15. Household baptism in Acts is based on household belief. See Alan J. Thompson, *The Acts of the Risen Lord Jesus: Luke's Account of God's Unfolding Plan*, ed. D. A. Carson, New Studies in Biblical Theology (Downers Grove, Ill.: IVP Academic, 2011), pp. 142-43 n. 60.

[6]Eckhard J. Schnabel, *Early Christian Mission*, Vol. 2, *Paul and the Early Church* (Downers Grove, Ill.: IVP Academic, 2004), p. 1439.

[7]Thessalonica, Corinth and Ephesus (1 Thessalonians 2:9; Acts 18:3; 1 Corinthians 9:12; Acts 20:33–34). See Ben Witherington, *The Acts of the Apostles: A Socio-Rhetorical Commentary* (Grand Rapids: Eerdmans, 1997), p. 547.

[8]Abraham J. Malherbe, *Paul and the Thessalonians: The Philosophic Tradition of Pastoral Care*, Proclamation Commentaries (Mifflintown, Penn.: Sigler Press, 1987, 2000), pp. 17-18.

[9]Witherington, *Acts*, pp. 574-75.

[10]Lydia was prosperous. As a merchant in purple cloth, she dealt with aristocracy but was not one of them. Purple cloth was highly valued, but the process of dyeing involved the use of animal urine. F. Scott Spencer, *Journeying Through Acts: A Literary-Cultural Reading* (Grand Rapids: Baker Academic, 2004), p. 175.

[11]See Meeks, *First Urban Christians*, p. 62.

[12]See Witherington, *Acts*, pp. 403-4 and Eckhard Schnabel, *Paul the Missionary: Realities, Strategies and Methods* (Downers Grove, Ill.: IVP Academic, 2008), p. 264.

[13]See Peter T. O'Brien, "Caesar's Household," in *Dictionary of Paul and His Letters*, ed. Ralph P. Martin, Gerald F. Hawthorne and Daniel G. Reid (Downers Grove, Ill.: IVP Academic, 1993), pp. 83-84.

[14]Meeks, *First Urban Christians*, pp. 21-22.

Chapter 15: One Gospel

[1]John McRay, *Paul: His Life and Teaching* (Grand Rapids: Baker, 2007), p. 159.

[2]See Eckhard J. Schnabel, *Early Christian Mission*, Vol. 2, *Paul and the Early Church* (Downers Grove, Ill.: IVP Academic, 2004), pp. 1392-1404.

[3]Robert L. Plummer, *Paul's Understanding of the Church's Mission: How Did the Apostle Paul Expect the Early Christian Communities to Evangelize?* Paternoster Biblical Monographs (Eugene, Ore.: Wipf & Stock, 2006), p. 52.

Chapter 16: The Obedience of Faith

[1]Ephesians 4:1; Colossians 1:10; 1 Thessalonians 2:12; Galatians 5:16-26; 2 Corinthians 5:15.

Chapter 17: When You Come Together

[1]For this section see John McRay, *Paul: His Life and Teaching* (Grand Rapids: Baker, 2007), pp. 390-401; and Paul Barnett, *Messiah* (Nottingham, U.K.: Inter-Varsity Press, 2009), pp. 182-85.

[2]Eckhard Schnabel, *Paul the Missionary: Realities, Strategies and Methods* (Downers Grove, Ill.: IVP Academic, 2008), p. 300.

[3]Acts 16:15, 33; 18:8; 1 Corinthians 1:16; 16:15.

[4]Barnett, *Jesus the Messiah*, p. 177.

[5]See Schnabel, *Paul the Missionary*, p. 236.

[6]See Gordon D. Fee, *Paul, the Spirit and the People of God* (Peabody, Mass.: Hendrickson, 1996); and Robert Banks, "Church Order and Government," in *Dictionary of the Later New Testament and Its Developments,* ed. Gerald F. Hawthorne, Ralph P. Martin and Daniel G. Reid (Downers Grove, Ill.: IVP Academic, 1993); and Don N. Jr. Howell, "Confidence in the Spirit as the Governing Ethos of the Pauline Mission," in *The Holy Spirit and Mission Dynamics,* ed. C. Douglas McConnell, Evangelical Missiological Series (Pasadena, Calif.: William Carey Library, 1997), pp. 36-65.

[7]1 Thessalonians 5:19-21; Acts 21:9; 1 Corinthians 11:5; 12:7-11; 13:2; 14:3, 24, 29.

[8]Romans 8:26-27; Ephesians 5:18-20; 6:18-20; Colossians 3:16-17.

[9]See Eckhard J. Schnabel, "Evangelism and the Early Church: What Do We Know About the Disciples as Missionaries?" *Trinity Magazine* (2005): 21-23, www.tiu.edu/files/tiu/trinitymagazine/evan05sp.pdf.

[10]Romans 12:10, 16; 13:8; 15:7; Galatians 5:13; 6:2; Ephesians 4:2, 32; Colossians 3:13; 1 Thessalonians 5:11.

[11]See Colin Kruse, "Ministry in the Wake of Paul's Mission," in *The Gospel to the Nations: Perspectives on Paul's Mission,* ed. Peter Bolt and Mark Thompson (Downers Grove, Ill.: IVP Academic, 2001), pp. 205-20; and Roland Allen, *Missionary Methods: St Paul's Or Ours?* 4th ed. (London: World Dominion Press, 1912), p. 168.

[12]See Banks, "Church Order and Government."

[13]Dean S. Gilliland, *Pauline Theology and Mission Practice* (Grand Rapids: Baker, 1983), p. 216. Acts 14:21-22; 15:4, 32-35; 16:5; 18:23; 20:2.

[14]For more on various leadership roles see McRay, *Paul,* pp. 374-90.

[15]Acts 20:28; Philippians 1:1; 1 Corinthians 16:15-16; Ephesians 4:11-13; 1 Timothy 3:1-13; Titus 1:5-9.

[16]Eckhard J. Schnabel, *Early Christian Mission,* Vol. 2, *Paul and the Early Church* (Downers Grove, Ill.: IVP Academic, 2004), p. 1493.

Chapter 18: Nothing Left to Do

[1]Estimates vary from 22,000 to 65,000. John McRay, "Antioch," in *Dictionary of Paul and His Letters,* ed. Gerald F. Hawthorne and Ralph P. Martin (Downers Grove, Ill.: IVP Academic, 1993).

[2]The name caught on. The Roman historian Tacitus reported that in A.D. 64, following the six-day fire in Rome, Nero brutally executed "Christians." See Eckhard J. Schnabel, *Early Christian Mission,* Vol. 1, *Jesus and the Twelve* (Downers Grove, Ill.: IVP Academic, 2004), p. 793.

[3]See Eckhard Schnabel, *Paul the Missionary: Realities, Strategies and Methods* (Downers Grove, Ill.: IVP Academic, 2008), pp. 66-71.

[4]Authority is not conveyed by the church or churches but by the apostolic call to spread the gospel. See Eckhard J. Schnabel, *Early Christian Mission,* Vol. 2, *Paul and the Early Church* (Downers Grove, Ill.: IVP Academic, 2004), p. 1428; Harold R. Cook, "Who Really Sent the Missionaries?" *Evangelical Missions Quarterly* 13 (October 1975): 233-39; Joseph and Michele C. [surname withheld], "Field-Governed Mission Structures, Part 1: In the New Testament," *International Journal of Frontier Missions* 18, no. 2 (Summer 2001): 59-66.

[5]See the references to "we" in Acts and 2 Corinthians 1:1; Philippians 1:1; 2:19-30; Colossians 4:7-14. See Schnabel, *Early Christian Mission,* 2:1425-45; E. Earle Ellis, "Paul and His Co-Workers," *New Testament Studies* (1970): 437-52.

[6]1 Thessalonians 2:9; 2 Thessalonians 3:8; 2 Corinthians 6:5; 11:23, 27; 1 Corinthians 3:8; 2 Corinthians 10:15; 1 Thessalonians 3:5; 1 Corinthians 15:58; 1 Thessalonians 1:3; 1 Timothy 5:17.

[7]The text is disputed. The weight of evidence favors "Junia" as a woman who served as a pioneering missionary with her husband. For a discussion see Stephen B. Addison, *The Continuing Ministry of the Apostle in the Church's Mission,* D.Min. diss., Pasadena, Calif., Fuller Theological Seminary, 1995, pp. 109-11, online at www.movements.net/2011/06/17/apostolic-ministry.html.

[8]See Wayne A. Meeks, *The First Urban Christians: The Social World of the Apostle Paul* (New Haven, Conn.: Yale University Press, 1983), p. 59.

[9]Andreas J. Köstenberger and Peter T. O'Brien, *Salvation to the Ends of the Earth: A Biblical Theology of Mission,* ed. D. A. Carson, New Studies in Biblical Theology (Downers Grove, Ill.: IVP Academic, 2001), p. 152.

[10]As usual Paul was not ministering alone. During his mission to Ephesus his coworkers included Epaphras (Colossians 1:3-8; 4:13), Philemon (Philemon 1-2), Aristarchus from Macedonia (Acts 19:29; 20:4; 27:2; Philemon 23), Gaius from Corinth (Acts 19:29; 1 Corinthians 1:14), and Tychicus and Trophimus (Acts 20:4; Colossians 4:7). Aquila, Priscilla and Timothy were with Paul from the beginning of his mission in Ephesus (1 Corinthians 16:10). Stephanas, Fortunatus and Archaicus visited him (1 Corinthians 1:17).

[11]Robert Maddox, *The Purpose of Luke-Acts,* ed. John Riches (Edinburgh: T & T Clark, 1982), p. 11.

[12]A figure not matched by any other Western world city until London reached one million in the eighteenth century. Schnabel, *Early Christian Mission,* p. 559.

[13]Paul's second letter to Timothy was also written from prison, but at a time when Paul expected to face death.

[14]Ben Witherington, *The Acts of the Apostles: A Socio-Rhetorical Commentary* (Grand Rapids: Eerdmans, 1997), p. 816.

[15]Ben Witherington, *New Testament History* (Grand Rapids: Baker Academic, 2003), pp. 199, 319-26.

[16]See Maddox, *Purpose of Luke-Acts,* p. 77.

Interlude: Julius Ebwongu Shifts the Paradigm

[1]Sources for this chapter included interviews and email correspondence with Bill Smith and Ray Belfield; and Robert A. Shipley, "Rabbit Churches: An Inquiry into the Enabling Assumptions of the Uganda Assemblies of God Church Planting Movement" (Pan-Africa Theological Seminary, September 2010).

[2]See Shipley, "Rabbit Churches," pp. 155-57.

Chapter 19: Seeing the End

[1]We don't normally associate "learning" with Jesus, but the writer of Hebrews (Hebrews 5:8) does.

[2]David Lawton, "Augie Joshua Interview," www.movements.net/2010/07/22/i-love-this-guy .html (accessed July 22, 2010).

[3]Ibid.

Chapter 20: Connecting with People

[1]For more on this method of connecting with Muslims see Kevin Greeson, *The Camel: How Muslims Are Coming to Faith in Christ!* (Midlothian, Va.: WIGTake Resources, 2007). Also Kevin Greeson, "Movements Audio Podcasts," www.movements.net/resources/the-movements-podcast (accessed December 5, 2011).

[2]Tim Scheuer, "Movements Audio Podcasts," www.movements.net/resources/the-movements-podcast (accessed December 5, 2011).

Chapter 21: Sharing the Gospel

[1]See the Implementation Guide for more details on how to train people to share their story, how to share Jesus' story and how to make disciples using the discovery Bible study approach.

Chapter 22: Training Disciples

[1]See David Watson, "Discovering God: Field Testing Guide v2.0," www.cpmtr.org/wp-content/plugins/downloads-manager/upload/2008%20Discovering%20God%202.0.pdf (accessed December 5, 2011).

[2]For the *Seven Commands of Christ* see Nathan and Kari Shank, *The Four Fields: A Manual for Church Planting Facilitation,* www.churchplantingmovements.com (accessed December 5, 2011).

Chapter 24: Multiplying Workers

[1]Sources for the story of Brother Haik: Felix Corley, "Obituary: Haik Hovsepian Mehr," *The Independent,* www.independent.co.uk/news/people/obituary-haik-hovsepian-mehr-1391238.html (accessed January 26, 2012); Karen Hartley, "Biography of Haik Hovsepian-Mehr," *Truett Journal of Church and Mission* 2, no. 1 (2004): 43-57.

[2]John and Keith Castle Bellamy, "2001 Church Attendance Estimates," *NCLS Occasional Paper* 3 (2004): 13.

Chapter 25: Starting Somewhere

[1]Dave Lawton and his workers use an inductive Bible study method developed by David Watson called *Discovering God.* For more information visit www.cpmtr.org.

[2]See David Lawton, "Movements Audio Podcasts," www.movements.net/resources/the-movements-podcast (accessed December 5, 2011).

Implementation Guide

[1]Tim Scheuer, "Share Jesus Without Fear," adapted from William Fay, *Share Jesus Without Fear* (Nashville: Broadman & Holman, 1999). Accessed October 8, 2012, www.movements.net/wp-content/uploads/2012/03/SJWF-simplified.pdf.

Movements That Change the World: Five Keys to Spreading the Gospel

"A thoroughly readable description of the dynamics of missionary movements, as well as how to initiate, maintain and extend them."

Alan Hirsch, *coauthor of* The Permanent Revolution

"Every so often a book comes along that fuels the flame that was started in my heart years ago when I was a young and on-fire world changer. I love this book!"

Floyd McClung, *author of* Follow: A Simple and Profound Call to Live Like Jesus

Steve Addison's *Movements That Change the World* draws from biblical, historical and contemporary case studies to isolate the essential elements of a dynamic missionary movement.

The church fulfills its mission today to the extent that it honors these essential elements, modeled perfectly in Jesus' missionary enterprise:

- white-hot faith
- commitment to the cause
- contagious relationships
- rapid mobilization
- adaptive methods

Jesus calls us to participate in a missionary movement that will one day reach every tribe, every language, every people and every nation. These five characteristics point the way to how we can obey his call.

To find out more, visit the Movements website:
www.movements.net